Arkansas in the Civil War: 1861

By Ron Kelley

O God of battles! steel my soldiers' hearts;
Possess them not with fear; take from them now
The sense of reckoning, if the opposed numbers
Pluck their hearts from them.

-William Shakespeare
(Spoken by Henry, Henry V, Act IV Scene 1)

Arkansas Toothpick Publishing- Helena, Arkansas

www.arkansastoothpick.com

Preface

As I sat down to gather my notes for this volume, there was one pressing question I sought the answer to more than any: what documents can I find to help tell the whole story of Arkansas in 1861 of why she left the Union? I began with the usual sources and compiled newspaper accounts, mostly Little Rock and Memphis-based. The reason Memphis papers were sought in my searches for documents is because Memphis was a proverbial "Limbo" of sorts for some Arkansas soldiers leaving their homes and gathering in Memphis until they left for the seat of war, then in Virginia.

Other sources were obvious to the general Arkansas Civil War reader, including the Ordinance for Secession on May 6. Other sources were brought in as they were reacted to in Arkansas, namely Abraham Lincoln's first inaugural address; this is the document that Arkansas began reacting to in fear of having to give up their economic machine of slavery as the abolition party of Lincoln threatened the very institution on which wealth was largely based in the South.

A letter from a soldier in Little Rock in May to his wife and children give us a personal insight into the lives of those that really wrote this "Diary" of sorts. Legal documents give the reader a better sense in context in this volume to better understand the story of a rebelling state in a turning point in her history. There is even evidence of strings being pulled behind the scenes during the Little Rock Arsenal crisis noted in the opening pages of this book. Documents in a string of chronology help interpret the drama in January and February as steamboats were being pulled over along the Arkansas River.

This is also the story of how a frontier state with relatively very little infrastructure rose to the challenge and supplied two armies and its intrinsic population while providing much-needed valuable natural resources. This is also the story of how women selflessly and energetically provided for the war effort in supplying the Arkansas boys the best of homespun uniforms and under garments. Editorials galore spiced up the pages of Arkansas newspapers while the population braced for an inevitable clash between the "Lincolnites" and the people of Arkansas. Arkansas troops saw their first battle at the Battle of Manassas and shortly afterwards at Wilson's Creek in the summer of 1861.

The summer of 1861 was marked chiefly by flag presentations and the mustering of units for Confederate service. With two major engagements having been fought, both of which were resounding

Confederate victories, the stage was set for what they thought would be a short war. Battles as epic as Shiloh or Gettysburg were not a part of the soldiers' psyche as the war dragged on to the winter months. The first year of the war is laid out before the reader like never before in a timeline of Arkansas primary source documents, awaiting interpretation. Some of the documents you will read have never been published, and most that have been published are available now for the first time in a while.

By the time I spent hundreds of hours in archives, transcribing one hundred and fifty year old newspapers, editing them all together, and finally stepping back and looking at the complete puzzle, a new picture emerges of why the Civil War began, how the country split, and most importantly, what was it that caused Arkansas to leave the Union and what did she do when she joined the Confederate States?

To spare the reader my personal thoughts of interpretation of the following pages, I urge them to instead draw their own conclusions based on the chronology of events and rhetoric contained herein. I was able to pull from a variety of sources to give, in some instances, conflicting views in the 1861 politico from which so many heated arguments arose.

I do hope the reader will notice the content index following a list of both federal and state congresses as *Diary of a State: 1861* opens. To those countless Arkansas men, women, and children that paid the ultimate sacrifice during the Civil War, this volume is dedicated to you.

Ron Kelley
Public Historian

Thirty-Sixth Congress
(United States)
(March 4, 1859-March 3, 1861)

Senate	William K. Sebastian	Helena
Senate	Robert Ward Johnson	Pine Bluff
House	Thomas Carmichael Hindman	Helena (Dist. 1)
House	Albert Rust	Little Rock (Dist. 2)

Thirteenth General Assembly
(November 5, 1860 to January 21, 1861;)
(Special Sessions: November 4-18, 1861; March 5-22, 1862)

<u>Senate:</u>

President- Thomas Fletcher
Secretary- John D. Kimbell

Arkansas, Desha, Jefferson Counties	Thomas Fletcher
Benton, Madison	M. Douglas
Carroll, Newton	W.W. Watkins
Chicot, Drew, Ashley	L.H. Besler
Clark, Polk, Pike	A.A. Pennington
Conway, Perry, Yell	G.W. Lemoyne
Crawford, Franklin	Jesse Miller
Dallas, Bradley	Joseph Gray
Hempstead, Sevier, Lafayette	A.H. Carrigan
Hot Spring, Montgomery, Saline	J.F. Fagan
Independence	J.S. Trimble
Izard, Van Buren	S.E. Rosson
Johnson, Pope	A.M. Ward
Lawrence, Fulton	Z.P. McAlexander
Marion, Searcy	W.C. Mitchell
Mississippi, Crittendon	Thomas B. Craighead
Ouachita, Calhoun	J.B. McCulloch
Phillips, Monroe	O.H. Oates
Pulaski, Prairie	F.A. Terry
Randolph, Greene	J.F. Davies
St. Francis, Poinsett	W.A. Jones

Scott, Sebastian	G.J. Clark
Union, Columbia	J.H. Askew
White, Jackson	D.McCreary

House of Representatives:

Speaker- Bradley Bunch
Clerk- Samuel M. Scott

County	Representative
Arkansas	John T. Gibson
Ashley	Robert Tucker
Benton	J. Dunnagin, J.P. Putnam
Bradley	A. McLean
Calhoun	Elam Williams
Carroll	B. Bunch, J. Childers
Chicot	Bat Jones
Clark	Charles Cargile
Columbia	D.L. Kilgore, A.C. Wheeler
Conway	Robert N. Harper
Craighead	Vacant
Crawford	J.M. Brown, Andrew Morton
Crittenden	B.L. Armstrong
Dallas	Edward M. Harris
Desha	James P. Clayton
Drew	W.M. Harrison, C.F. Hemingway
Franklin	John P. Humphreys
Fulton	J.W. Ware
Greene	L.L. Mack
Hempstead	R.K. Garland, O. Jennings
Hot Spring	Jas. M. Sanders
Independence	J.F. Saffold, W.B. Padgett, W.B. Massey
Izard	Thos. W. Edmondson
Jackson	W.H. Stone
Jefferson	F.F. Yell, James H. Hudson
Johnson	J.E. Cravens, L. Robinson
Lafayette	Robert P. Crowell
Lawrence	W. Ferguson, W. Sharp
Madison	J.C. Montgomery, S.E. Kenner

Marion	E.H. Messeck
Mississippi	John R. Acree
Monroe	Z.P.H. Farr
Montgomery	D.A. Wollard
Newton	Thos. Raines
Ouachita	Carnal H. Thorn
Perry	F.R. Janes
Phillips	J.C.O. Smith, Thomas J. Key
Pike	Willis Jones
Poinsett	Phillip Van Patten
Polk	Peter B. Allen
Pope	J.S. Bowden
Prairie	John C. Davis
Pulaski	John T. Trigg, W.Q. Pennington
Randolph	James H. Perkins
St. Francis	G.W. Seaborn, J.W. Landrum
Saline	Robert Murphy
Scott	James J. Lee
Searcy	B.F. Stephenson
Sebastian	John T. Loudon, B.T. Duval
Sevier	A.T. Pettus, W.D.S. Cook
Union	D.R. Coulter, T.F. Nolen
Van Buren	J.B. Lewis
Washington	John Crawford, B.F. Boone, J. Mitchell, L.M. Bell
White	No record
Yell	John H. Jones

CONTENT INDEX FOR
DIARY OF A STATE: 1861

	(Washington, D.C.)	Johnson to John Pope.
30	February 8, 1861 (Washington, D.C.)	Dispatch from R.W. Johnson and T.C. Hindman to Governor Rector.
30	February 9, 1861 (Washington, D.C.)	Dispatch from R.W. Johnson to R.H. Johnson.
30	February 10, 1861 (Little Rock, Ark.)	Dispatch from Totten to Cooper.
31	February 12, 1861 (Little Rock Arsenal)	Orders No. 6.
31	February 12, 1861 (Little Rock Arsenal)	Dispatch from Totten to Cooper (Includes Inclosures B, C, D, E, F).
36	February 12, 1861 (Fort Smith, Ark.)	Report No. 2 (J. McKinstry to Captain S. Williams).
37	February 16, 1861 (Little Rock, Ark.)	Arkansas Correspondence.
38	February 21, 1861 (Little Rock, Ark.)	An act to provide for defraying the expenses of commissioners to purchase arms.
39	February 22, 1861 (Little Rock, Ark.)	Dispatch to the Secretary of War from Geo. Ruddy.
40	February 24, 1861 (Little Rock, Ark.)	LITTLE ROCK LETTER.
43	March 2, 1861 (Little Rock, Ark.)	Proclamation of the Governor.
43	March 4, 1861 (Washington, D.C.)	President Abraham Lincoln's First Inaugural Speech.
52	March 4, 1861 (Little Rock, Ark.)	DISPATCH FROM LITTLE ROCK.
52	March 4, 1861 (Little Rock, Ark.)	Arkansas State Convention.
53	March 5, 1861 (Little Rock, Ark.)	Second Day.
54	March 6, 1861 (Little Rock, Ark.)	Arkansas State Convention.

55	March 6, 1861 (Little Rock, Ark.)	Arkansas State Convention.
59	March 9, 1861 (Pine Bluff, Ark.)	Dispatch from Read Fletcher to Governor Rector.
59	March 9, 1861 (Little Rock, Ark.)	Arkansas State Convention.
61	March 10, 1861 (Little Rock, Ark.)	Special Correspondence of the *Avalanche.*
64	March 10, 1861 (Memphis, Tenn.)	HON. THOMAS C. HINDMAN.
65	March 11, 1861 (Little Rock, Ark.)	Special Correspondence of the *Avalanche.*
69	March 11, 1861 (Little Rock, Ark.)	WILL ARKANSAS SECEDE?
69	March 11, 1861 (Little Rock, Ark.)	Editorial.
70	March 12, 1861 (Little Rock, Ark.)	Arkansas State Convention.
72	March 16, 1861 (Little Rock, Ark.)	Military.
73	March 23, 1861 (Jefferson County, Ark.)	Description of a ball held in Pine Bluff with the Jefferson Guards in attendance.
74	March 29, 1861 (Pulaski County, Ark.)	Free Barbecue in Lefevre Township.
74	April 5, 1861 (Des Arc, Ark.)	Cavalry Company.
75	April 13, 1861 (Johnson County, Ark.)	From Johnson County. Tremendous Excitement Large and Enthusiastic Meeting.
76	April 15, 1861 (Washington, D.C.)	BY THE PRESIDENT OF THE UNITED STATES: A PROCLAMATION.
79	April 16, 1861 (Montgomery, Ala.)	Dispatch from L.P Walker to Thomas C. Hindman.
81	April 17, 1861 (Montgomery, Ala.)	Dispatch from L.P. Walker to Governor Rector.

82	April 19, 1861 (Fort Smith, Ark.)	Report No. 3 (Report of Captain William W. Burns, commissary of subsistence, U.S. Army, of the seizure of subsistence stores at Pine Bluff, Ark.
82	April 19, 1861 (Dardanelle, Ark.)	For the *True Democrat.*
83	April 20, 1861 (Clarksville, Ark.)	From Johnson County.
84	April 20, 1861 (Little Rock, Ark.)	Military Ball.
84	April 20. 1861 (Little Rock, Ark.)	Proclamation.
85	April 20, 1861 (Clark County, Ark.)	Clark County.
86	April 20, 1861 (Hot Spring County, Ark.)	Drums.
86	April 21, 1861 (Napoleon, Ark.)	Dispatch from William W. Burns to Colonel Jos. Taylor.
87	April 21, 1861 (Nashville, Tenn.)	Dispatch from S.R. Cockrell to General Walker.
88	April 22, 1861 (Montgomery, Ala.)	Dispatch from L.P. Walker to Governor Rector.
89	April 22, 1861 (Little Rock, Ark.)	Dispatch from Governor Rector to Simon Cameron.
89	April 23, 1861 (Little Rock, Ark.)	Dispatch from T.B. Flournoy to L.P. Walker.
89	April 23, 1861 (Little Rock, Ark.)	Dispatch from Governor Rector to L.P. Walker.
90	April 24, 1861 (Fort Smith, Ark.)	Report of Major Richard C. Gatlin, Fifth U.S. Infantry, of the seizure of Fort Smith, Ark.
90	April 24, 1861 (Little Rock, Ark.)	Dispatch from T.B. Flournoy to L.P. Walker.
91	April 24, 1861 (Little Rock, Ark.)	Report of Captain Alexander Montgomery, assistant quartermaster, U.S.

		Army, of the seizure of Fort Smith, Ark.
92	April 25, 1861 (Little Rock, Ark.)	Dispatch from T.B. Flournoy to L.P. Walker.
92	April 25, 1861 (Little Rock, Ark.)	Editorial. (Ladies making uniforms for the Prairie company).
93	April 27, 1861 (Pulaski County, Ark.)	Announcement. Raising of a secession pole.
93	April 29, 1861 (Little Rock, Ark.)	Dispatch from Governor Rector to L.P. Walker.
93	May 1, 1861 (Washington, Ark.)	Dispatch from Benj. P. Jett to Jefferson Davis.
94	May 4, 1861 (Cairo, Ill.)	Query.
94	May 6, 1861 (Little Rock, Ark.)	Address of S.H. Hempstead to the Arkansas secession convention.
97	May 6, 1861 (Little Rock, Ark.)	Ordinance No. 2 (Secession Ordinance).
100	May 7, 1861 (Little Rock, Ark.)	Letter from Billy to Martha.
101	May 8, 1861 (Fort Smith, Ark.)	Dispatch from B. Burroughs to Governor C. Harris.
102	May 10, 1861 (Fort Smith, Ark.)	From Fort Washita.
103	May 11, 1861 (Little Rock, Ark.)	Advice to Volunteers. How to Prepare for the Campaign.
103	May 15, 1861 (Mound City, Ark.)	Flag Presentation.
104	May 15, 1861 (Mound City, Ark.)	Flag Presentation at Camp Rector.
104	May 15, 1861 (Mound City, Ark.)	Another Flag Presentation at Camp Rector.
104	May 21, 1861 (Camp on Walnut Creek)	Report No 8. Report of Major Samuel D. Sturgis, Fourth U.S. Cav.
105	May 25, 1861	From Conway County.

	(Lewisburg, Ark.)	
106	May 28, 1861 (Memphis, Tenn.)	Reported Invasion.
107	May 28, 1861 (Little Rock, Ark.)	Letter from Little Rock.
107	May 30, 1861 (Little Rock, Ark.)	Notice. Citizens should organize a guerilla band.
107	June 1, 1861 (Little Rock, Ark.)	Flag Presentation.
108	June 1, 1861 (Mound City, Ark.)	Presentation of Banners to the Jefferson Guards – Patriotic Compliments from abroad.
111	June 11, 1861 (Memphis, Tenn.)	Arkansas Volunteers.
111	June 13, 1861 (Little Rock, Ark.)	Fast Day.
111	June 13, 1861 (Little Rock, Ark.)	Soldiers' Health. Interesting Suggestions and Recommendations.
115	June 13, 1861 (Pocahontas, Ark.)	An Arkansas Heroine.
116	June 22, 1861 (Little Rock, Ark.)	A Card.
116	June 22, 1861 (Little Rock, Ark.)	Flag presentation to the Dixie Grays.
119	June 23, 1861 (Memphis, Tenn.)	Grateful Acknowledgements.
119	June 27, 1861 (Little Rock, Ark.)	Address to the Ashley Volunteers.
121	July 3, 1861 (Memphis, Tenn.)	Report. To the Executive Committee of the Southern Mothers.
124	July 3, 1861 (Ultimathule, Ark.)	Sevier County Star company left for Fort Smith.
124	July 3, 1861 (Memphis, Tenn.)	Harry Macarty.

124	July 4, 1861 (Little Rock, Ark.)	Constitution of the Stay at Home Guards.
126	July 4, 1861 (Carroll County, Ark.)	Flag presentation to Captain Smith.
128	July 4, 1861 (Little Rock, Ark.)	Announcement. John C. Peay is candidate for Sheriff of Pulaski County.
128	July 4, 1861 (Little Rock, Ark.)	Hempstead County Davis Blues.
129	July 4, 1861 (Little Rock, Ark.)	Our Paper.
130	July 4, 1861 (Little Rock, Ark.)	A Song for the Arkansaw Boys. By Lillian Montecalm.
131	July 4, 1861 (Searcy, Ark.)	Searcy Girls.
131	July 4, 1861 (Little Rock, Ark.)	The Ladies of Little Rock.
132	July 6, 1861 (Little Rock, Ark.)	Military Barbecue & Flag Presentation.
134	July 9, 1861 (Quitman, Ark.)	Letter to the editor (flag presentation to the Quitman Rifle Company).
134	July 11, 1861 (Benton, Ark.)	Address of Miss Frank J. Pack, Delivered in presenting a flag to the "Saline Rifle Rangers," at Benton, Arkansas, July 11th, 1861.
136	July 11, 1861 (Memphis, Tenn.)	Southern Mothers' Association.
136	July 11, 1861 (Little Rock, Ark.)	Presentation of a Flag to Hot Springs Rifle Company. By Miss Ann Bennet, on behalf of the Ladies of Ouachita and surrounding townships.
138	July 17, 1861 (Memphis, Tenn.)	To the Ladies of the Society of Southern Mothers.
139	July 18, 1861 (Union County, Ark.)	County Script Called In.
140	July 18, 1861	Flag Presentation.

		(Sulphur Rock, Ark)
141	July 20, 1861 (Little Rock, Ark.)	Socks for the Soldiers.
142	July 20, 1861 (Little Rock, Ark.)	Col. Cleburne's Regiment.
142	July 25, 1861 (Little Rock, Ark.)	An Arkansas Farewell.
144	July 30, 1861 (Springfield, Ark.)	Our Correspondents.
147	August 1, 1861 (Calhoun County, Ark.)	Presentation Address of the Flag to the Moro Grays, Calhoun County, Ark. By Miss Lucy Lorraine Adams.
148	August 1, 1861 (Jackson County, Ark.)	Speech of Miss Elizabeth Higginbotham.
150	August 8, 1861 (Little Rock, Ark.)	Proclamation by the Governor.
151	August 8, 1861 (Little Rock, Ark.)	A Chance for the Girls- Gold Medals for the Most Industrious.
151	August 8, 1861 (Little Rock, Ark.)	Development of the Resources of Arkansas.
153	August 12, 1861 (Little Rock, Ark.)	To the Voters of the 5th Judicial District of the State of Arkansas, composed of the counties of Conway, Prairie, Dallas, Hot Spring, Saline and Pulaski.
153	August 12, 1861 (Springfield, Mo.)	Report of Major General Sterling Price, commanding Missouri State Guard, of operations from July 25 to August 11.
159	August 14, 1861 (Helena, Ark.)	Shoemakers Wanted Immediately.
159	August 15, 1861 (Little Rock, Ark.)	Direct Taxation.
161	August 15, 1861 (Little Rock, Ark.)	Lead.
162	August 15, 1861 (Fort Smith, Ark.)	GEN. N.B. Pearce.

162	August 15, 1861 (Long View, Ark.)	Letter to the Editor (Ferry in Moro).
163	August 20, 1861 (Little Rock, Ark.)	Clothing for the Soldiers Circular Letter from the Military Board.
165	August 21, 1861 (Pond Springs, Mo.)	Extract of a Letter from Capt. Galloway.
165	August 22, 1861 (Little Rock, Ark.)	Address of Mrs. W. M. Aikin to the Izard Volunteers.
167	August 22, 1861 (Little Rock, Ark.)	Clothing for the Soldiers.
168	August 22, 1861 (Little Rock, Ark.)	Lieut. Lockman recruiting for his Co.
168	August 22, 1861 (Fort Smith, Ark.)	News from Missouri.
168	August 22, 1861 (Little Rock, Ark.)	The Call for More Troops.
169	August 22, 1861 (Little Rock, Ark.)	Executive Office.
171	August 24, 1861 (Little Rock, Ark.)	Clothing for the Soldiers.
171	August 24, 1861 (Humboldt, Tenn.)	Death of a Soldier.
172	August 28, 1861 (Van Buren, Ark.)	Letter from Camp Frank Rector.
173	August 29, 1861 (Little Rock, Ark.)	Clothing for the Soldiers Again.
174	August 29, 1861 (Little Rock, Ark.)	THE WAR- WHEN WILL IT CEASE?
177	August 29, 1861 (Little Rock, Ark.)	Arms Wanted.
177	August 29, 1861 (Little Rock, Ark.)	PRESIDENTIAL AND CONGRESSIONAL ELECTIONS.
177	August 29, 1861 (Little Rock, Ark.)	War Coffee.

178	September 3, 1861 (Jefferson County, Ark.)	To the Ladies of Jefferson County.
179	September 3, 1861 (Pittman's Ferry, Ark.)	Clothing for the Soldiers.
182	September 3, 1861 (Lewisburg, Ark.)	Letter regarding how volunteers are being clothed.
182	September 5, 1861 (Memphis, Tenn.)	A GALLANT ARKANSAS YOUTH.
183	September 5, 1861 (Little Rock, Ark.)	Announcement for Guns.
183	September 19, 1861 (Memphis, Tenn.)	Camden Knights reached Memphis.
184	September 12, 1861 (Little Rock, Ark.)	Letter to the Editor from the Camden Knights Company.
185	September 12, 1861 (Little Rock, Ark.)	Clothing for the Soldiers of the Hot Spring Rifle Company "E." 12th Regiment Arkansas Volunteers.
185	September 12, 1861 (Little Rock, Ark.)	Capital Guards.
187	September 12, 1861 (Little Rock, Ark.)	Office Military Board.
188	September 12, 1861 (Little Rock, Ark.)	Clothing for the Army.
188	September 12, 1861 (Little Rock, Ark.)	For the Soldiers.
189	September 19, 1861 (Little Rock, Ark.)	To the people of Ashley, Desha, Drew, Dallas, Hot Spring and Union counties, Arkansas.
190	September 19, 1861 (Memphis, Tenn.)	Announcement of a flag presentation to the 9th Arkansas.
190	September 21, 1861 (Little Rock, Ark.)	Little Rock Arsenal now has machinery to fix guns.
190	September 26, 1861 (Little Rock, Ark.)	The Preacher's Regiment.
192	September 26, 1861	Military companies have strange names.

	(Little Rock, Ark.)	
191	October 3, 1861 (Little Rock, Ark.)	Clothing ready for Columbia County volunteers.
192	October 3, 1861 (Little Rock, Ark.)	Soldiers' Clothing.
192	October 3, 1861 (Little Rock, Ark.)	Soldiers Aid Society.
192	October 5, 1861 (Memphis, Tenn.)	Arkansas Items.
193	October 9, 1861 (Jacksonport, Ark.)	Arkansas Items.
193	October 9, 1861 (Helena, Ark.)	Arkansas Items.
194	October 10, 1861 (Union County, Ark.)	Socks, Clothing, etc.
194	October 10, 1861 (Little Rock, Ark.)	The Concert.
195	October 11, 1861 (Van Buren, Ark.)	Arkansas Items.
195	October 14, 1861 (Pitman's Ferry, Ark.)	Letter from Camp Holmes.
197	October 17, 1861 (Camden, Ark.)	Patriotic Ladies.
197	October 18, 1861 (Little Rock, Ark.)	Barbecue and Flag Presentation.
200	October 24, 1861 (Chicot County, Ark.)	Value of the voluntary contributions to the army…
200	October 27, 1861 (Memphis, Tenn.)	A Card.
202	October 28, 1861 (Holly Springs, Ark.)	Clothing made for soldiers in Holly Springs.
202	October 31, 1861 (Little Rock, Ark.)	Arkansas penitentiary useful.
203	November 5, 1861	"Here's Your Mule."

		(Little Rock, Ark.)	
203	November 5, 1861 (Van Buren, Ark.)	Arkansas Intelligence.
203	November 7, 1861 (Little Rock, Ark.)	Let Us Rejoice.
204	November 7, 1861 (Little Rock, Ark.)	Exiles.
205	November 8, 1861 (Little Rock, Ark.)	Complimentary.
207	November 21, 1861 (Little Rock, Ark.)	Dallas Rifles.
208	November 21, 1861 (Camp Beauregard, Ark.)	Magruder Guards Thanks.
208	November 28, 1861 (Little Rock, Ark.)	Secret Lincoln organization.
208	December 11, 1861 (Little Rock, Ark.)	Ball given by the colored population.
209	December 15, 1861 (Little Rock, Ark.)	More of the Conspirators.
209	December 17, 1861 (Fort Smith, Ark.)	Troubles in the Indian Territory.
210	December 17, 1861 (Little Rock, Ark.)	The Conspirators.
211	December 25, 1861 (Little Rock, Ark.)	Christmas Day.

JEFFERSON COUNTY, Ark.,
January 10, 1861.[1]

Headquarters 24th Regiment
Arkansas Militia Pine Bluff March 4/61

I, Donelson McGregor Colonel Commandant of the 24th Regiment of Arkansas Militia, do hereby certify to his Excellency Henry M. Rector Governor and Commander in Chief of the Militia of the said State that at the election held by Company A in 1st Battalion of 24th Regiment of the Militia of said State in Jefferson County on the 10th day of January AD 1861, Lewis S. Reed was duly elected 2nd Lieutenant of said Company and is entitled to his commission for the same according to Law.

Donelson McGregor
Col. Commandant
24th Regiment
Ark Militia

LITTLE ROCK, Ark.
January 15, 1861.

AN ACT
TO PROVIDE FOR A
STATE CONVENTION.[2]

SECTION 1. Be it enacted by the General Assembly of the State of Arkansas, that the governor shall issue his proclamation, ordering an election in all the counties in this state, submitting to the people the question of "convention" or "no convention," to be held on the eighteenth day of February, 1861, which election shall be conducted as state elections are now conducted;
Provided, The sheriffs of the several counties shall be required to give but ten days' notice of said election.
SEC. 2. Be it enacted, That, at said election, the people shall also vote for a delegate or delegates to said convention, and each delegate elected shall be made a special returning officer, and shall bring up the

---

[1]   Jefferson County
2   Journal of The Convention of the State of Arkansas, Little Rock, Ark., 1881, pp. 3-4.

13

certified vote of his county on the question of convention or no convention, which vote from all the counties, shall be opened by the governor, auditor, treasurer and secretary of state, or any three of them, on the second day of March, 1861; and if, on counting the vote of all the counties of this state, it shall appear that a majority of all the votes cast are for a convention, then the governor shall immediately issue his proclamation, requiring the delegates elected as aforesaid to convene in the capitol on the following Monday, and organize themselves into a state convention, by the election of a president, and such other officers as may be required, and, in case of sickness, or any other unavoidable cause, to prevent any delegate to the convention from getting to the capital, he shall have power to send up the returns of his county by a special messenger, selected by himself.

SEC. 3. Be it further enacted, That the delegates, or special returning officers, shall be paid mileage at the same rate that members of the General Assembly are paid, to be certified by the president of the convention, if one be organized, and if not, the auditor is required to issue his warrant for the same, taking the mileage accounts of the members of the General Assembly as a guide to regulate the amount to which the delegate, or delegates, coming from the same county, may be entitled.

SEC. 4. Be it further enacted, That the officers and members of said convention, if it shall be organized, shall be paid the same per diem pay that the officers and members of this General Assembly are paid: their accounts therefore to be certified by the president of the convention, and the secretary shall certify the account of the president.

SEC. 5. Be it further enacted, That each county in this state shall be entitled to elect as many delegates to said convention as it is now entitled to members in the lower branch of the General Assembly, and the qualifications for a delegate shall be the same as now required for a member of the House of Representatives.

SEC. 6. Be it further enacted, That fifty members of said convention shall be necessary to constitute a quorum to transact business.

SEC. 7. Be it further enacted, That if any seat in the convention, hereby provided for, be contested, the convention shall have power to determine such contest, as the General Assembly has to determine contests for seats in either house, in the manner now prescribed by law.

SEC. 8. Be it further enacted, That upon the organization of said convention, it shall take into consideration the condition of political affairs, and determine what course the State of Arkansas shall take in the present political crisis.

SEC. 9. *Be it further enacted,* That a sufficient amount of money be, and the same is, hereby appropriated out of the state treasury to pay the necessary expenses of said convention, should one be held.

SEC. 10. *Be it further enacted,* That this act shall take effect and be in force from its passage. Approved, January 15th, 1861.

LITTLE ROCK ARSENAL, January 29, 1861.

Report Number 1.[3]

Reports of Captain James Totten, Second U. S. Artillery, of the seizure of the U. S. Arsenal at Little Rock, Ark.

SIR: I have the honor herewith to inclose a copy of a communication received this day from his Excellency Henry M. Rector, governor of the State of Arkansas, and also a copy of my reply to his Excellency's communications.

Please submit both these communications to the Secretary of War for the decision of the President of the United States, with the request that instructions be sent me as to my future action in the premises. I also request that means and money may be sent me to carry out the orders I may receive.

I forward, in the same mail with this, copies of the communications, herein mentioned, to the general commanding the Department of the West. I deem it necessary in this connection respectfully to inform the authorities concerned that, in my opinion, most positive and unequivocal instructions are called for, in order that I may not mistake the intentions of the administration regarding the matter at issue. I believe there is trouble ahead for this command, and that by the 4th day of March coming decided action will be absolutely imperative in the officer who may then command this arsenal, and, if left to his own discretion, he may not in everything correspond with the wishes of the Federal authorities.

---

3   *War of the Rebellion,* ser.1, 1:638 [hereafter referred to as OR; all references to series 1 unless otherwise noted]

Whatever orders may be given, I respectfully ask that they may be sent by a reliable agent, and not by mails, as there appears to be some reason in believing that they are not entirely trustworthy at present. I would not myself, in the present instance, trust to this doubtful medium of communication if I had means at my disposal of sending an officer to Washington, and, indeed, if I can procure the necessary funds, I may yet forward copies of the various communications now inclosed by such an agent as indicated.

I am, sir, very respectfully, your obedient servant,
JAS. TOTTEN,
Captain, Second Artillery, Commanding Post.

Colonel S. COOPER,
Adjutant-General U. S. Army, Washington City, D. C.

[Inclosure A.]

THE STATE OF ARKANSAS,
Executive Department, Little Rock, January 28, 1861.

CAPTAIN: The public exigencies require me to make known to you that the U. S. Arsenal at this place will be permitted to remain in the possession of the Federal officers until the State, by authority of the people, shall have determined to sever their connection with the General Government, unless, however, wit should be thought proper to order additional forces to this point; or, on the other hand, an attempt should be made to remove or destroy the munitions of war deposited in said arsenal. Any assurances that you may be able to give touching the observance of these two latter conditions will greatly tend to quiet the public mind, and prevent a collision between the sovereign people of Arkansas and the Government troops now stationed at this point.

Respectfully,
HENRY M. RECTOR,
Governor of Arkansas and Commander-in-Chief.

Captain TOTTEN, *U. S. Army, Little Rock Arsenal.*

[Inclosure B.]

HEADQUARTERS LITTLE ROCK ARSENAL,
Little Rock, Ark., January 29, 1861.

SIR: I have to acknowledge the receipt of your communication of the 28th instant, which was handed to me this morning by your aide-de-camp, J. J. Gaines, esq., and in answer thereto, to say to your excellency that my understanding leads me to believe that the troops under my command were ordered here at the request of some of the members of Congress from this State, and several good citizens also, for what reasons, if any, I have not been apprised.

As you will readily understand, I cannot give your excellency any assurances as to what instructions may in the future be issued regarding this arsenal and the Federal troops now stationed here, but I can assure you that, so far as I am informed, no orders, such as you refer to in your two propositions, have been issued, nor do I believe, privately and unofficially, that any such orders will be given by the Federal Government. I have furthermore to remind your excellency that as an officer of the Army of the United states, my allegiance is due to that Government in whose [service] I am, and that I act by its authority and permission, and until absolved from the allegiance my honor is concerned in the faithful performance of what I may conceive to be my duty.

I shall forward your communication to the Secretary of War to be laid before the President of the United States, and ask instructions relative to the matter contained in it, and, if not prohibited by these authorities, I will cheerfully inform your Excellency what these instructions are.

In the meantime let me say, in conclusion, that I most cordially concur with your Excellency in the desire to avoid collision between the Federal troops under my command and the citizens of Arkansas, and shall do everything in my power which an honorable man in my position can or dare do to prevent so deplorable an event.

I am, respectfully,
JAS. TOTTEN,
Captain, Second Artillery, U. S. Army.
Commanding Little Rock Arsenal.

His Excellency HENRY M. RECTOR,
Governor of Arkansas and Commander-in-Chief.

17

LITTLE ROCK, Ark.,
January 29, 1861.[4]

THE STATE OF ARKANSAS, EXECUTIVE DEPARTMENT,
To His Excellency JOHN ROSS,
Principal Chief Cherokee Nation: SIR: It may now be regarded as almost certain that the States having slave property within their borders will, in consequence of repeated Northern aggressions, separate themselves and withdraw from the Federal Government.

South Carolina, Alabama, Florida, Mississippi, Georgia, and Louisiana have already, by action of the people, assumed this attitude. Arkansas, Missouri, Tennessee, Kentucky, Virginia, North Carolina, and Maryland will probably pursue the same course by the 4th of March next. Your people, in their institutions, productions, latitude, and natural sympathies, are allied to the common brotherhood of the slaveholding States. Your country is salubrious and fertile, and possesses the highest capacity for future progress and development by the application of slave labor. Besides this, the contiguity of our territory with yours induces relations of so intimate a character as to preclude the idea of discordant or separate action.

It is well established that the Indian country west of Arkansas is looked to by the incoming administration of Mr. Lincoln as fruitful fields, ripe for the harvest of abolitionism, freesoilers, and Northern mounte-banks.

We hope to find in your people friends willing to co-operate with the South in defense of her institutions, her honor, and her firesides, and with whom the slaveholding States are willing to share a common future, and to afford protection commensurate with your exposed condition and your subsisting monetary interests with the General Government. As a direct means of expressing to you these sentiments, I have dispatched my aide-de-camp, Lieutenant Colonel J. J. Gaines, to confer with you confidentially upon these subject, and to report to me any expressions of kindness and confidence that you may see proper to communicate the governor of Arkansas, who is your friend and the friend of your people.

Respectfully, your obedient servant,
HENRY M. RECTOR,
Governor of Arkansas.

---

4   OR,1(1):683-4

**PINE BLUFF, Ark.,
January 31, 1861.**[5]

OUTRAGE COMMITTED BY THE MOB AT PINE BLUFF, THE FIRST OUTBREAKS IN THE STATE- JOINED BY A PARTY FROM HELENA, PROCEEDED TO CAPTURE THE ARSENAL AT LITTLE ROCK.

Sometime about the last of January 1861, the people still showing but little disposition to take action, the mob began to be more open and furious, and became so bold at Pine Bluff as even to attack and rob steamboats at the wharf. This was about the time the incendiary, exciting, and false reports were being sent out from Little Rock, alluded to in a former chapter. In those orders and reports it was stated, that the Government was sending re-enforcements, and a large amount of commissary supplies for the Arsenal at Little Rock, and the forts up the Arkansas River. This was enough for the excited rabble at Pine Bluff, who had been drilling and organizing from the time Mr. Lincoln's election had been announced. One company indeed had been organized during the Presidential campaign, styled the "Jefferson Guards." It was made up of the young hot-spurs and principal bloods of the town, who boasted and swaggered of their bravery and prowess, until one might have thought the Devil himself would have left town in fear and disgust.

They were ready at any moment to aid or assist in the prosecution of any measure looking to the rupture then imminent, between the two sections of the country. Accordingly, when in addition to their own conceived designs, and the will of the leaders about Pine Bluff, they received intimations of co-operation at these points, they determined upon aggressive action.

An opportunity soon offered in some boats ascending the Arkansas river freighted with Government stores. It was represented and urged, that these stores were intended to supply troops sent into Arkansas to subjugate her people to the rule and dominion of Lincoln, and that the safety of their property and liberties demanded prompt and decisive action. A caucus held for the purpose, decided to stop the Boats and seize

---

5   Demby, *The War in Arkansas, or A Treatise on the Great Rebellion of 1861; Its Progress, and Ultimate Results Upon the Destinies of the State,* 60-64.

their cargoes. There were several boats, and the freight consisted of army commissary supplies.

This notorious robbery was the first violent measure of the gathering mob. When they boarded the Boats, and were inquired of as to their authority for their proceedings, by the commanders, they pointed to their guns and pistols- remarking "that was the law and authority now in Arkansas." As resistance could not be made, and as no civil authority could or would interfere- nothing remained for the Masters of the Boats but to acquiesce the best they could.

The cargoes were stored on shore in ware-houses, and wherever else they could be put away. They were of the finest and best quality, such flour, and other articles of provision had never before been seen in Pine Bluff. Many had a desire to test the quality, and made free to help themselves to what they wished, especially the fine liquors. Ex-governor John Selden Roane, one of the chief leaders in the enterprise, had a good supply of it sent over to his residence on the opposite side of the river, as was said, for safe keeping. It was supposed others of like "kith and kin," such as Gen. James, Bocage, Bell, the Raglands, etc., took and possessed themselves of their respective portions for a like purpose. They all lived high while it lasted, and the old saying of "come light go light," was fully verified. They boasted much of their achievement, and how they had disappointed "ole Abe" in his expectations. "Old Abe's menials" they said, "were to be fed and liquored on the best while they were robbing and coercing the South." All this too, before Mr. Lincoln was inaugurated, the better to conceal their nefarious designs against the Government. Everything was attributed to him, of a detestable character, in order to arouse a feeling of hatred akin to madness. Such were the intensity and maliciousness of the manner of the mob toward the Government, that it was even dangerous to speak of it in respectable terms. The most contemptuous epithets that could be imagined were substituted for the Government and its representatives whenever spoken of. And what is still more remarkable, little or nothing were said of, or attributed to Mr. Buchanan, who was still at the head of the Government, but the whole attack seemed aimed directly at Mr. Lincoln as though he was then directing affairs. This may be accounted for on the ground, that as Mr. Lincoln was the chief object to be destroyed in achieving their designs, they had no ammunition to waste on others of less importance.

They constantly bandied around such complimentary epithets as, "Old Abe," the "Ape," "King Abraham the first," "Lincoln Government," the "Rump Government," "Abolitionist," "the Yanks," or "the Dutch," "Goths and Vandals," etc. In all their conversation these sweet morsels were spiced and flavored with a variety of course wit and humor suitable as side dishes, and all relished with a gusto unappreciated by any but those who witnessed it, and were prepared to observe impartially. If this had only been true of the ill-bred rabble enlisted in this tumult and blackguardism, it would not have been so remarkable, but those who were considered the elite and intelligent of society - men and women - led off in front, and brandished those vulgarisms around in every circle.

Quite an excitement was created over this robbery of the Boats. And no little degree of praise and encomiums were lavished upon the perpetrators of this chivalrous achievement. Much curiosity was gratified in looking over and examining the goods and the marks on the boxes by the throng visiting the wharf and ware-houses. The mark "A.C.S" elicited much inquiry, few, if any, seemed to understand it.

John W. Barnhill, the town Marshall, was the person who had charge of the storing away of this plunder, and he, it was said, discovered the meaning of the mysterious mark, designed on purpose, as they thought, as a disguise and trick to pass the goods to their destination. He announced to the astonished and wonder-stricken crowd, that the letters "A.C.S." stood for "Abe's Children South." This of course was satisfactory. This adventure was conscientiously opposed by some who were in favor of secession. They contended that, inasmuch as the people had taken no steps towards seceding, and as we were yet a portion of - what they pleased to call - "the old compact of a rotten thing, called a Government," the move was premature, and could be considered in no other light than an outrage. Some who were outspoken against it, were reminded of their lack of prudence, in being told that no opposition would be tolerated for a moment.

The leading spirits of the mob were aware of the apathy and unwillingness on the part of the people to do anything rashly, and as their cause was a desperate one, they at once resolved upon desperate measures, as the most effectual means of involving the whole in common with themselves in such a manner as to force action and co-operation on the entire people of the state.

No sooner had this brilliant achievement of robbery at Pine Bluff been consummated, than the mob at Helena, with a similar spirit longing for plunder, determined upon the capture of the Arsenal at Little Rock. They embarked on boats for that purpose, and by the time they reached

Pine Bluff, on their way up the Arkansas river, the chivalric and invincible boat-robbing crowd, flushed with recent success, were enthusiastic to join in the proposed attack. Men and boys of all grades and ages, capable of bearing shot guns, butcher knives, and a certain portion of whiskey, were seen running with maddened excitement in every direction, preparing to join in the enterprise that was to make each participant a hero to be read of in all time among the brave and chivalrous sons of Arkansas.

Accordingly they proceeded to Little Rock, all together in high glee, well stimulated with Yankee whiskey - perhaps a portion of that just captured was distributed for the occasion. They reached Little Rock without difficulty.

PINE BLUFF, Ark.,
February 5, 1861.[6]

Gov. Rector,

I hastened from Little Rock with all dispatch and arrived here last evening- found the rumors as to troops on the S.H. Tucker false- gotten up by a Bar Keeper to create excitement and cause a run. This morning a boat passed here without landing and rumor says fired cannon (I certainly heard the report) and pursued the boat but found nothing suspicious on board of her- There is great excitement here- Gen Yell and WP Grace were nominated on Saturday as secession candidates- for the convention and will undoubtedly be elected by overwhelming majorities. This will be handed by Mr. Hicks- who I employed to bring me here- and to whom I now given an order directed to you for thirty dollars for three days him of horse and buggy.

Very respectfully,
Willow Williams Jr.

---

6   Letter written by Willow Williams, Jr. to Governor Henry Massie Rector, Governor of Arkansas, regarding the steamboat S.H. Tucker being pulled over in Pine Bluff.

LITTLE ROCK ARSENAL,
February 6, 1861.[7]

LITTLE ROCK, *February* 6, 1861.
I have to inform the authorities that companies of armed citizens from various section of this State have already arrived, and it is said there will soon be five thousand here for the express purpose of taking this arsenal. Instructions are urgently and immediately asked. Collision seems inevitable if this arsenal is to be held.

JAMES TOTTEN,
Captain, Second Artillery, Commanding Post.
Colonel S. COOPER, *Adjutant-General U. S. Army.*

LITTLE ROCK ARSENAL,
February 6, 1861.[8]

SIR: I have the honor herewith to inclose a copy of a communication just received from H. M. Rector, governor of the State of Arkansas, demanding the surrender of this arsenal to the State authorities. As I have already written and telegraphed you for the information of the President, I am perfectly in the dark as to the wishes of the administration, from the want [of] instructions how to meet such a crisis as at present. If I had positive orders to cover the case in point I should obey them implicitly; but I have nothing whatever, within my knowledge, indicative of the course the Government wishes its agents to pursue, and I am therefore left to act as my judgment and my honor as a Federal officer dictate under the present trying circumstances. I inclose also copies of certain resolutions, passed by the citizens of Little Rock, and of the common council of said city, explanatory of the circumstances under which the matter above referred to had been brought about.

I am, very respectfully, your obedient servant,
JAS. TOTTEN,
Captain, Second Artillery, Commanding Post.

Colonel S. COOPER,
Adjutant-General U. S. Army, Washington, D. C.

---

7   OR,1(1):639
8   OR,1(1):640-642

[Inclosure A.]

EXECUTIVE OFFICE,
Little Rock, Ark., February 6, 1861.

SIR: There is now in this city a considerable number of the citizens of this State who have come here, under arms, with the avowed purpose of taking possession of the U. S. Arsenal.

Reliable information has been received that a large force of citizens are on the march to this place for the same purpose. This movement is prompted by the feeling that pervades the citizens of this State that in the present emergency the arms and munitions of war in the arsenal should be under the control of the State authorities, in order to their security. This movement, although not authorized by me, has assumed such an aspect that it becomes my duty, as the executive of this State, to interpose my official authority to prevent a collision between the people of the State and the Federal troops under your command.

I therefore demand in the name of the State the delivery of the possession of the arsenal and munitions of war under your charge to the State authorities, to be held subject to the action of the convention to be held on the 4th of March next. This course is the only one which can possibly prevent the effusion of blood and the destruction of the property of the citizens and the Government. I beg leave to assure you that the steps which the citizens have seen fit to take is not prompted by any personal distrust of you, but the jealousy which naturally exists towards the authorities of the United States under the present unhappy condition of the country.

This communication will be handed you by T. D. Merrick, General of First Division of the Arkansas Militia, who will call on you personally, accompanied by his staff, and who will receive from you your response.

Respectfully, your obedient servant,
HENRY M. RECTOR,
Governor of Arkansas.

Captain TOTTEN,
Commanding U. S. Arsenal, Little Rock, Ark.

This is the paper marked "A."

HENRY M. RECTOR,
Governor of Arkansas.
JAMES TOTTEN,
Captain, Second Artillery.

[Inclosure B.]
COUNCIL CHAMBER,
Little Rock, Ark., February 5, 1861-3 o'clock p. m.

Resolved as a sense of this council, That if there be any impending danger or necessity which requires the seizure of the U. S. Arsenal at head of the State, to order such seizure to be made by the organized military power of the State. But that all unauthorized attempts to seize the arsenal by persons without orders from the governor is an insult to his station and authority, and deserves the reprehension of all our people, and calculated to injure the cause of States rights, and we earnestly recommend the governor to interpose his authority to check any such movements if unauthorized by him.

Resolved, That a copy of these resolutions be immediately communicated to the governor, and that a committee, to consist of the whole council, be appointed for that purpose, and the same committee to communicate with the leaders of such movement.

C. P. BERTRAND,
Mayor pro tem.

Attest:
A. J. SMITH, *City Recorder.*

[Inclosure C.]
COUNCIL CHAMBER,
Little Rock, Ark., February, 6, 1861.

At a called meeting of the city council, held at 4 o'clock p. m. of this day-

Present: Charles P. Bertrand, mayor pro tem., and Aldermen Waid, Peary, Tucker, Watkins, Henry, Robins, and George-

The following preamble and resolutions were introduced by Alderman Geo. C. Watkins:

"Whereas an armed force of about four hundred men from different parts of this State are assembled at Little Rock for the purpose of seizing the U. S. Arsenal at this place, under the apprehension that the arsenal and the arms and the munitions of war stored therein may at no distant day be used to the injury of the people of this State, and it is reasonably certain that such force will soon be increased to one thousand men, or to five thousand, if necessary for the purpose designed;

"And whereas the governor of the State has on this day officially assumed the responsibility of said movement, and has made a demand in the name and by authority of the State upon the officer in command of the arsenal to surrender the same to the authorities of the State;

"And whereas the arsenal is so located that any attack or defense of it would involve the destruction of much of the property of private citizens of Little Rock, and the loss of many lives of our citizens, and the probable sacrifice of the officers and their command in charge of the arsenal: Therefore,

"*Resolved*, That this council do earnestly deprecate a hostile collision in their midst between the forces of the State and the United States troops stationed at the arsenal, and hope that same may be avoided if it can possibly be done consistently with a proper sense of duty and honor on the part of those upon whom rests the responsibility of a collision and the deplorable consequences that would inevitably result from it.

"*Resolved further*, That a copy of these resolutions be furnished to the governor of the State, and also a copy of the same of the officer in command of the arsenal at this place."

A true copy from the record:

Attest:
GORDON W. PEARY,
Acting Recorder pro tem.

[Inclosure D.]

"Whereas many good citizens of this State have come to Little Rock in obedience to what they supposed to be the orders of the governor, to assist in taking the U. S. Arsenal at this place; and whereas the governor disavows such orders as being without his authority or sanction: Therefore,

"*Resolved*, As the opinion of this meeting, that it is the duty of the governor to assume the responsibility of this movement or to interpose his authority and influence to prevent it.

"*Resolved further,* That in case there be, in opinion of the governor, any danger or necessity for seizing the arsenal, we earnestly recommend him, as the only way to prevent the effusion of blood, to order the same to be done in his official capacity and in the name and by authority of the State, and to that end that he make an official demand upon the officers in charge of the arsenal to surrender the same to the State authorities.

"*Resolved further,* That in our opinion the governor, as the executive head of the State, may rely upon the sympathy and co-operation of all good citizens in what he may do by authority of the State and her organized military power.

"The foregoing resolutions were, this 6th day of February, 1861, unanimously adopted by a mass meeting of the citizens of Little Rock, Arkansas.

"RICH'D H. JOHNSON,
"*Chairman.*

"JOHN D. KIMBELL, *Secretary.*"

CHOCTAW NATION,
February 7, 1861.[9]

We copy from the *South Western Democrat* resolutions passed by the General Council of the Choctaw Nation. We are glad to see our neighbors taking such a bold and manly position, and think that some of our own people might learn a lesson from them. The message of James Hudson, the principal chief, is an able paper, and we regret that we have not space to republish it. It takes the position boldly and unequivocally that in the event of a dissolution of the Union the Choctaw Nation will go with the Southern States. Read the resolutions below from the *South Western Democrat.*

Resolutions.

Expressing the feelings and sentiments of the General Council of the Choctaw Nation, in reference to the political disagreement existing between the northern and southern States of the American Union.

Resolved by the General Council of the Choctaw Nation, assembled,

---

9   *Arkansas Daily True Democrat,* March 12, 1861, Little Rock, Ar.

That we view with deep regret and great solicitude, the present unhappy political disagreement between the northern and southern States of the American Union, tending to a permanent dissolution of the government, and the disturbance of the various important relations existing with that government, by treaty, stipulations and international laws, portending much injury to the Choctaw government and people.

Resolved, further, that we express the earnest desire and ready hope entertained by the entire Choctaw people, that any and all political disturbances agitating and dividing the people of the various States may be honorably and speedily adjusted; and the example and the blessing, and fostering care of the general government, and the many and friendly social ties existing with their people, continue for the enlightenment in moral and good government; and prosperity in the material concerns of life, to our whole population.

Resolved, further, That in the event of a permanent dissolution of the American Union takes place, our many relations with the general government must cease, and we shall be left to follow the natural affections, education, institutions, and interest of our people, which indissolubly bind us in every way to the destiny of our neighbors, and brethren of the southern states; upon whom we are confident we can rely for the preservation of our rights, of liberty and property, continuance of friendship, general counsel and fraternal support.

Resolved, further, That we desire to assure our immediate neighbors, the people of Arkansas and Texas, of our determination to observe amicable relations in every way so long existing between us, and the firm reliance we have, that amid any disturbance with other States, the rights and feelings so sacred to us will remain respected by them, and be protected from the encroachment of others.

Resolved, further, That his excellency, the principal chief, be requested to enclose, with an appropriate communication from himself, a copy of these resolutions to the Governors of the southern States, with the request that they be laid before the State convention of each State, as many as have assembled at the date of their reception; and that in such as have not, they be published in the newspapers of the State.

Further enacted, That these resolutions take effect, and be in force from and after their passage. Approved Feb. 7th, 1861.

WASHINGTON, D.C.,
February 7, 1861.

CONFEDERATE CORRESPONDENCE, ETC.[10]

U. S. SENATE, Washington, February 7, 1861.
His Excellency H. M. RECTOR, Little Rock, Ark.:
The motives which impelled capture of forts [in] other States do not exist
in ours. It is all premature. We implore you prevent attack on arsenal if
Totten resists.

R. W. JOHNSON.
W. K. SEBASTIAN.

WASHINGTON, D.C.,
February 7, 1861.[11]

R. H. JOHNSON, JAMES B. JOHNSON, Little Rock:
Southern States which captured first were in the act of seeding, were
threatened with troops, and their ports and commerce endangered. Not so
with us. If Totten resists, for God's sake deliberate and go stop the
assault.

R. W. JOHNSON.

WASHINGTON, D.C.,
February 7, 1861.[12]

JOHN POPE, Esq., Little Rock, Ark.:
For God's sake to do not complicate matters by an attack. It will be
premature and do incalculable injury. We cannot justify it. The reasons
that existed elsewhere for seizure do not exist with us.

ALBERT PIKE.
R. W. JOHNSON.

---

10   OR,1(1):681
11   OR,1(1):681-82
12   OR,1(1):682

WASHINGTON, D.C.,
February 8, 1861.[13]

His Excellency Gov. HENRY M. RECTOR, Little Rock:
Don't attack arsenal unless success is certain. Repulse would be disgraceful. Pledge might be required not to remove or injure arms and munitions without notice. Please telegraph us.

R. W. JOHNSON.
T. C. HINDMAN.

WASHINGTON, D.C.,
February 9, 1861.[14]

U. S. SENATE, February 9, 1861.
R. H. JOHNSON, Little Rock, Ark.:
Arsenal yours. Thank God! Hold it. My address mailed to-night. Publish it quick. Peace Congress no use; failure.

R. W. JOHNSON.

LITTLE ROCK ARSENAL,
February 10, 1861.[15]

SIR: In answer to your telegram dated Washington, February 9, 1861, I this morning answered by telegraph as follows:
"I have retired with my command from Little Rock Arsenal, and the governor of Arkansas, in the name of the United States, has charge of all the public property, to hold the same until legally absolved from the trust. I have reported particulars by mail, and shall duplicate them, and explain the whole matter thoroughly. I shall order and proceed with my command to Saint Louis, where I beg that orders may be sent me for my future guidance."

I am, very respectfully, your obedient servant,
JAS. TOTTEN,
Captain, Second Artillery.
Colonel S. COOPER,
Adjutant-General U. S. Army, Washington City, D. C.

---

13   OR,1(1):683
14   OR,1(1):683
15   OR,1(1):646

LITTLE ROCK, Ark.,
February 12, 1861.[16]

ORDERS No.6

CAMP AT FLETCHER'S LANDING,
Vicinity of Little Rock, Ark., February 12, 1861.

This command, consisting of Company F, Second Artillery, and the enlisted men of the Ordnance Department formerly garrisoning Little Rock Arsenal, will embark to-day on the steamboat *Madora*, and proceed direct to Saint Louis, Mo., and report to the general commanding the Department of the West for orders as to its future movements.

JAMES TOTTEN,
Captain, Second Artillery, Commanding.

LITTLE ROCK ARSENAL,
February 12, 1861.[17]

LITTLE ROCK, ARK., *February* 12, 1861.

SIR: I have the honor herewith to inclose for the information of the President the originals of four papers relative to my withdrawal from Little Rock Arsenal with my command of the 8th instant.

I forwarded by mail copies of these papers on the 9th of this month, and now inclose the originals by General S. H. Hempstead, of Little Rock, a reliable gentleman, who has politely offered to deliver to you any communication I may wish to send.

For any additional information concerning my retiring from Little Rock I have the honor to refer you to my letters of previous dates. I shall also be most happy to explain any point relative to the matter which may not appear clear already from my past communications.

I beg also to refer to Adjutant-General to the bearer of this, General Hempstead, for much information which it did not appear to me necessary to make known officially. I refer more particularly here to the rumored action taken by the governor of Arkansas to collect forces at Little Rock for the purpose of seizing the arsenal, and also to the views of his conduct and that of his friends and counsellors, taken by the city of

---

[16]   OR,1(1):646
[17]   OR,1(1):642

Little Rock in its public meetings and the meetings of its council very recently.

I inclose a copy of my letter of transmittal of the 9th instant (inclosed then), with the copies of the original papers now forwarded. [Inclosure E.]

Very respectfully, your obedient servant,
JAS. TOTTEN,
Captain, Second Artillery.

ADJUTANT-GENERAL U. S. ARMY.

[Inclosure B.]

LITTLE ROCK ARSENAL,
Little Rock, Ark., February 6, 1861.

SIR: In the present trying circumstances by which the undersigned finds himself surrounded, as a Federal officer, he is anxious to learn officially from your excellency, before answering your demands for the surrender of the U. S. Arsenal at this place, the following important points, viz:

1st. If this arsenal and all the munitions of war stored therein are left instant as at the hour of 3 o'clock p. m. to-morrow, by the United States forces now in charge of them, will the governor of the States of Arkansas officially take charge of said arsenal and munitions of war in the name of the United States Government, and hold them in that light until future circumstances shall legally absolve him from the responsibility?

2nd. If the United States forces now garrisoning Little Rock Arsenal evacuate said post, and leave the munitions of war intact as at the hour of 3 o'clock p. m. to-morrow, will the governor of the State of Arkansas officially guarantee to said forces an unmolested passage through the State in any direction the officer commanding said troops may elect, and guarantee, moreover, to said forces that right of carrying with them all the public and private property they brought with them to said arsenal, all which has been purchased for or by them, and all which has been sent to them since stationed at said arsenal, consisting of ordnance and ordnance stores, clothing, camp and garrison equipage, and barracks and mess furniture, as also provisions and all their individual or private property.

3rd. If the arsenal and munitions of war stored therein are left intact as at the hour of 3 o'clock p. m. to-morrow, will the governor of Arkansas, in his official capacity, guarantee to the United States forces

32

now in charge therefore the right of marching away from said place with all the honor due to them as Federal officers and soldiers who do not surrender their trust, but simply evacuate a post for want of instructions from their superiors in office, and in doubt as to the propriety of bringing on civil war among their fellow-countrymen?

Explicit and entailed answers to each and every one of these questions will have great influence upon the undersigned in his answer to the communication of the governor of Arkansas, which is promised by 3 o'clock p. m. to-morrow.

I am, very respectfully,
JAMES TOTTEN,
Captain, Second Artillery, Commanding Post.

His Excellency HENRY M. RECTOR, *Governor of Arkansas.*

[Inclosure C.]
EXECUTIVE OFFICE,
Little Rock, Ark., February 7, 1861.

Captain JAMES TOTTEN, U. S. Army,
In charge of U. s. Arsenal, Little Rock:

SIR: Your communication of the 6th instant (yesterday), propounding to myself certain propositions, explicit and detailed answers to which would have great influence upon you in your answer promised the governor of Arkansas by 3 p. m. to-day, was received at about 11 o'clock this morning.

After mature reflection I propose to accept your first, second, and third propositions, with the following understanding: That being informed your command brought no cannon with you-so none are to be taken away. You shall have a safe passage out of the State in any direction you may please with your command, provided, however, you do not station yourself within the limits of the State of Arkansas or on the borders thereof.

Whatever your command, either of private or public property, brought with them you will be permitted to take away.

I have the honor to be, Captain, respectfully, your obedient servant,

HENRY M. RECTOR,
Governor of Arkansas.

[Inclosure D.]

LITTLE ROCK, ARK., *February* 8, 1861.
Memorandum this day made and signed by James Totten, Captain of Second Artillery, in the Army of the United States, and Henry M. Rector, governor of the State of Arkansas. This paper, marked A,*[see inclosure A Totten to Cooper, February 6, p. 640] signed by us, is the demand made by the governor upon Captain Totten for the delivery of the U. S. Arsenal at this place to the State authorities. The paper marked B, signed by us, is a copy of the response of Captain Totten to that communication. The paper marked C, signed by us, is the response of the governor accepting, as therein stated, the terms of the paper B.

It is further witnessed, that on this day, at the hour of 12 m., said Captain Totten, with his command, doth retire from said arsenal, and delivered the same, with all its stores, arms, and munitions of war, intact, to the governor of Arkansas, pursuant to the tenor and purport of said papers A, B, C. And the said Captain James Totten protests that he had thus acted because in the presence of a greatly superior armed force, and which he became satisfied would soon become overwhelming by re-enforcements in case of resistance, involving the sacrifice of his command, without regard to the probable loss of life on the part of the assailants; because any defense of the arsenal in the city of Little Rock, whether successful or unsuccessful, would necessarily involve, to a greater or less extent, the destruction of property in the city, and the loss of lives of the peaceful citizens and families dwelling therein; because, being without instructions from his Government, he took, of necessity, the responsibility of doing what he thought proper and best under all the circumstances, desiring to avoid cause of civil war in this Government, by the first instance of a hostile and bloody collision, yet protesting for himself and in the name of his Government against events beyond his control, and which have actuated him to this course.
(Signed in duplicate.)

HENRY M. RECTOR,
Governor of Arkansas.
JAS. TOTTEN,
Captain, Second Artillery, Commanding Little Rock arsenal.

LITTLE ROCK, ARK., *February* 9, 1861.

SIR: I have the honor herewith to inclose for the information of the President copies of four distinct papers relative to a solemn and ever-to-be-regretted act which had been force upon me through the necessities of the circumstances surrounding me. The papers marked A, B, C, and D explain the whole sad affair from beginning to end, in connection with information previously communicated, and comment on my part, therefore, seems unnecessary at present. I have been forced, as the inclosed papers will show, to retire with my command from Little Rock Arsenal, and yield my charge into the hands of Henry M. Rector, governor of the State of Arkansas, who has taken charge of the same in the name of the United States, to hold it in that light until legally absolved from the trust.

I hope I have acted in the whole matter in a manner which will meet the approbation of the Federal authorities. My object throughout these trying circumstances has been to avoid bringing about bloodshed and civil war in this immediate vicinity among peaceable, law-abiding, and loyal citizens of the United States. In doing so, I sincerely believe, in the absence of all instructions, I have only done what appears to be the course indicated by the present administration in this past course, so far as I am informed. It gratifies me beyond measure to be able, on this occasion, to bear honest testimony to the honorable, high-toned, loyal, and law-abiding action taken by the great majority of the most respectable citizens of Little Rock. From the richest to the poorest, I am happy to say, there was but one sentiment, and that was in opposition to the course of the governor and those who counseled and aided him in the deed done.

I am, very respectfully, your obedient servant,
JAS. TOTTEN,
Captain, Second Artillery, Commanding.

Colonel S. COOPER,
Adjutant-General U. S. Army, Washington City, D. C.

[Inclosure F.]

ORDERS No.3
HEADQUARTERS LITTLE ROCK ARSENAL,
Little Rock, Ark., February 8, 1861.
The troops of this command, consisting of Company F, Second Artillery, and all the enlisted men of the Ordnance Department, will be prepared to move to-day from this post to a camp to be selected by the commanding officer on the banks of the Arkansas River.

The command will depart as soon as the necessary transportation can be provided.

By order of Captain Totten:

ST. CLAIR DEARING,
Second Lieutenant, Second Artillery, Post Adjutant.

FORT SMITH, Ark.,
February 12, 1861.

No. 2.[18]

Report of Major Justus McKinstry, quartermaster, U. S. Army, of the seizure of U. S. ordnance stores at Napoleon, Ark.

ASSISTANT QUARTERMASTER'S OFFICE,
Saint Louis, Mo., February 12, 1861.
CAPTAIN: I have the honor to report, for the information of the general commanding, that I am in receipt of a telegram from Captain Montgomery, A. Q. M. at Fort Smith, Ark., informing me that a considerable amount of ordnance stores (list herewith inclosed), shipped by me on the 16th and 21st ultimo to Napoleon, Ark., en route for the posts on the Arkansas River, have been seized by certain individuals pretending to act for the State of Arkansas. As the State in question has passed no act of secession, or announced her withdrawal from the Union, I would respectfully recommend that orders be issued to my agents at Napoleon to take legal steps to recover the stores lost.

Very respectfully, your obedient servant,
J. MCKINSTRY, A. Q. M.

---

18   OR,1(1):646

Captain S. WILLIAMS, *Asst. Adjt. General,*
Headquarters Department of the West.

Shipment to Napoleon, Ark, per steamboat *Sunshine*, January 15, 1861:

Fourteen boxes, containing-

83 saddles; 166 stirrups; 83 saddle bags; 83 girths; 83 surcingles; 83 bridles, complete.

Shipment January 21, 1861, per steamboat *Southwester*:

One hundred and nineteen boxes [containing]-

40,000 .58 elongated-ball cartridges, percussion; 10,000 .58 rifle-musket blank cartridges, percussion; 20,000 Sharps' carbine-ball cartridges; 50,000 Colt's pistol-ball cartridges, R. B; 10,000 Colt's pistol blank cartridges.

J. MCKINSTRY, A. Q. M.
ASSISTANT QUARTERMASTER'S OFFICE,
February 12, 1861.

LITTLE ROCK, Ark.,
February 16, 1861.

Arkansas Correspondence.[19]

To the Editors of the Avalanche:

In redemption of the premise I made when I left your city, I proceed to drop you the first of a series of letters; although, at this moment, I have nothing of especial interest, not having had time to look around and see "how the land lies." At this momentous crisis in affairs of State, it seems idle to write of anything that has not a bearing upon the questions of secession, coercion, submission and civil war. But I trust you will permit me to drop a few words commendatory of our good boat, the *Fredric Notrebe*, and her worthy and gentlemanly officers, Capt. R. Haines, Messrs. Ed. W. Parker, E. G. Allen and E. S. Adams, her clerks. These gentlemen are the most courteous, attentive and accommodating that I have ever travelled with on any steamer. The *Notrebe* is of the largest class of stern-wheelers – entirely new, and well adapted for the trade she is in. She is well finished and furnished, and her cabin tastefully carpeted and decorated. Her state-rooms are large and airy, the

---

19   *The Avalanche*, February 16, 1861, Memphis, Tenn.

bedding clean and comfortable. As to her cuisine, I must say, emphatically, that she has as good a table as any craft afloat or ashore, hotel or steamer. We experienced all the comforts of a home, the disagreeable weather to the "contrary notwithstanding." Left Memphis at midnight on the 12th, and landed at Little Rock last night a little after dark. Laid by most of one night in Arkansas river on account of foul weather, and the other nights we were compelled to run slow on account of the innumerable obstructions to navigation in the shape of snags, or "Arkansaw tooth-picks," sand-bars, etc. The Arkansas is the grave-yard of steamboats, I should say, from the number of wrecks we passed, and places pointed out where others had perished. I noticed the wrecks of the *Frontier City, New Cedar Rapids, and Quapaw*, standing in water up to their cabin floors, at various places, some considerable distance apart.

In the spring time, a trip on this river must be one of considerable interest to the tourist. This is my first sight of Little Rock. I find the city to be much the same that I had expected to find it - not large, scattering, and covering space enough for a very populous city. The houses are quite small, and many of them wear the dingy marks of time.

On Monday, the election of delegates, and for a State Convention, occurs. If the Convention carries, provision has been made for its assembling on the Monday following (25th.) I hear that the Southern half of Arkansas is strong for immediate secession. If the movement is defeated, it will be in consequence of the apathy of the other part. But I hope and believe that Arkansas will show more pluck than did Tennessee; that she will be true to herself and her seceded sisters, and declare her independence before the 4th of March. More anon.

RAMROD.

LITTLE ROCK, Ark.,
February 21, 1861.[20]

An act to provide for defraying the expenses of commissioners to
purchase arms.

Whereas, the General Assembly has passed an act appointing a commission to purchase arms, accoutrements and so forth, for the State of Arkansas: And whereas, in passing said act no provision was made to pay such commissioners through the discharge of the duties imposed

---

[20]   Records of the General Assembly of Arkansas, 1861.

upon them by law, the commissioners must, of necessity, spend considerable amounts of money; Therefore, Be it enacted by The General Assembly of the State of Arkansas, That a sufficient sum be, and the same is hereby, appropriated out of any money in the treasury not otherwise appropriated by law, to defray the necessary expenses of said commissioners incurred in the discharge of duties imposed by law, and that the certificate of the Governor, or either of the commissioners, to the effect that he has actually expended the sums mentioned in their respective accounts in the discharge of the duties imposed upon him by law, shall be a sufficient authority for the Auditor to issue his warrant on the treasury in payment of the same.

Bradley Bunch
Speaker of the House of Representatives
Hon. Fletcher
President of the Senate

LITTLE ROCK, Ark.
February 22, 1861.[21]

To the SECRETARY OF WAR, *City of Washington, D.C.:*

We, the undersigned, citizens of Arkansas, learn with deep regret that the post of Fort Smith is to be abandoned by the General Government. It is fair to suppose that this order has been determined upon in consequence of the action of a mob in Little Rock and the unfortunate course of the governor in demanding from the United States officer, the arsenal.

The late decision of the people at the ballot-box has proved beyond question the almost unanimous voice in the counties adjoining Fort Smith for Union as against violence, mob law, and secession. We, therefore, in the name of the people, the whole people, ask a suspension of this movement until the decision of the State by its convention is known.

GEO. RUDDY *et al.*

---

21   OR,1(1):655

LITTLE ROCK, Ark.,
February 24, 1861.

LITTLE ROCK LETTER[22]

Puissant *Avalanche*: Again do I take my pen up to jot you down a few desultory lines, from the screaming State of Arkansas. I have been here in her capital nine days, and have rambled over much of the town. At the risk of repeating what others may have said, I will say something relative to the city. Little Rock is commandingly seated on an elevated, undulating tract on the south side of that crooked and treacherous river, the Arkansas, which at this point is about 400 yards wide, and maintains that width until somewhere towards its mouth, where it does not appear to be half so wide but much deeper. As to its buildings, they are as good as could be expected for a frontier town, though generally small and presenting a dingy appearance. When the railroad connections are completed, the rather Sleepy-Hollowish air that now seems to repose over it will be dispelled, every department of business quickened and re-animated, and large buildings supplant the small ones of the *ancien regime.*

The population of Little Rock I judge to be six or seven thousand. Its present growth has been attained without those powerful and life-giving accessories, railroads. The State continues to be deplorably deficient in facilities for travel, intercommunication, etc. It was but a few weeks since, (thanks to the enterprise and energy of H. A. Montgomery,) that this place was put in telegraphic connection with the rest of the world. There are, however, not a few commodious stores and warehouses, as well as large and handsome private mansions. Worthy of note among the latter are the residences of Mrs. Chester Ashley, and Captain Pike, of legal, literary, and martial fame. The Arsenal of our late Uncle Sam is back in the suburbs, half a mile from the river, in a southeastern direction and is the handsomest situation I have noticed. The buildings are of brick, substantially built, stuccoed, and of the usual castellated style of a spacious plot, tastefully laid off with walks and drives, sown in grass and ornamented with pine, aspen, sycamore, arbor vitae, etc.

---

22   *The Avalanche*, March 2, 1861, Memphis, Tenn.

It is still in the custody of the redoubtable militia of Arkansas – one company garrisoning it. The stars and stripes no longer wave over its ramparts. On the ever-glorious anniversary of Washington's birth, the volunteer military paraded the streets, (a company of horse and one of foot,) and at noon a salute of fifteen guns were fired at the Arsenal. Let us, amid all our troubles and vicissitudes, and transformations, ever honor and cherish the name, the memory, the immortal deeds of that great Southerner.

The State-house stands on the bank of the river; is a two-story edifice, stuccoed, of moderate proportions for its character, and in somewhat of a dilapidated condition. In the line of churches, there are many – every denomination, I believe, being represented. Hotels are numerous, but of a small class, yet equal, I imagine, to the demands of the public. There are at this time only three newspapers published here – the *True Democrat*, Secession; the *State Gazette*, Union; and the *Arkansas Baptist*. Each of these have an excellent outfit of cylinder presses, jobbers, etc., and are in a prosperous condition. Other newspapers that were commenced here recently have *caved*.

The shipping interest of this port is more extensive than I had imagined. Last week there was scarcely a day that I did not observe at least a half dozen steamboats at the landing, discharging dry goods, groceries and produce, and receiving "the staple." Some of these are large, commodious side-wheel boats, with elegant cabins, and capable of carrying 3,500 bales of cotton – such as the *Judge Fletcher, Tycoon* and *35th Parallel*.

There are lines to Memphis, St. Louis, Louisville and Cincinnati, and New Orleans. That in the Little Rock and Memphis trade is too well known to you to require further mention, besides I have paid them my compliments in a former letter. My favorite, the *Fred. Notrebe*, arrived to-day and leaves tomorrow morning. I commend the boat, the officers, and her fare to the traveling public as *au fait*. The Arkansas is now in excellent boating order.

The State Convention assembles here on the 4th March. There is more of the submission sentiment in this city than elsewhere in the State, much more than I had anticipated. They say they think they have carried the State, but I do not think so, and certainly hope not. If they have, they have placed Arkansas in a false, disgraceful attitude. Her interests are entirely bound up with those of the Southern Confederacy, more especially with New Orleans; and surely if Louisiana could take the step,

41

Arkansas need not hesitate. In doing so she had to make sacrifices and dare consequences, which, in extent and character, are common to no other one of the seceding States.

Look at what she risked and dared. In allying her fortunes to those of a Southern Confederacy, the policy of which is free trade or a greatly modified tariff system, Louisiana foresaw the probable sacrifice of her staple interest of agriculture and industry, sugar production and manufacture – liberally protected and encouraged by the tariff of the late Union. Her sugar planters recked not of this, but patriotically put in their straight Secession co-operation tickets, ignoring the consideration of millions of dollars assured them by the late regime.

That is what was directly sacrificed, and what was risked more. The interests of New Orleans – the commercial metropolis alike of Louisiana and the South – are inseparably connected with those of the West and Northwest.

By this connection her commerce thrives, wealth increases, population grows. Separation from those producing regions risks the vast considerations involved in such interests, and yet New Orleans returned an overwhelming majority of straight out Secessionists – five to one. The citizens of New Orleans, constituting about one-third of the population of the State, felt all the ties of commercial relations and social intercourse with the citizens of the West and Northwest, and yet they went for co-operation with their brethren of the South, five to one. They risked the prosperity of their vast foreign commerce and all the dependent interests of their great emporium, and yet they went with the other Southern States by five to one.

Why, then, should Arkansas or Tennessee hesitate? From their geographical situation they have not, nay, nothing like the responsibility, the sacrifice to make that Louisiana had. But let us hope that they will soon burst the bonds of apathy and lethargy, and, rising in their sovereignty, appreciating fully the dangers that confront them, nobly assert their independence, and with those gallant States whose destines... are mutual, congenial, and homogeneous.

RAMROD.

LITTLE ROCK, Ark.
March 2, 1861.
PROCLAMATION BY THE GOVERNOR.[23]
STATE OF ARKANSAS.

To the Delegates elected to the State Convention
in said State- GREETING:

Whereas, The General Assembly of the State of Arkansas, on the 15th day of January, 1861, passed an act entitled "An act to provide for a State Convention," to be held in the capitol, on the 4th of March, 1861; provided, a majority of all the votes cast on the 18th day of February, 1861, the day of election designated by said act, should be for a convention; *And whereas,* in pursuance of said act, and a proclamation of the governor, issued to the sheriffs of the several counties in this state, on the 16th day of January, 1861, said election was held on the 18th day of February, 1861; *And whereas,* it appears upon counting the votes cast, that a majority of eleven thousand five hundred and eighty-six are "for convention."

Therefore, I, Henry M. Rector, in virtue of authority in me vested by said act, authorize and direct said delegates elected for the several counties, to assemble in convention at the capitol, on the 4th day of March, 1861, for the objects and purposes, by said act of the General Assembly, intended.

In testimony whereof, I have hereunto set my hand, and caused the seal of the State of Arkansas to be affixed at Little Rock, this 2d day of March, A.D. 1861.

HENRY M. RECTOR

WASHINGTON, D.C.,
March 4, 1861.
President Lincoln's First Inaugural Address.

Fellow-citizens of the United States: In compliance with a custom as old as the government itself, I appear before you to address you briefly, and to take in your presence the oath prescribed by the Constitution of the United States to be taken by the President "before he enters on the execution of his office."

---

23   "Journal of The Convention of the State of Arkansas", Little Rock, Ark., 1881, p. 5

I do not consider it necessary at present for me to discuss those matters of administration about which there is no special anxiety or excitement.

Apprehension seems to exist among the people of the Southern States that by the accession of a Republican administration their property and their peace and personal security are to be endangered. There has never been any reasonable cause for such apprehension. Indeed, the most ample evidence to the contrary has all the while existed and been open to their inspection. It is found in nearly all the published speeches of him who now addresses you. I do but quote from one of those speeches when I declare that "I have no purpose, directly or indirectly, to interfere with the institution of slavery in the States where it exists. I believe I have no lawful right to do so, and I have no inclination to do so." Those who nominated and elected me did so with full knowledge that I had made this and many similar declarations, and had never recanted them. And, more than this, they placed in the platform for my acceptance, and as a law to themselves and to me, the clear and emphatic resolution which I now read:

Resolved, That the maintenance inviolate of the rights of the States, and especially the right of each State to order and control its own domestic institutions according to its own judgment exclusively, is essential to that balance of power on which the perfection and endurance of our political fabric depend, and we denounce the lawless invasion by armed force of the soil of any State or Territory, no matter under what pretext, as among the gravest of crimes.

I now reiterate these sentiments; and, in doing so, I only press upon the public attention the most conclusive evidence of which the case is susceptible, that the property, peace, and security of no section are to be in any wise endangered by the now incoming administration. I add, too, that all the protection which, consistently with the Constitution and the laws, can be given, will be cheerfully given to all the States when lawfully demanded, for whatever cause - as cheerfully to one section as to another.

There is much controversy about the delivering up of fugitives from service or labor. The clause I now read is as plainly written in the Constitution as any other of its provisions:

No person held to service or labor in one State, under the laws thereof, escaping into another, shall in consequence of any law or regulation therein be discharged from such service or labor, but shall be delivered up on claim of the party to whom such service or labor may be due.

It is scarcely questioned that this provision was intended by those who made it for the reclaiming of what we call fugitive slaves; and the intention of the lawgiver is the law. All members of Congress swear their support to the whole Constitution - to this provision as much as to any other. To the proposition, then, that slaves whose cases come within the terms of this clause "shall be delivered up," their oaths are unanimous. Now, if they would make the effort in good temper, could they not with nearly equal unanimity frame and pass a law by means of which to keep good that unanimous oath?

There is some difference of opinion whether this clause should be enforced by national or by State authority; but surely that difference is not a very material one. If the slave is to be surrendered, it can be of but little consequence to him or to others by which authority it is done. And should anyone in any case be content that his oath shall go unkept on a merely unsubstantial controversy as to how it shall be kept?

Again, in any law upon this subject, ought not all the safeguards of liberty known in civilized and humane jurisprudence to be introduced, so that a free man be not, in any case, surrendered as a slave? And might it not be well at the same time to provide by law for the enforcement of that clause in the Constitution which guarantees that "the citizen of each State shall be entitled to all privileges and immunities of citizens in the several States."

I take the official oath to-day with no mental reservations, and with no purpose to construe the Constitution or laws by any hypercritical rules. And while I do not choose now to specify particular acts of Congress as proper to be enforced, I do suggest that it will be much safer for all, both in official and private stations, to conform to and abide by all those acts which stand unrepealed, than to violate any of them, trusting to find impunity in having them held to be unconstitutional.

It is seventy-two years since the first inauguration of a President under our National Constitution. During that period fifteen different and greatly distinguished citizens have, in succession, administered the executive branch of the government. They have conducted it through many perils, and generally with great success. Yet, with all this scope of precedent, I now enter upon the same task for the brief constitutional term of four years under great and peculiar difficulty. A disruption of the Federal Union, heretofore only menaced, is now formidably attempted.

I hold that, in contemplation of universal law and of the Constitution, the Union of these States is perpetual. Perpetuity is implied, if not expressed, in the fundamental law of all national governments. It is safe to assert that no government proper ever had a provision in its organic law for its own termination. Continue to execute all the express provisions of our National Constitution, and the Union will endure forever—it being impossible to destroy it except by some action not provided for in the instrument itself.

Again, if the United States be not a government proper, but an association of States in the nature of contract merely, can it, as a contract, be peaceably unmade by less than all the parties who made it? One party to a contract may violate it - break it, so to speak; but does it not require all to lawfully rescind it?

Descending from these general principles, we find the proposition that, in legal contemplation the Union is perpetual confirmed by the history of the Union itself. The Union is much older than the Constitution. It was formed, in fact, by the Articles of Association in 1774. It was matured and continued by the Declaration of Independence in 1776. It was further matured, and the faith of all the then thirteen States expressly plighted and engaged that it should be perpetual, by the Articles of Confederation in 1778. And, finally, in 1787 one of the declared objects for ordaining and establishing the Constitution was "to form a more perfect Union."

But if the destruction of the Union by one or by a part only of the States be lawfully possible, the Union is less perfect than before the Constitution, having lost the vital element of perpetuity.

It follows from these views that no State upon its own mere motion can lawfully get out of the Union; that resolves and ordinances to that effect are legally void; and that acts of violence, within any State or States, against the authority of the United States, are insurrectionary or revolutionary, according to circumstances.

I therefore consider that, in view of the Constitution and the laws, the Union is unbroken; and to the extent of my ability I shall take care, as the Constitution itself expressly enjoins upon me, that the laws of the Union be faithfully executed in all the States. Doing this I deem to be only a simple duty on my part; and I shall perform it so far as practicable, unless my rightful masters, the American people, shall withhold the requisite means, or in some authoritative manner direct the contrary. I trust this will not be regarded as a menace, but only as the declared purpose of the Union that it will constitutionally defend and maintain itself.

In doing this there needs to be no bloodshed or violence; and there shall be none, unless it be forced upon the national authority. The power confided to me will be used to hold, occupy, and possess the property and places belonging to the government, and to collect the duties and imposts; but beyond what may be necessary for these objects, there will be no invasion, no using of force against or among the people anywhere. Where hostility to the United States, in any interior locality, shall be so great and universal as to prevent competent resident citizens from holding the Federal offices, there will be no attempt to force obnoxious strangers among the people for that object. While the strict legal right may exist in the government to enforce the exercise of these offices, the attempt to do so would be so irritating, and so nearly impracticable withal, that I deem it better to forego for the time the uses of such offices.

The mails, unless repelled, will continue to be furnished in all parts of the Union. So far as possible, the people everywhere shall have that sense of perfect security which is most favorable to calm thought and reflection. The course here indicated will be followed unless current events and experience shall show a modification or change to be proper, and in every case and exigency my best discretion will be exercised according to circumstances actually existing, and with a view and a hope of a peaceful solution of the national troubles and the restoration of fraternal sympathies and affections.

That there are persons in one section or another who seek to destroy the Union at all events, and are glad of any pretext to do it, I will neither affirm nor deny; but if there be such, I need address no word to them. To those, however, who really love the Union may I not speak?

Before entering upon so grave a matter as the destruction of our national fabric, with all its benefits, its memories, and its hopes, would it not be wise to ascertain precisely why we do it? Will you hazard so desperate a step while there is any possibility that any portion of the ills you fly from have no real existence? Will you, while the certain ills you fly to are greater than all the real ones you fly from - will you risk the commission of so fearful a mistake?

All profess to be content in the Union if all constitutional rights can be maintained. Is it true, then, that any right, plainly written in the Constitution, has been denied? I think not. Happily the human mind is so constituted that no party can reach to the audacity of doing this. Think, If you can, of a single instance in which a plainly written provision of the Constitution has ever been denied. If by the mere force of numbers a majority should deprive a minority of any clearly written constitutional right, it might, in a moral point of view, justify revolution - certainly would if such a right were a vital one. But such is not our case. All the vital rights of minorities and of individuals are so plainly assured to them by affirmations and negations, guarantees and prohibitions, in the Constitution, that controversies never arise concerning them. But no organic law can ever be framed with a provision specifically applicable to every question which may occur in practical administration. No foresight can anticipate, nor any document of reasonable length contain, express provisions for all possible questions. Shall fugitives from labor be surrendered by national or by State authority? The Constitution does not expressly say. *May* Congress prohibit slavery in the Territories? The Constitution does not expressly say. *Must* Congress protect slavery in the Territories? The Constitution does not expressly say.

From questions of this class spring all our constitutional controversies, and we divide upon them into majorities and minorities. If the minority will not acquiesce, the majority must, or the government must cease. There is no other alternative; for continuing the government is acquiescence on one side or the other.

If a minority in such case will secede rather than acquiesce, they make a precedent which in turn will divide and ruin them; for a minority of their own will secede from them whenever a majority refuses to be controlled by such minority. For instance, why may not any portion of a new confederacy a year or two hence arbitrarily secede again, precisely as portions of the present Union now claim to secede from it? All who cherish disunion sentiments are now being educated to the exact temper of doing this.

Is there such perfect identity of interests among the States to compose a new Union, as to produce harmony only, and prevent renewed secession?

Plainly, the central idea of secession is the essence of anarchy. A majority held in restraint by constitutional checks and limitations, and always changing easily with deliberate changes of popular opinions and sentiments, is the only true sovereign of a free people. Whoever rejects it does, of necessity, fly to anarchy or to despotism. Unanimity is impossible; the rule of a minority, as a permanent arrangement, is wholly

48

inadmissible; so that, rejecting the majority principle, anarchy or despotism in some form is all that is left.

I do not forget the position, assumed by some, that constitutional questions are to be decided by the Supreme Court; nor do I deny that such decisions must be binding, in any case, upon the parties to a suit, as to the object of that suit, while they are also entitled to very high respect and consideration in all parallel cases by all other departments of the government. And while it is obviously possible that such decision may be erroneous in any given case, still the evil effect following it, being limited to that particular case, with the chance that it may be overruled and never become a precedent for other cases, can better be borne than could the evils of a different practice. At the same time, the candid citizen must confess that if the policy of the government, upon vital questions affecting the whole people, is to be irrevocably fixed by decisions of the Supreme Court, the instant they are made, in ordinary litigation between parties in personal actions, the people will have ceased to be their own rulers, having to that extent practically resigned their government into the hands of that eminent tribunal. Nor is there in this view any assault upon the court or the judges. It is a duty from which they may not shrink to decide cases properly brought before them, and it is no fault of theirs if others seek to turn their decisions to political purposes.

One section of our country believes slavery is right, and ought to be extended, while the other believes it is wrong, and ought not to be extended. This is the only substantial dispute. The fugitive-slave clause of the Constitution, and the law for the suppression of the foreign slave-trade, are each as well enforced, perhaps, as any law can ever be in a community where the moral sense of the people imperfectly supports the law itself. The great body of the people abide by the dry legal obligation in both cases, and a few break over in each. This, I think, cannot be perfectly cured; and it would be worse in both cases after the separation of the sections than before. The foreign slave-trade, now imperfectly suppressed, would be ultimately revived, without restriction, in one section, while fugitive slaves, now only partially surrendered, would not be surrendered at all by the other.

Physically speaking, we cannot separate. We cannot remove our respective sections from each other, nor build an impassable wall between them. A husband and wife may be divorced, and go out of the presence and beyond the reach of each other; but the different parts of our country cannot do this. They cannot but remain face to face, and intercourse, either amicable or hostile, must continue between them. Is it possible, then, to make that intercourse more advantageous or more satisfactory after separation than before? Can aliens make treaties easier than friends can make laws? Can treaties be more faithfully enforced between aliens than laws can among friends? Suppose you go to war, you cannot fight always; and when, after much loss on both sides, and no gain on either, you cease fighting, the identical old questions as to terms of intercourse are again upon you.

This country, with its institutions, belongs to the people who inhabit it. Whenever they shall grow weary of the existing government, they can exercise their constitutional right of amending it, or their revolutionary right to dismember or overthrow it. I cannot be ignorant of the fact that many worthy and patriotic citizens are desirous of having the National Constitution amended. While I make no recommendation of amendments, I fully recognize the rightful authority of the people over the whole subject, to be exercised in either of the modes prescribed in the instrument itself; and I should, under existing circumstances, favor rather than oppose a fair opportunity being afforded the people to act upon it. I will venture to add that to me the convention mode seems preferable, in that it allows amendments to originate with the people themselves, instead of only permitting them to take or reject propositions originated by others not especially chosen for the purpose, and which might not be precisely such as they would wish to either accept or refuse. I understand a proposed amendment to the Constitution - which amendment, however, I have not seen - has passed Congress, to the effect that the Federal Government shall never interfere with the domestic institutions of the States, including that of persons held to service. To avoid misconstruction of what I have said, I depart from my purpose not to speak of particular amendments so far as to say that, holding such a provision to now be implied constitutional law, I have no objection to its being made express and irrevocable.

The chief magistrate derives all his authority from the people, and they have conferred none upon him to fix terms for the separation of the States. The people themselves can do this also if they choose; but the executive, as such, has nothing to do with it. His duty is to administer the present government, as it came to his hands, and to transmit it, unimpaired by him, to his successor.

Why should there not be a patient confidence in the ultimate justice of the people? Is there any better or equal hope in the world? In our present differences is either party without faith of being in the right? If the Almighty Ruler of Nations, with his eternal truth and justice, be on your side of the North, or on yours of the South, that truth and that justice will surely prevail by the judgment of this great tribunal of the American people.

By the frame of the government under which we live, this same people have wisely given their public servants but little power for mischief; and have, with equal wisdom, provided for the return of that little to their own hands at very short intervals. While the people retain their virtue and vigilance, no administration, by any extreme of wickedness or folly, can very seriously injure the government in the short space of four years.

My countrymen, one and all, think calmly and well upon this whole subject. Nothing valuable can be lost by taking time. If there be an object to hurry any of you in hot haste to a step which you would never take deliberately, that object will be frustrated by taking time; but no good object can be frustrated by it. Such of you as are now dissatisfied, still have the old Constitution unimpaired, and, on the sensitive point, the laws of your own framing under it; while the new administration will have no immediate power, if it would, to change either. If it were admitted that you who are dissatisfied hold the right side in the dispute, there still is no single good reason for precipitate action. Intelligence, patriotism, Christianity, and a firm reliance on Him who has never yet forsaken this favored land, are still competent to adjust in the best way all our present difficulty.

In your hands, my dissatisfied fellow-countrymen, and not in mine, is the momentous issue of civil war. The government will not assail you. You can have no conflict without being yourselves the aggressors. You have no oath registered in heaven to destroy the government, while I shall have the most solemn one to "preserve, protect, and defend it."

I am loath to close. We are not enemies, but friends. We must not be enemies. Though passion may have strained, it must not break our bonds of affection. The mystic chords of memory, stretching from every battle-field and patriot grave to every living heart and hearthstone all over this broad land, will yet swell the chorus of the Union when again touched, as surely they will be, by the better angels of our nature.

LITTLE ROCK, Ark.,
March 4, 1861.

DISPATCH FROM LITTLE ROCK[24]

To the Editors of the Avalanche:

Convention met at nine A.M. A temporary organization effected. During the roll call proceedings were suspended in consequence of a tie vote in Fulton county. Mr. Turner is President pro tem. Although the convention was carried by upwards of 11,000 majority, there is a small majority of Union delegates. But it is confidently expected that a secession ordinance will pass. Adjourned at one o'clock, to meet tomorrow morning.

Brewer.

LITTLE ROCK, Ark.,
March 4, 1861.

Arkansas State Convention.[25]

To the Editors of the Avalanche:

Our State Convention assembled at the capitol to-day at 10 o'clock, and organized without little difficulty…Generally classed, the members may be said to stand thus: Thirty-five unconditional Secessionists and forty Union men. Among this latter class, however, there are many, who are styled "conditional Secessionists" – this is to say, men whose future action, in reference to secession, will depend much upon the happening of events which may transpire during the session of the Convention.

For the purpose of organizing, the Union men of all shades caucused and acted together, and succeeded in electing a President and all the other officers of the Convention. Hon. David Walker, of Washington, was chosen as President. He is rather a strong Union man; and all the other officers elected are of the same stripe.

This preliminary action of the Convention, however, is not disheartening to the secession men, for, as I said before, there are many among the Union men who, it is well known, can and will be brought to vote for an ordinance of Secession whenever it can be demonstrated, as soon it must be to every intelligent mind, that there is no longer a hope of getting a recognition and enforcement of our rights from Mr. Lincoln's Administration or the people of the North in the old Union.

---

24   *The Avalanche,* March 5, 1861, Memphis, Tenn.
25   *The Avalanche,* March 9, 1861, Memphis, Tenn.

The unfortunate and unexpected course of your State has had its legitimate effect upon the minds and action of our people; but we hope to see that soon overcome by the more powerful counteraction which we are led to expect from Virginia and the other border States.

I shall endeavor to keep you posted with regard to the more important doings of the Convention.

Yours truly,
PALMETTO.

LITTLE ROCK, Ark.,
March 5, 1861.

Second Day.[26]

To the Editors of the Avalanche:

Most of the session to-day was consumed in perfecting organization. On the question of appointing committees, and as to the extent of their duties, a desultory debate ensued, which gave some indication of the speaking talent of the Convention. The Secessionists, though numerically in a small majority, have a vast preponderance in point of talent and ability. Among the most prominent members on that side may, without invidious distinction, be named Messrs. Adams and Hanley of Phillips; Grace and Yell, of Jefferson; Flannigan, of Clark; Gould, of Bradley; Patterson, of Jackson; Johnson, of Desha; Hilliard, of Chicot, and others. On the side of the Union members, there are but few prominent and well known men of the State, Messrs. Thomason and Turner, of Crawford; Walker, of Washington, and Garland, of Pulaski, being about all they can muster under that head. There are many other good speakers, however, on both sides.

The Union men, both in and out of the State, are making strong efforts to defeat the secession of the State. The Hall to-day was flooded with printed copies of a telegraphic dispatch from Memphis, signed by D. C. Cross, W. H. Carroll, and J. H. McMahon, and addressed to Thos. H. Bradley, Union delegate from Crittenden county. The dispatch is dated 5th of March, and reads as follows: "Lincoln's Inauguration is decidedly and clearly peaceful. True copy of Peace Congress adjustment shows it reasonable and just. Tennessee Commissioners sanguine that Rhode Island, New Jersey, Pennsylvania, Ohio, Indiana, Illinois, and

---

26   *The Avalanche,* March 5, 1861, Memphis, Tenn.

New York will adopt the adjustment. Union members of the Virginia Convention satisfied." When you receive this you can better judge of the truth of this dispatch, and if the justness of the influence which it was designed to exert. We have much to fear from the officious intermeddling of these outside busy-bodies...

LITTLE ROCK, Ark.,
March 6, 1861.

Arkansas State Convention.[27]

To the Editors of the Avalanche

Nothing was done yesterday in the Convention, the preliminary business, organization etc., being on hand. A committee of thirteen was appointed to consider and report what action is proper in the disturbed condition of the country, that Arkansas should take.

This morning the Convention was called to order at 10 A.M. After prayer by the chaplain, the President laid before the body the credentials of Commissioner Spain, from South Carolina, to this Convention. Accompanying his credentials were the ordinance of secession and other documents. On motion the documents were read and laid on the table to be considered when the Convention shall be thoroughly organized, which will be to-morrow or the day after. The Commissioner was invited to a seat on the floor and a committee appointed to wait upon him and inform him of the action of the Convention.

The President then presented similar papers from the Commissioner of the State of Georgia, and the same action was had thereon, and similar courtesies extended. The Commissioner from Georgia is Mr. D. P. Hill. These gentlemen will doubtless address the Convention to-morrow, or at an early day. The report of the committee appointed yesterday to prepare rules for the government of the body was then made. Most of the time was consumed by members in discussing the various rules. The "previous question" machinery, which is a part of all the codes for parliamentary government, was left out, or ignored in the report...

RAMROD.

---

27   *The Avalanche*, March 11, 1861, Memphis, Tenn.

**LITTLE ROCK, Ark.,
March 6, 1861.**

Special Correspondence of the *Avalanche*
Arkansas State Convention. [28]

To the Editors of the Avalanche:

The Convention met at 10 A.M. After some debate on the rules as published, the President announced the Committee. Three to wait on the Governor for information as to the condition of State and Federal affairs.

A resolution was offered that the Committee on Federal Relations be instructed to report immediately on Ordinance of Secession.

Mr. Hanley moved that it be made the special of the day for Tuesday next.

The Delegate from Desha was for immediate action. They were sent here to pass an ordinance; the sentiment of the people; in his opinion, was at this moment ripe for it, and nothing less, he thought, would satisfy a majority of the people of Arkansas. What has this Convention to do? For what was it called? Certainly not to change the Constitution of Arkansas. We have seen the Inaugural of Lincoln. Boldly has he shown his hand, and the friends of Southern rights, Southern citizens had nothing whatever to expect from his moderation or conservatism. That conservatism was all imaginary. A rabid and radical, revolutionary, abolition administration was now organizing, and in his opinion, in ten days, civil war, with all its dark train of attendant horrors and calamities dire, would be precipitated on the country. The gentlemen of the other side of the Convention were as well prepared, he believed, as they ever would be. The country is in great peril, and the people of Arkansas were anxious that something decisive should be done. He was opposed to deferring until Tuesday. Let us go to work to-day.

Mr. Cypert said that he was for immediate action. The next breeze that sweeps from the North may bring the clash of contending foeman, and the peaceful waters of Charleston harbor be stirred by hostile fleets. The momentous time has arrived, and gentlemen intend to vote for the ordinance to take Arkansas out of the Union, let them say so at once.

---

28   *The Avalanche*, March 13, 1861, Memphis, Tenn.

One of the delegates from Washington advocated delay, but gave a different reason from those usually advocating it; the voting down of an ordinance at this stage, he said, would have a baneful influence at the North. If we do it, let us do it after a full... rate consideration of the question in all its hearings. He did not believe there was a member of this Convention who indorsed the Republican party, or sympathized with it in the remotest degree.

One of the delegates from Hempstead replied to a remark made by a delegate as to waiting to investigate, to confer, and to inquire into the resources of Arkansas. He wanted to know what the gentlemen meant? Does he mean that if we find ourselves poor we must submit? He could say for himself that he was for immediate and unconditional secession. He wished to unite the destinies of Arkansas with those of her sister States of the sunny South.

Mr. Patterson, of Jackson, (Secessionist) said that his mind was completely made up. He was ready to act now; yet he thought precipitation impolitic. So anxious was he for the success of the Secession Ordinance that he was unwilling to do anything that might endanger its fate. If gentlemen of the other side had not, like him, decided what course to take in this vital matter, he was for yielding [his] time. As for himself, he was for secession firmly, thoroughly, boldly. He thought our friends on the other side came here for the same great and patriotic purpose that we did – for the welfare, the safety and honor of Arkansas. Towards them he counseled conciliation. We are acting for the final destiny of a great State, and upon our action depends the welfare and happiness of generations yet unborn. If there was any reason why this debate should be deferred, we should listen to it. But when gentlemen were ready to act, he was ready to go as far as the farthest. He would like, in passing this momentous measure, to have it done unanimously, if possible. Once and for all, he was for secession.

Mr. Garland, of Pulaski, offered a resolution that the committee on Ordinances and Resolutions be instructed to report their views as to the proper course it is the duty of Arkansas to pursue, in the present condition of national affairs, as early as practicable which, after some debate, he withdrew.

A delegate said that the resolution offered yesterday by Fishback, to the effect that we would resist coercion, amounted to nothing; he was opposed to dealing in generalities. Mr. Thomason, of Crawford, (Unionist,) combatted the ideas of those who proclaimed that their minds were made up. He was also ready at any moment for the question. A delegate from Philips, said that whilst his own mind was made up, whilst he deemed it the only course, constituent with her safety and honor, for Arkansas to secede from the late Union, yet he was in favor of granting to the other side ample time for deliberation. He wished not to see precipitation, as it was a matter of more importance and gravity than any we had ever acted upon, or probably ever would.

Mr. Garland, of Pulaski, was ready to vote now, and to vote with great joy against any secession – was, however, for delay, at the instance of others. Another delegate declared with some vehemence, that he was for immediate action, so far as he was individually concerned. He represented a constituency who were nearly unanimous for secession, and that instantly, he was prepared to vote for the Ordinance – he would consider it the proudest moment of his life. In doing so, he would leave a monument that his children and posterity would honor.

Mr. Yell, of Jefferson, urged deliberation. He wanted our Union friends to make up their minds and go along with us. He was for making the Ordinance of Secession the order of the day for Tuesday next. He remarked on the great importance of the issue.

A delegate said the people of Arkansas never would submit to the program of Lincoln. The sentiment was loudly applauded in the gallery and lobby. He said, we are called upon to take common ground against a common enemy. We shall see in less than sixty days a people unanimous in sentiment and in arms, ready to resist to the last extremity, the fantastical, tyrannical despotism which has seized the Federal Government, and now wields it for the destruction and degradation of the Southern people. The Ordinance of Secession was made the special order for the next Tuesday.

Mr. Garland moved that the use of the Hall be tendered to certain distinguished gentlemen from other Southern States, at present in the city, who were desirous of addressing the Convention and citizens upon the great issue of the day. Motion agreed to unanimously.

Messrs. Spain, of South Carolina, and Hill, of Georgia, Commissioners, and Col. R. G. Payne, of Tennessee, are the gentlemen expected to make addresses. I learn that Col. Payne will speak to-night in the Representatives Hall.

The Arkansas delegation in Congress are looked for daily. By resolution, they were voted seats within the bar.

Mr. Laughinghouse, of St. Francis, offered the following, which was referred to the Committee on Federal Relations:

"Resolved, That in the opinion of this Convention, any attempt on the part of the Federal Government to retake the forts, arsenals, or public property, to collect the revenue, or to enforce the laws in any of the Sates that have seceded or withdrawn from the Federal Union, will amount to coercion on the part of the Federal Government, and will justify or warrant resistance by those States, and will meet with the unqualified disapprobation of this Convention and the people of this State, justifying as fully in our own consciences, and, as we believe, in the estimation of the civilized world, in severing the ligaments which unite us to a Government so unjust and so unmindful of its obligations to those governed, and so disposed to usurp and assume the exercise of powers not delegated by the Constitution under which it arrogates to act."

The following is a copy of an ordinance of secession, introduced in the Arkansas Convention to-day (March 8th) by Mr. Floyd, of Johnson:

AN ORDINANCE- To dissolve the Union between the State of Arkansas and the other States united with her under the company entitled "The Constitution of the United States."

We, the people of the State of Arkansas in Convention assemble, do declare and ordain, and is hereby declared and ordained, that the acceptance of the compact by the General Assembly of Arkansas, approved on the 18th of October, A.D., 1836, in pursuance of an act of the Congress of the United States of America, which was approved on the 23rd of June, A.D., 1836, and authorized by the people of the State of Arkansas, by which the sovereign State of Arkansas became a party to the Federal Compact under the Constitution of the United States of America, and all laws and ordinances by which the State of Arkansas became a member of the Federal Union, be, and the same are hereby repealed and abrogated, and that the Union now subsisting between the State of Arkansas and other States, under the name of the United States of America, is hereby dissolved.

We do further declare and ordain, that all rights required and vested under the Constitution of the United States, or any act of Congress, or treaty, or under any law of this State, and not incompatible with this ordinance shall remain in full force and have the same effect as if this ordinance had not been penned.

Without debate, the ordinance was referred to the Committee on Federal Relations, and the Convention adjourned at three o'clock.

PINE BLUFF, Ark.,
March 9, 1861.[29]

Gov H.M. Rector
    Dear Sir, [Mr.] Fish, having resigned his position as Lieut. Col. of 24th Regiment, I ordered in pursuance of Statewide requirement an election to fill the vacancy - said election was held on the 9th inst; due proclamation having been made and the election in all things conducted according to law. The result of the election I am happy to say resulted in the election of our gallant friend John McNaly.

By order of Col. Commandant
Read Fletcher-Adjutant

LITTLE ROCK, Ark.,
March 9, 1861.

Special Correspondence of the Avalanche.[30]
Arkansas State Convention

    Lincoln's Inaugural, in full, has been received and read by our people. They regard it as a programme more brutal and bloody than the famous Rochester Manifesto of the tyrant's prime-minister, the arch-devil Seward. This authoritative exposition of the views and policy of Mr. Lincoln, in the present trying crisis, has had a powerful effect upon the popular mind, but I am sorry to say that the Union members of the Convention have received it with that stolid, infatuated submissiveness which a man, robbed of every instinct of humanity, might display in witnessing the last act of degradation that could be heaped upon his mother.
    The people are fast outstripping, in the progress of secession sentiments, their representatives in the Convention. This requires some explanation. It is owing to the fact, which the outside world ought to know, that the Union members of the Convention are, with but one or two exceptions, old Whig Federalists, who are glued together by their old

29   Jefferson County, Ark. Records, Jefferson County Library.
30   *The Avalanche*, March 14, 1861, Memphis, Tenn.

anti-Democratic prejudices, and who see, in the inauguration of a Black Republican Administration, the consummation of one of their life-long desires – the death of the Democratic party; and whose native impulses of patriotic devotion to the rights, interests, and honor of their section are chilled and paralyzed by the controlling fear, that in the construction of a Southern Confederacy, the Democratic element might be predominant. It is humiliating to think that men, upon such great questions and in such fearful crisis as the present, should suffer themselves to be actuated by such paltry and sordid considerations, but we are forced to the painful conclusion that such is the case.

The people have been deceived; we already begin to hear their murmurs of dissatisfaction and complaint; through false representations they were wrongfully influenced to vote for these old antiquated fossil remains of Federalism, and they begin to appreciate their mistake. But they have been sold out to the Hindoos [sic], and I fear the Hindoos are determined to hold them to their bargain, so far as their action in the Convention is concerned. I do not wish to be understood, however, as intimating that all Whigs in the State are Submissionists, far from it; some of the ablest members of the Convention, together with a large body of the old Whigs of the country, are strong Secessionists and brightest ornaments of the sacred cause. A day or two ago, there seemed to be no doubt of the willingness of a large majority of the Convention to vote for an ordinance of secession, with the proviso that it should be submitted to the people for their ratification or rejection; this was based upon the conviction, then very generally entertained, that the people would reject it, but since the great reaction in popular sentiment, occasioned by the reception of Lincoln's Inaugural, the old Federal fogies of the Convention, who have a keen scent for the fleshpots, have strengthened their upper lips and seemed determined to vote down all resolutions and ordinances that would be at all displeasing to Mr. Lincoln. My opinion now is that this Convention will adjourn without doing anything; and that the people will have to hold a new Convention to obtain what they are determined to have, THEIR RIGHTS IN OR OUT OF THE UNION.

The Convention has been occupied all day in discussing a resolution introduced by Mr. Echols, of Calhoun, recognizing the legal existence of the Confederate States of America. Able speeches in support of that resolution were made by Messrs. Grace and Yell of Jefferson, Laughinghouse of St. Francis, Smoot of Columbia, and others. A few miserably weak remarks were offered on the Union side by gentlemen, whose names, for the sake of posterity, ought not to be published. The Convention adjourned without taking a vote on the resolution. Governor Rector, on the call of a Convention, sent in a message, communicating certain information in regard to the political condition of the State, of which I send you a copy. He strongly favors and urges the adoption of an ordinance of secession.

Yours, truly,
PALMETTO.

LITTLE ROCK, Ark.,
March 10, 1861.

Special Correspondence of the *Avalanche*.[31]

The last petty, contemptible subterfuge has been taken from the Union-submissionists. "Honest Abe" has been safely delivered of his Inaugural, is snugly quartered in the White House, with Gen. Scott's Pretorian guards to protect him, and legions of hungry Wide Awakes and Abolitionists thronging around Washington, its purieus, the Capitol, and Departments, seeking the offices in his bestowal.

The Inaugural, in full, was first ventilated here yesterday morning, in the *True Democrat*. It is universally conceded here, as elsewhere, by every man that "knows a hawk from a bandy saw," that if he carries out the programme there laid down, war is inevitable. Indeed, I expect the ball has already been opened at Charleston and Pensacola. Gen. Jeff. Davis is not the man to be taken by surprise or delay till his enemy gains an advantage over him. If anything of this kind is done, he himself is the man to do it.

Now, what will this impracticable, intractable majority of temporizers and Submissionists do in the Convention? I believe that a sufficient number of them will unite with us to pass the secession ordinance. But there are some of whom there is no hope whatever – Union men under all circumstances. The *Democrat* of this morning says: "The overwhelming vote for a Convention can mean nothing else than a

31   *The Avalanche*, March 14, 1861, Memphis, Tenn.

full adjustment of our rights in the Union, or secession from it. Many of the delegates were immediate Secessionists, and a majority of them advocated secession in case something was not done by the fourth of March. That time has arrived, but it has brought no peace to the country, and the cloud that gathered above us still lowers there in murkier gloom. The Peace Congress has failed completely. The plan submitted, though not even acceptable to the South, was voted down by the Black Republicans. The policy of Lincoln, as foreshadowed in his Inaugural, is coercion. In view of these facts, we do not hesitate to say that the people of Arkansas are overwhelmingly in favor of secession. The vote for a Convention proves this. The increasing feeling all over the State shows that the people are getting impatient at the degradation of submitting longer to the domineering insolence of Lincoln and his myrmidons. We have seen the feeling in our own town, once so very conservative. Men here have declared for immediate secession, who, two weeks ago, were the strongest Union men in the State. In some sections the Union men are coming over *en masse*, and we verily believe, that in six weeks a Submissionist would not be tolerated in a majority of the counties of this State. In view of these facts, why does the Convention longer hesitate? Are we to be humiliated and disgraced as Tennessee has been? Are we to have revolution and anarchy in our midst by the inaction of the only body that can give us peace and quiet? The State is impatient. The people are satisfied that all hope of compromise is at an end. They will soon begin to murmur at the inaction of the Convention, which, while it hesitates to act, has no hesitation about consuming four or five hundred dollars per day of the people's money. We believe that a large majority of the Convention are good and true men, and our only regret is that a few Submissionists are allowed to delay the action of the body. For God's sake, give us an ordinance of secession. It is our last, our only resort – it is a necessity.

But these old-fogy Submissionists never will be prepared to act. They are not men of the right metal. Had such men predominated in the colonies, in the days that tried men's souls, freedom would never have been won – never; but we should now be the vassals of England. I think the Convention will act decisively one way or the other next week. If the ordinance is not passed, I believe that the people of Arkansas will do like those of Texas – take the matter into their own hands, call another Convention, elect a majority of Secessionists, and instantly cease to be the tail-end of a damned Black Republican monarchy. If something

62

decisive is not done soon, Arkansas may prepare to lose her Southern tier of counties and those on the river, as they will annex themselves to Louisiana.

On Friday night Col. R. G. Payne, of Memphis, delivered an able, profound, comprehensive and eloquent address in the Hall of Representatives, to a crowded audience, in which were many ladies and delegates of the Convention. For its length – two hours – he held spellbound the large assemblage, who were now convulsed with laughter at his humorous and sarcastic hits at the psalm-singing, canting, hypocritical, dollar-worshiping, nigger-loving, puritanical Yankees; now wrought up to the highest pitch of enthusiasm by his vivid flashes of electrifying eloquence. He depreciated the deplorable and disgraceful position in which Tennessee had been placed, but thought a revolution was actively going on there in the minds of her citizens; and I doubt not such is the fact. Let her rally once more, pick her flint, and try it again.

In the Convention yesterday morning, (6th day,) a resolution was introduced "that the State of Arkansas recognize the independence of the Confederate States of America." A debate of an animated nature ensued, which consumed all of the forenoon. In the midst of it, a communication from the Governor was received and read. It was in response to the resolution requesting him to lay before the Convention such information as he had of State and Federal affairs, and the seizure of the United States Arsenal at Little Rock. I will endeavor to send you a copy with this.

Mr. Grace, of Jefferson, spoke warmly in favor of prompt action and secession. When he ceased, Mr. Fishback, (Submissionist,) jumped up and poured forth a stream of Union twaddle, concluding by shouting that when he recorded his vote against secession, he wanted the whole universe to look on and behold him! It will be a sublime spectacle. Vive nincompoop! Fiddlesticks.

Mr. Laughinghouse, (Phoebus, what a name!) next addressed the Convention. If his name does sound a little queer to a stranger, I am happy to say he is a trump – his heart is right. He delivered a brief, emphatic, fervid speech for Southern independence. He said that seven of the grand columns that supported the great edifice of constitutional liberty had been knocked from under it, and now were again placed in their proper positions – supporting a new temple – an edifice – a glorious fabric – dedicated to the honor, liberty, welfare and independence of the Southern people. He claimed to be an American citizen; had been as strong as a Union man as any other, but now there is no Union, and since there is not, he was for forming a new one – one in which there was a mutuality of interest, a congeniality of sentiment, a common and kindred interest; and, come weal or woe, he would stand by the South to the last hour of his existence.

A Union-shrieker took the floor and let off in the spread-eagle style, referring to the position of Tennessee and Virginia, and the tombs of Washington, Jackson and Polk. Fiddlesticks! What do such men care for the memories of Jackson and Polk?

Mr. Patterson, of Jackson, said that he had always been considered the hottest-headed man in the world, ready to pull down the Government; acknowledged that he was impulsive and enthusiastic, especially when impressed that he was in the right cause, as he now was. He expressed strong secession sentiments, and declared that if Arkansas remained in the disunited States, under the baleful and odious despotism of Lincoln, Seward, Sumner, Chase, Lovejoy, Giddings & Co., he would leave the State to find a more congenial Government. In this he will find many sympathizers who will go with him. I hear planters daily pronounce similar sentiments…

RAMROD.

MEMPHIS, Tenn.,
March 10, 1861.

HON. THOMAS C. HINDMAN.[32]

This distinguished champion of Southern honor and rights, passed through the city, yesterday, on his way from the scene of his public duties at Washington to his residence in Helena. We had the pleasure of a short visit from him. He left on the *H. D. Mears*, expecting to reach home by midnight, and to start to-morrow for Little Rock, where we expect to hear of good results from the developments he will be able to make of the purposes of the Administration of Abraham Lincoln, which, he informs us, are in his opinion, bent upon an attempted consummation of the theory of the President's entire political life and of the bloody and coercive sentiments of his Inaugural Address.

---

32   *The Avalanche*, March 11, 1861, Memphis, Tenn.

LITTLE ROCK, Ark.,
March 11, 1861.[33]

The Convention met Monday morning, and was opened with prayer. Some of the Union-savers showed their hands to-day in an unmistakable manner, and fully entitled themselves to the title of "Submissionists." Such sentiments as I heard uttered by these gentlemen to-day in the State-house of Arkansas, I was not prepared for, I must confess. I infer from what transpired that no ordinance will be passed - certainly not unless there can be found four men on the other side who will go with us. Of this there is some hope, but quite feeble. Say what they may, I cannot believe they reflect the sentiment and will of their constituents, even as that will and sentiment stood at the time of their election – must assuredly not at this time. Since the 4th, events have transpired which must have wrought a great and decided change in the sentiment of those counties who have sent up Union delegates.

This morning the President laid before the Convention the correspondence between Gov. Rector and Capt. Totten, U.S.A., relative to the United States Arsenal at this place. Referred to Committee on State Affairs.

Resolutions and motions of various kinds were offered, not, however, of much consequence. One of them was against coercion – to resist any attempt on the part of the Federal Government to retake any of the forts, arsenals, or public property in the States which have seceded, or to levy men, money, etc., in those States and Arkansas. Referred.

Mr. Thomasson, (Submissionist,) offered a long preamble and resolutions setting forth the grievances of the South – the wrongs and outrages inflicted by the North electing a sectional President, and winding up with a remedy for everything complained of. And what do you suppose it was? The calling of a Convention of all the States (thirty-four) to amend the Constitution of the United States! Oh, most lame and impotent conclusion.

On motion the resolutions were received, and 200 copies ordered to be printed for the use of the Convention. A delegate offered a strong Secession resolution, which was referred.

Mr. Turner, (Submissionist and peace man,) offered resolution remonstrating against the border States, including North Carolina,

33   *The Avalanche*, March 14, 1861, Memphis, Tenn.

Tennessee and Arkansas, taking any part in movements for recapturing forts in the seceded States and recommending a pacific adjustment of all difficulties.

Mr. Adams, of Phillips, offered a resolution that the State will hold the Little Rock arsenal and not permit the forces of the United States, to retake it or be quartered therein.

The report of the committee in the tie-vote case of Fulton county was read. They take issue with the Governor for refusing to issue his proclamation for an election, and indulge some very tart language in their comments upon the Governor's notion of the relative powers and prerogatives of himself and the Convention.

Mr. Yell moved that the President of the Convention order an election to be held, saying that it was manifestly his duty so to do.

The resolution that the State of Arkansas recognize the nationality and independence of the "Confederate States of America," was called up, and gave rise to a debate which lasted during the balance of the session.

Judge Batson, of Johnson, in discussing it, said that while we remain an integral part of the United States we cannot enter into a treaty with any foreign government. This resolution does not contemplate anything of that sort. He thought we had power to pass the resolution and could do so without violating our duties towards the Federal Government. We had a right to express our sympathy for the oppressed, and to speak out against the oppressor. If we vote down this resolution, it struck him that it would be indorsing the odious dogma of coercion. We desired to give the influence of name and sanction to the new government rising into sovereignty.

Judge Adams, of Phillips, addressed the House in a brief but forcible speech in favor of the resolution. This Convention owed no allegiance to any power on earth. If they do the people can never assemble in their primary capacity to assert their rights for any cause whatever. This right was not subject to any law. He then alluded to a scene which occurred in this city a few nights since when the Commissioners from South Carolina were on the point of returning, the deep and heart-felt solicitude they expressed as to the action of Arkansas. They counted confidently upon having her united with the States of the Southern Confederacy.

Mr. Turner, of Crawford, said "He was surprised to hear delegates claiming such extraordinary powers for this Convention; to hear gentlemen declare that we were above and superior to all other powers.

66

When did we sever our connection with the Federal Government? The Southern Confederacy did not send Commissioners here to Arkansas to ask a recognition of their independence. They had sent Commissioners to Washington for that purpose. Their independence has not yet been recognized by any power on earth. What right has this State to do so? There is no propriety in it. I hold that we have a Government; and yet the doctrines advanced here are that we have no Government. I thank God that this dark tide of revolution which has swept over the Gulf States has been arrested by the Border States. Let the gentlemen bring up their ordinance of secession; we shall vote it down. It is a new-fangled, modern doctrine, originating in the school of John C. Calhoun. We recognize no such doctrine. We wish to be respectful to the gentlemen, but are not prepared for any such extraordinary doctrine. Do we know that this so-called Confederate States of America is an independent Government? We know it only from telegraphic dispatches and the newspapers. But we do owe allegiance to the Federal Government, and I am not prepared to yield it. Gentlemen call it a tyrannical Government. It is gross perversion of language. The Federal Government is a kind and beneficent Government, and has always been so. I revere it and intend to sustain it to the best of my ability; I love and venerate it." His speech was an old-fogy affair and full of coercion doctrine, or strongly squinted at it.

Judge Adams responded. The Confederate States were a living reality; they were an actual living, existing nationality. The allegiance we owe to the State was nothing but a legal fiction. We are the representatives of the sovereignty of the people, in Convention assembled. As to the Government of the United States, although I have loved it, and battled for it, as late as last summer, for one I am willing to dissolve our connection with it and unite with the Southern Confederacy.

Mr. Stillwell, of Pulaski, said the liberties of Rome were once preserved by the cackling of geese. We must remember, also, that they were destroyed by the babbling of men. And Mr. S. proceeded to "babble" for the Union. He combatted the arguments of Judge Adams; harped upon his oath to support the Constitution of the United States: referred to the recognition of our independence by England and France. It was only done after long delay and until they had clearly established their independence. It was one of the reserved powers of the Federal Government. Arkansas was not a separate, independent nationality. What power or right has she to take this step of recognizing the independence of States and empires? There was no such antagonism in society North

67

and South, as was alleged. Granting there was a dissolution was not [to] remedy it, but only make matters worse. He objected to the resolution, because it was a direct indorsement of the doctrine of secession. The same variety of interests existed in the Gulf States as in all the States. South Carolina is a free-trade State, and Louisiana a sugar-producing State, requiring a protective tariff. Arkansas will find it to her interest to establish manufactures, and will require protection to her cotton. They will secede among themselves. He did not suppose they would keep together three years. He thought Arkansas would divide into two or four parts if the secession doctrine prevailed. Portions of the gentleman's remarks, relative to the graves of his relatives in Arkansas, were pathetic and touching...Mr. Cypert, of White, replied in a doleful tone, deploring the recklessness of gentlemen advocating secession. His remarks were unimportant.

Mr. Grace again spoke in favor of the resolution. He showed cause why we should secede, and showed, also, the remedies in secession for the ills to which we are now subject. It requires sixty millions to administer the Federal Government. The Southern Confederacy can be administered for half that amount. We could save thirty millions per annum, now paid as tribute to the free States. If our property must be stolen, let it not be done by those living on our bounty and hospitality. Our allegiance is due first to Arkansas. If the Convention has the power to alter and amend the Constitution of Arkansas, we are superior to that Constitution. Some gentlemen of the other side desired that men can be found at this late day to entertain an idea so preposterous? Did not ex-President Tyler and some of the first intellects of the country try? What did even Crittenden accomplish? All compromises were rejected. Government was not instituted for the protection of majorities, but of minorities. Majorities never revolutionize. Revolution is a right- a natural, inalienable right; in it like here in [the] South [is]our only safety. The cotton States have organized a government – they have declared themselves an independent sovereignty – they have seceded – the fact is known to us, and soon will be to the universe, and their independence acknowledged. Arkansas has common grievances with them to redress, and it is a sufficient reason why we should co-operate with them. The action which Arkansas may take may strengthen the hands of the Black Republican President...

RAMROD.

LITTLE ROCK, Ark.,
March 11, 1861.

WILL ARKANSAS SECEDE?[34]

There is much speculation [as] to what the Convention now in session at Little Rock will do. Since the dotards and cowards have a majority on joint ballot, we can hope from them nothing – expect nothing. They seem incapable of appreciating the reaction that has taken place in the public mind since their election, and more particularly since the publication of Lincoln's Inaugural. A few days since we cherished the fond hope that the proud young Commonwealth across the river would be rescued from the polluting clutches that held Tennessee in ignominious thralldom, but we are doomed to sad disappointment. Craven and cowardly submission has been burnt deep into the brow of a majority of the delegates, and Arkansas will be forced to kiss the hand that smites her. Without pledges for the safety of her property or the security of her honor she has marched into Seward's Confederacy as quietly as the sheep goes to the shambles. As a general thing "misery loves company," but we must confess that we were unwilling to see Arkansas degrade herself by bad associations, but she has linked her destiny with that of Tennessee, and like a yoke of trusty oxen they bend their jaded necks in dragging the chariot in which Seward, Lincoln and Chase are riding. Like well-broke dray horses they are tugging at the wheel while the whip of coercion is being cracked over their backs.

LITTLE ROCK, Ark.,
March 11, 1861.[35]

A large number of resolutions, embodying the different views of members touching the great questions of the day – one of which, recognizing the doctrine and right of a State to secede from the Federal Union whenever, in the opinion of the people of that State, the safety of their rights and vital interests require it – were offered and referred to appropriate committees. The Committee on Federal Relations, to-day made a report, substantially to the effect that it is the right and duty of

---

34   *The Avalanche*, March 11, 1861, Memphis, Tenn.
35   *The Avalanche*, March 11, 1861, Memphis, Tenn.

Arkansas, to the extent of her ability, to resist all and every attempt of the Federal Government to coerce any of the seceded States back into the Union; and that any attempt to retake any of the captured forts, arsenals or dock-yards in said seceded States, or to reinforce any of said works in said seceded States, now in possession of the United States forces, will be regarded as attempts at coercion and resisted accordingly. Inasmuch as a majority of this committee are Union men, their report is regarded as indicative of the return of better feeling on the part of the Union side of the Convention. The debate on the resolution recognizing the legal existence of the Confederate States, postponed from Saturday, was continued to-day and took up most of the morning session. In the discussion of this resolution the best talent of the Convention was called out, and we were favored with some noble and eloquent speeches. Among the orators of the day, on the Secession side, I cannot forbear to mention the name of Hon. Mr. Grace, of Jefferson, who made the best speech of the session. He stirred the embers of Southern feeling in the hearts of his auditors to such an extent as to cause them to burn forth into irrepressible flames of enthusiastic applause. He is a noble and gallant defender of their rights, interests, and honor of the South. Judge Adams, of Phillips and Judge Floyd, of Johnson, also made able and convincing speeches. A few stale Union-shrieking harangues were howled from the other side and echoed by appropriate hisses in the galleries...

LITTLE ROCK, Ark.,
March 12, 1861.
> Special Correspondence of the *Avalanche*.[36]
> Arkansas State Convention

The convention met at 10 A.M. Prayer. Mr. Fishback offered a resolution to appoint a commissioner to each of the slaveholding States, to consult together as to a settlement of resolutions of yesterday. I regard both as impracticable.

Mr. Mayo, a resolution which was ordered to be printed. There being no reports from committees, the special order of the day was taken up – the resolution that "the Committee on Ordinances" be instructed to report, as early as practicable, an ordinance for the immediate secession of Arkansas from the Union.

---

36   *The Avalanche*, March 15, 1861, Memphis, Tenn.

Mr. Slemons, of Drew, (Secession) said that he had not heretofore participated in debate – not that he felt no interest – not that his constituents felt none. They do feel vitally interested. The time has come when the people of Arkansas must act, and act promptly and decisively. He had loved the Union, and her flag, as dearly as any man on this floor. Kindred blood of his had sprinkled every battle field of Mexico, from Palo Alto to Churabusco. But those stars and stripes are now disgraced. They were now the symbol of Abolition power and dominion. We have met here, not to sing Te Deums and hosannas to the Union, not to eulogize the patriots of the Revolution, but to provide for the present. The man who shuns the adjustment of this question now, entails it upon his posterity. It must be met, and now is the proper time. There is a revolution going on, even in our borders, and the first gun fired by this Black Republican Government at a citizen of any Southern State, will be the signal for ten thousand armed Arkansians to rush to the field, ready for the fray. He gave a flattering account of the vast resources of Arkansas. He refuted the silly charge of the allies of Lincoln, that we want to set up a nigger oligarchy or aristocracy. Gentlemen boast here of the State of his birth, (although a Southern State) nor particularly proud of Arkansas. He was not consulted as to where he should first see the light of day. We are told that Arkansas must wait for Tennessee; that Tennessee is a great State. But she has also a Johnson and an Etheridge, traitors who have misled many honest or ignorant men. Must we wait for her? Must we wait for Virginia, which John Brown captured and held for twenty-four hours? Maryland is to be waited for- the home of that vile traitor, Winter Davis; and Missouri, which has a rank Abolitionist for a representative in Congress, and is a semi-Abolitionism State at best; and old Kentucky, which tolerates in her midst such fanatics as Cassius M. Clay, and like Virginia and Maryland, had a Lincoln electoral ticket last election, and voted several hundred Lincoln votes. Poor little Arkansas was to wait for these and pattern after them. Never, gentlemen, never! They must set better examples first. She has pure patriots, as brave men, as gallant soldiers as any State, and let her act for herself on her own responsibility. His remarks were quite racy and original, and elicited some laughter and applause.

Mr. Smoot, (Secessionist) of Columbia, said that if President Davis and the members of the Southern Congress were rebels and traitors, they should be hung, and their followers dispersed. It was a logical deduction, if we believed Lincoln's Inaugural and the assumptions of the Union-savers. If we believe that the Southern Confederacy is a failure, and that those seceded States still are a part of this Union, we must be coercionists and submissionists. It is a logical conclusion. But we all agree as to the outrages of the North upon the South and that some remedy should be adopted.

How can we do it but by revolution or secession? Where is the evidence that the Republicans intend to grant us our rights, and justice, and equality hereafter in the Union? Their whole history shows they will not. Convention after convention had been called; remonstrance after remonstrance had been made. When old Virginia humiliated herself by getting on her knees and humbly begging for justice, they threw her petition back in her face. He would like to know what Arkansas could do but secede. We are compelled to do it, and therefore he was for passing this resolution. Nothing can save the Union apart of Omnipotence Himself. No paper compromises can do it. Every possible consideration of interest and honor tell us Arkansas should secede...

LITTLE ROCK, Ark.,
March 16, 1861.

Military.[37]

As a decided Military spirit seems to pervade, we would suggest that there are four good military companies in Little Rock, any of which afford ample inducements to the citizen of military tastes or inclinations:

Capt. Churchill's Cavalry, is a fine company, well officered and will soon be well armed. In it there are some vacancies, and we would like to see its ranks well filled.

Capt. Peay's Capital Guards, is a first rate Infantry company, as well commanded as any company in the State, and the ranks are not yet full.

Capt. Woodruff's Artillery; is a new company, well officered and appointed, with room in the ranks for yet a few more.

Capt. Franklin's Rifles, a new company, is organized and in the tide of successful experiment. Sharp shooters can have a chance in that company.

Gentlemen desirous of attaching themselves to Cavalry, to Infantry, or to Artillery service, have, in Little Rock, superior advantages in all respects.

---

37   *Weekly Arkansas Gazette*, March 16, 1861, Little Rock, Ark.

JEFFERSON COUNTY, Ark., March 23, 1861.[38]

On Saturday, the 23d, the ball was opened at Pine Bluff in Good earnest, by the secessionists. Hon. R. W. Johnson and Gen. James Yell were escorted to the Court-house from the Fennerty House, by the Jefferson Guards, with bayonets bristling from their guns, and keeping step to martial music. From the spectacle an outsider might have inferred that it was necessary for those gentlemen to have a body-guard even in this strong hold of secessionism. But this is by no means the case. Our citizen soldiery here are invincible in peace, and they merely wished to render military honors to a General and a Colonel who desired to point out to them "the wisest and safest policy for the interest, the honor, and the future security of "Arkansas." Such wisdom does not need a body guard to quell opposition to it. The secessionists have laid down their programme, the stakes are all set, and now if they can work up to them they say they will be the proudest and the happiest people on earth in a Southern Confederacy. They promised that the people shall be exempt from the burdens of a tariff of duties, and only be subjected to a few cents direct tax to support the government. They promise that all shall be peace and prosperity as soon as Arkansas secedes from the Union. Their last great battle will be fought on the soil of Arkansas. Having given up all hopes of success in any other Southern State yet remaining in the Union, all their energies and efforts are to be expended in Arkansas. They tell us that the States already out of the Union will remain out, and that all hope of or labor for, a reconstruction of the government will be useless. From indication in Louisiana, Mississippi, Texas, Alabama and other localities, I am induced to believe that things are not going on so prosperously in the Confederate States as some of the secessionists here would have us believe. It is not my purpose to condemn the course of the seceded States, but I am clearly of the opinion that, if Arkansas and other border slave States get proper guaranties from the government in the shape of Constitutional amendments, every State which is now a member of the Southern Confederacy will come back into the Union in the course of twelve months. Therefore, I work against precipitation and separate State action, and favor cooperation and reconstruction.

R.

---

38   *Weekly Arkansas Gazette*, April 7, 1861, Little Rock, Ark.

PULASKI COUNTY, Ark.,
March 29, 1861.

Free Barbecue in Lefevre Township.[39]

The citizens of Lefevre township, Pulaski county, having determined to give a barbecue and raise a secession flag, met at Mound Church on the 29th March, to make necessary arrangements.

The meeting was well attended. D. M. Thomson, esq., was chosen president, and Maj. W. W. Morrow, acted as secretary. A committee [was] appointed to arrange and procure all necessaries.

Committee of Arrangements. J. D. Amos, Leon Lefevre, S. S. Smith, A. L. Lefevre, Sr., L. Thomson, Jesse Hill, J. Deihl, T. J. Churchill, W. F. Ford, and Wm. Faulkner.

Committee to Procure a Pole, etc. Jos. Adams, W. A. Martin, J. A. Wright, W. B. Lefevre, Robt. Owens, and B. F. Vaughn.

Committee to Invite Orators. D. M. Thomson, Jas. Harper, and W. W. Morrow.

Saturday, the 27th day of April, was chosen for the barbecue, on which occasion a secession pole will be raised, upon which the ladies will hoist a blue flag. There will be several orations on the present impending questions, and also a good band of music will be in attendance. A large and sumptuous dinner will be given, and a sufficiency of good water.

A cordial invitation is extended to all.

D. M. Thomson, Pres't.

W. W. Morrow, Sec'y.

DES ARC, Ark.,
April 5, 1861.

Cavalry Company.[40]

This corps, at their last meeting, adopted as their name, The Des Arc Rangers. On last Saturday they paraded through our streets, for the first time, in their uniforms, presenting quite a soldier-like appearance. The uniform adopted by the Rangers is a red flannel shirt, with a deep blue breast and back, blue cuffs and black velvet collar, with three rows of

---

39   *Arkansas True Democrat*, April 11, 1861, Little Rock, Ark

40   *The Constitutional Union*, April 5, 1861, Des Arc, Ark.

brass buttons in front; black pants, with red stripes up the sides; United States cavalry fatigue cap, with ostrich plume, with colt's Navy repeaters and United States dragoon sabers.

JOHNSON COUNTY, Ark.,
April 13, 1861.

From Johnson County.
Tremendous Excitement Large and Enthusiastic Meeting.[41]

On Saturday the 13th of April at the battalion muster, on the parade ground, near the residence of Maj. James B. Wilson, on Horse Head Creek, besides the Battalion who had assembled for the purpose of military drill, there was an immense concourse of ladies and gentlemen present to hear of, and learn the stirring events that are fast transpiring around us.

At 10 o'clock the crowd that had assembled learned that the flag of the Confederated States, with a full band of music was nearby coming from Clarksville. The gallant Maj. A. C. Jacobs of the 10th regiment, within ten minutes had 800 men mounted to go out and meet and salute the white man's flag. In full gallop, at a half mile they met the band and flag, and the echoes of their cheerings was heard bounding from hill side to the mountain top, that swelled and gladdened the heart of the patriot to see the flag of the Confederated States high up floating in the clear sun light of heaven as it came over the crest of the hill, and the full band playing the Southern Marseilles, and three hundred stout hearts as a guard of honor erecting the emblem of southern liberty to the parade ground. The infantry was formed and presented arms with open columns for the flag and escort to pass through. After countermarching, and the line of horsemen formed, Maj. Jacobs ordered three cheers for President Davis and the Confederate States, which was done with most hearty good will by the whole mass present, both mounted men and infantry, and the *ladies*, God bless them, by the waiving of handkerchiefs and tossing to the gallant knights of chivalry and valor, their lovely bouquets, as tokens of their heartfelt approbation...

Bozarias.

---

41   *Arkansas True Democrat*, April 25, 1861, Little Rock, Ark.

WASHINGTON, D.C.,
April 15, 1861.
BY THE PRESIDENT OF THE UNITED STATES:
A PROCLAMATION.

Whereas the laws of the United States have been for some time past and now are opposed and the execution thereof obstructed in the States of South Carolina, Georgia, Alabama, Florida, Mississippi, Louisiana, and Texas by combinations too powerful to be suppressed by the ordinary course of judicial proceedings or by the powers vested in the marshals by law:

Now, therefore, I, Abraham Lincoln, President of the United States, in virtue of the power in me vested by the Constitution and the laws, have thought fit to call forth, and hereby do call forth, the militia of the several States of the Union, to the aggregate number of 75,000, in order to suppress said combinations and to cause the laws to be duly executed.

The details of this object will be immediately communicated to the State authorities through the War Department.

I appeal to all loyal citizens to favor, facilitate, and aid this effort to maintain the honor, the integrity, and the existence of our National Union, and the perpetuity of popular government, and to redress wrongs already long enough endured.

I deem it proper to say that the first service assigned to the forces hereby called forth will probably be to repossess the forts, places, and property which have been seized from the Union, and in every event the utmost care will be observed, consistently with the objects aforesaid, to avoid any devastation, any destruction of or interference with property, or any disturbance of peaceful citizens in any part of the country.

And I hereby command the persons composing the combinations aforesaid to disperse and retire peaceably to their respective abodes within twenty days from date.

Deeming that the present condition of public affairs presents an extraordinary occasion, I do hereby, in virtue of the power in me vested by the Constitution, convene both houses of Congress.

Senators and Representatives are therefore summoned to assemble at their respective chambers at twelve o'clock noon on Thursday, the fourth day of July next, then and there to consider and determine such measures as in their wisdom the public safety and interest may seem to demand.

In witness whereof I have hereunto set my hand and caused the seal of the United States to be affixed.

Done at the city of Washington this fifteenth day of April, in the year of our Lord one thousand eight hundred and sixty-one, and of the Independence of the United States the eighty-fifth.

By the President:
ABRAHAM LINCOLN.

WILLIAM H. SEWARD,
Secretary of State.

———

WAR DEPARTMENT,
Washington, April 15, 1861.

SIR: Under the act of Congress "for calling forth the militia to execute the laws of the Union, suppress insurrections, repel invasions," &c., approved February 28, 1795, I have the honor to request Your State the quota designated in the table below, to serve as infantry or riflemen, for the period of three months, unless sooner discharged.

Your Excellency will please communicate to me the time at or about which your quota will be expected at its rendezvous, as it will be met as soon as practicable by an officer or officers to muster it into the service and pay of the United States. At the same time the oath of fidelity to the United States will be administered to every officer and man. The mustering officer will be instructed to receive no man under the rank of commissioned officer who is in years apparently over forty-five or under eighteen, or who is not in physical strength and vigor.

Maine	1 regiment; 37 officers; 743 men; 780 aggregate.
New Hampshire	1 regiment; 37 officers; 743 men; 780 aggregate.
Vermont	1 regiment; 37 officers; 743 men; 780 aggregate.
Massachusetts	2 regiments; 74 officers; 1486 men; 1560 aggregate.
Rhode Island	1 regiment; 37 officers; 743 men; 780 aggregate.
Connecticut	1 regiment; 37 officers; 743 men;

	780 aggregate.
New York	2 Major-Generals; 4 Brigadier-Generals; 17 regiments; 649 officers; 12,631 men; 13, 280 aggregate.
Pennsylvania	2 Major-Generals; 4 Brigadier-Generals; 16 regiments; 612 officers; 11,888 men; 12,500 aggregate.
New Jersey	1 Brigadier-Generals; 4 regiments; 151 officers; 2972 men; 3,123 aggregate.
Delaware	1 regiment; 37 officers; 743 men; 780 aggregate.
Maryland	1 Brigadier-Generals; 4 regiments; 151 officers; 2972 men; 13, 3123 aggregate.
Virginia	3 regiments; 111 officers; 2229 men; 2340 aggregate.
North Carolina	2 regiments; 74 officers; 1486 men; 1560 aggregate.
Tennessee	2 regiments; 74 officers; 1486 men; 1560 aggregate.
Arkansas	1 regiment; 37 officers; 743 men; 780 aggregate.
Kentucky	1 Brigadier-Generals; 4 regiments; 151 officers; 2972 men; 3,123 aggregate.
Missouri	1 Brigadier-Generals; 4 regiments; 151 officers; 2972 men; 3,123 aggregate.
Illinois	1 Brigadier-Generals; 6 regiments; 225 officers; 4458 men; 4683 aggregate.
Indiana	1 Brigadier-Generals; 6 regiments; 225 officers; 4458 men; 4683 aggregate.
Ohio	1 Major-General; 3 Brigadier-Generals; 13 regiments; 494 officers; 9659 men; 10, 153 aggregate.

Michigan	1 regiment; 37 officers; 743 men; 780 aggregate.
Wisconsin	1 regiment; 37 officers; 743 men; 780 aggregate.
Iowa	1 regiment; 37 officers; 743 men; 780 aggregate.
Minnesota	1 regiment; 37 officers; 743 men; 780 aggregate.
Total	5 Major-Generals; 17 Brigadier Generals; 94 regiments; 69, 842 men; 73, 391 aggregate.

The rendezvous for your State will be: Maine, Portland; New Hampshire, Portsmouth; Vermont, Burlington; Massachusetts, Boston; Rhode Island, Providence; Connecticut, New Haven; New York, New York, Albany, Elmira; Pennsylvania, Philadelphia, Harrisburg; New Jersey, Trenton; Delaware, Wilmington; Maryland, Frederick City, Baltimore; Virginia, Staunton, Wheeling, Gordonsville; North Carolina, Raleigh; Tennessee, Knoxville, Nashville; Arkansas, Little Rock; Kentucky, Lexington; Missouri, Saint Louis; Illinois, Springfield, Chicago, Indiana, Indianapolis; Ohio, Columbus, Cleveland; Michigan, Detroit; Wisconsin, Milwaukee; Iowa, Keokuk; Minnesota, Saint Paul.

I have the honor to be, very respectfully, your obedient servant,

SIMON CAMERON,
Secretary of War.

**MONTGOMENRY, Ala.,
April 16, 1861.**[42]

Honorable T. C. HINDMAN, Helena, Ark.:

SIR: In reply to your inquiries in regard to the policy of this Government on the subject of accepting military aid from Southern States which are not yet members of the Confederacy, and especially as to Arkansas, I beg leave to state that thus far this department has through proper to decline for the present all tenders from those States, simply because the forces easily and rapidly raised in convenient proximity to the scenes of operation have been ample for all the needs of the country.

---

42 OR,1(1):684-5

Since the forced surrender of Fort Sumter to the forces of the Confederate States, followed by a most warlike proclamation from the Executive of the Washington Government, the probability that serious and perhaps long-continued hostilities will ensue is greatly increased.

If the war shall be commenced with the spirit which seems to animate our enemies, there is every reason to anticipate the operations of both the belligerent will be conducted on a much more imposing scale than this continent has ever witnessed; and I may add that the general opinion preponderates strongly in that direction.

While this Government has an unfaltering confidence in the means and resources, pecuniary, moral, and military, of the Confederate States, as they now exist, to defend themselves against all assaults and to repel all their enemies, it yet by no means undervalues the assistance which it is in the power of the border slave States to render; and of these latter there is no one to which the people of this Confederacy have looked with more undoubting confidence for cordial sympathy and support than the State of Arkansas.

It is not possible yet to state absolutely that this Government will be in condition to need forces drawn from any State not in the Confederacy, but it is extremely probable that in the event of war (now, in its widest sense, apparently inevitable), which shall continue through the approaching summer, a brigade organized in conformity to the act of Congress "to provide for the public defense," will be gladly accepted at an early day in the next fall-say about the middle or last of August. Such a military organization, if required, as I think it will be, would be composed of course, as similar organizations will be, from the several Confederate States. It would be expected to elect its own officers, but would be subject to the control of such field officers as the President of the Confederate States might place over it.

All the signs of the times, as I view them, so conclusively favor the belief that war in its sternest phase is upon us, that I have not hesitated to intimate how strongly we rely on your State for active co-operation in what is, after all, a common defense. That she will prove true to herself, and so prove true to this Confederacy, I never for a moment have questioned.

Very respectfully, your obedient servant,
L. P. WALKER.

MONTGOMERY, Ala.,
April 17, 1861.[43]

WAR DEPARTMENT, C. S. A.,
Montgomery, April 17, 1861.

His Excellency Governor RECTOR, &c.:

SIR: War existing between this Government and that at Washington, forced by the perfidious conduct of the last, preparations are being made on both sides for the most active hostilities. Under these circumstances it is not improbable that forces will be sent from the North along the Ohio and Mississippi River to burn our cities and devastate our country. It becomes, therefore, the imperative duty of this Government to guard against these possible results by every means in their power. The defenses of the Mississippi require the erection of at least four additional batteries at eligible points along the banks of that river. It is proposed to construct one of these batteries at or near Helena, in the State of Arkansas, and I trust your Excellency will grant permission for the work to be done. I have the less hesitation in making this application to you, because I feel assured Arkansas will be identified with the States of this Confederacy, and that the danger which threatens is common to her as well as to ourselves. It cannot be that Mississippi, Louisiana, and Texas can be assailed in their political and material rights and interests without Arkansas being sensibly affected.

I trust, therefore, that through due regard to the exigencies and necessities of the times, the comity existing between Arkansas and the States of the Confederate Government, as well as their joint welfare and future relations, your Excellency will promptly accord to me the privilege of erecting, arming, and manning the battery to which I have referred at or near Helena. Events are hastening to a bloody issue, and there is no time to be lost in our movements.

I have the honor to be,
with the highest consideration and respect,
your obedient servant,
L. P. WALKER.

---

43   OR,1(1):685-6

FORT SMITH, Ark.,
April 19, 1861.

No. 3.[44]

Reports of Captain William W. Burns, commissary of subsistence, U. S.
Army, of the seizure of subsistence stores at Pine Bluff, Ark.

FORT SMITH, ARK., April 19, 1861.

[Major WAGGAMAN.]

MAJOR: Yours inclosing invoices of stores is received. The people of Arkansas are maddened by the seizure of their arms in Cincinnati, and I am assured by every one that these stores will be seized. I therefore start to-day down the river to meet them, hoping that I can get on the boat, and, by advising with the captain, avoid points and escape excitement. Please present the case to the general commanding, and send me the order of approval.

I am, sir, very respectfully, your obedient servant,

WM. W. BURNS,
Captain and C. S.

DARDANELLE, Ark.,
April 19, 1861.

For the *True Democrat.*[45]

Messrs. Johnson & Yerkes: I am truly gratified to know, and from the signs of the times I can confidently say, Yell county, is now aroused to a sense of her duty, and will be *all right* upon the all-important question of secession when she has a chance to cast her vote. . .

This morning we reared a pole, towering 110 feet, and from its lofty summit stretches out our southern flag, the star of Arkansas in the distance, like the swift comet, seeking to form one of those brilliant seven that are shedding light upon the independent pathway of our Confederacy. There were a great many people present from all parts of this (Pope and Perry,) the scene made an impression upon my mind never to be forgotten. As the flag was making its way swiftly aloft, ladies and gentlemen were thronging the side-walks, and amid the roar of the *anvils*, (not cannon,) and the enthusiastic tune of *Dixey*, played by the

---

44   OR,1(1):647
45   *Arkansas True Democrat*, May 2, 1861, Little Rock, Ark.

band of the Show-boat, *Wave*, Col. Lemoyne appeared upon the stand prepared for him, and in his usual manner, when appearing before an audience, seemed to take a survey of the entire crowd, and at the close of *Dixey*, addressed the ladies, complimenting their sex for the interest they always take in all important matters, illustrated by the effect that music and woman had upon the soldier. He then turned to the men and addressed them as the descendants of the revolutionary patriots, supporters, protectors and guardians of women and children, pictured to them the present state of things, compared it to the revolutionary crisis...

CLARKSVILLE, Ark.,
April 20, 1861.

From Johnson County.[46]

Messrs. Editors: This has been a glorious day for Johnson county. By appointment the people from the country flocked into town in large numbers; the ladies were all out, the business houses were closed; in short, everybody and his family were out to see the presentating of a large and handsome southern flag by Miss Sallie Robinson, who represented the ladies, to Dr. J. P Mitchell, the representative of the people of Johnson county. After the presentation of the flag of the Confederate States of America was hoisted to the masthead of a pole one hundred and two feet high, and was greeted with the enthusiastic cheers of the people - the salutes of the military and the firing of anvil artillery. Patriotic speeches were delivered by our legislators, Ward, Robinson and Cravens, and by our delegates, Batson and Floyd, amidst the waving of handkerchiefs and hats, three hearty huzzas were given for the Southern Confederacy. Soon afterwards dispatches were received announcing that Virginia had seceded, and that Kentucky, North Carolina, Virginia, Tennessee and Missouri had emphatically refused to furnish a single man, or any number of men, to fight under the black flag of abolitionism. I never have seen people so deeply excited - cheers loud and long rent the air, the artillery was again brought out and round after round was fired until the sky was almost darkened with the smoke. One more star was added to the flag and it was again sent home, where it waves over people who are determined to "do or die."

---

46   *Arkansas True Democrat*, April 25, 1861, Little Rock, Ark.

LITTLE ROCK, Ark.,
April 20, 1861.

Military Ball.[47]

The Ball given by the "Capital Guards," on Friday night of last week, was a brilliant affair, and went off in the most admirable manner. The supper, prepared by the ladies of the Episcopal Church, afforded ample evidence that they are judges of the good things of this life. The beaux, with their profusion of Military ornament, made a good display, but they were outshone by the sparkling eyes of the beauteous fair who graced the occasion. Being an invited guest, and having the run of the house, we "sloshed about," saw, and paid general attention to all, including, of course, the presiding divinity of the gallery, whom we regarded as among the chiefest of the attractions.

LITTE ROCK, Ark.
April 20, 1861.

Pursuant to a proclamation of the President of the convention, the convention assembled this day in the hall of the House of Representatives at 10 o'clock, which said proclamation is in words and figures as follows, to wit:

PROCLAMATION of the President of the Convention of the People of the State of Arkansas, reconvening the Convention.

WHEREAS, By an ordinance of the state convention, passed on the 21st day of March, A.D. 1861, it was ordained that the President of the convention be authorized and empowered to convene the convention at an earlier day than the 19th of August, A.D. 1861, if in his opinion an exigency should arise requiring the same.

And whereas, From reliable information, I am satisfied that preparations are being made for a war between the citizens of the free and slave states, in which the safety, peace and prosperity of the people of Arkansas are involved, and for the preservation of which we must provide; for which purpose, in my opinion, the convention should be

---

47   *Weekly Arkansas Gazette*, April 20, 1861, Little Rock, Ark.

convened at the earliest practicable time.

Now, therefore, I, DAVID WALKER, President of the Convention, under the authority, and in accordance with the provisions of said ordinance, do declare and make known that a convention will be held on Monday, the sixth day of May, A.D. 1861, at the city of Little Rock, when and where the delegates to said convention are notified to attend as required by the second section of said ordinance.

In testimony whereof, I have hereunto set my hand as such President, this 20th day of April, A.D. 1861.

DAVID WALKER.

By E.C. BOUDINOT,
   Secretary of Convention.

CLARK COUNTY, Ark.,
April 20, 1861.

Clark County.

We have been permitted to publish the following letter from a gentleman in Clark county to a citizen of this place:

Arkadelphia,
April 20, 1861.

I have this moment participated in raising the first flag that I ever did in my life, except that of the old thirteen stars; but this time I participated with as good a grace as ever I done anything in my life, and I am proud to say to you that I do not believe there is more than three men that now say they are for union. So when I tell you that one of the largest secession flags is now floating from the Bell pole, you will scarcely believe me, but nevertheless it is true. We had speeches from Messrs. Flannigan, Beard, Witherspoon, Dr. Huey of Camden, Parson Garrett, Col. Bozeman, etc. There [are] petitions unanimously signed to send to the president of the convention to call it at the earliest day possible. This is the first time I ever saw the people of Arkadelphia a unit in my life on any subject.

Yours in haste,
Old Nick.

HOT SPRING COUNTY, Ark.,
April 20, 1861.

Drums.

Mr. Henry C. Ward, of Hot Spring county, is in town offering his Drums for sale. They are a good article, and may be seen at the stores of S. H. Tucker & Co. and Burgevin & Field.

NAPOLEON, Ark.,
April 21, 1861.[48]

COLONEL: I received an invoice of stores (year's supply) from Major Waggaman on the 18th, and fearing, from information on the river, that some unauthorized person might interfere with them, I came down to meet them. On arriving at Little Rock I found military preparations made to intercept all boats loaded with U. S. stores. The steamboat *Sky Lark* had just passed, after having been boarded and the U. S. stores taken from her at Pine Bluff. I learned (from the paper and otherwise) that the *Silver Lake, Number 2*, would be seized if not taken at Pine Bluff (cannon were stationed for that purpose and cannoneers ready). I called upon some prominent citizens, heretofore Union men, who advised me to see the governor. I called, but did not find his Excellency at home. I very soon discovered that the revolution was general. Troops were enrolling to march on Fort Smith. The steamboat I came down on was charted. When I arrived at Pine Bluff I found the *Silver Lake, Number 2*, tied up and strongly guarded. The crew had left, the stores were placed in different houses in town, and the steamboat was to transport troops to Fort Smith. I learned from Mr. Bell, the agent (I believe) of the governor, that he had instructions to cause the stores to be sent, to Little Rock, part of them to be used in the expedition to Fort Smith, for which 5,000 troops were called out. I am on my way to Saint Louis to report to the commanding officer of [the] department, and advise, in concurrence with Colonel Emory, that stores be sent at once from Leavenworth, via Forts Scott and Gibson, to Washita.

I am, sir, very respectfully, your obedient servant,
WM. W. BURNS,
Captain and C. S.

Colonel JOS. TAYLOR, A. C. G. S., Washington, D. C.

---

48   OR,1(1):647

NASHVILLE, Tenn.,
April 21, 1861. [49]

General WALKER, *Montgomery*:

DEAR SIR: I arrived here to-day from the Arkansas River, and it is with pleasure that I report a complete revolution in public sentiment since I left. Tennessee is with the cotton States, and you may now consider the slave States a unit. "Armed neutrality" has no advocates, not even the authors of that card, which was conceived in error. The patriotism which would stand by unmoved and witness the murder of your neighbor's wife and children, because of an imaginary line, is not the growth of Tennessee, nor of any State where the rays of a genial sun shine.

The legislature meets next Thursday, and the plan is to pass the ordnance of secession and let the people ratify it, arm the State, and stand ready to march South or North.

Arkansas will go out 6th of May before breakfast. The Indians come next. Companies are forming rapidly, and I expect both my sons to go whenever the insolent invader shall tread a hostile foot upon our soil.

Arkansas and Tennessee are wild with indignation at the insolence and usurpation of the buffoon at Washington City. They are ready for the fight, every man, white and black. The blacks in Arkansas would be entirely reliable, if necessary, in defense. I know the fact is so. They are more obedient and loyal than ever before. When the fight is over, a separation of the free blacks from the slaves is the true plan to protect and guard the institution. It is one of the domestic relations that I have studied with much care.

I indorse without a proviso every act in the cotton States, done separately or together, by President, Congress, and Cabinet, and am ready to aid in all that may be necessary to accomplish what has been undertaken.

The stores for troops at Fort Smith were seized as they went up the Arkansas River and stored in Pine Bluff, one mile from my plantation. Flour and bacon chiefly. I think Arkansas, Virginia, and Tennessee will be represented in your next Congress, called for the 29th instant.

I don't think there is any danger of an overflow. The Mississippi is level full, but not against the levee above Napoleon. The Arkansas has a

---

49   OR,1(1):686-7

10-foot bank, and falling, when I came out a few days ago. The prospect for a corn crop fine. I planted one hundred acres for your army. The cotton crop is just coming up and promises well. With streamers gay push forward with sanguine cheer. The God of Battles must and will be with you. Success to the arm which strikes for our rights.

Very truly, your friend,
S. R. COCKRELL.

MONTGOMERY, Ala.,
April 22, 1861. [50]

Gov. HENRY M. RECTOR, Little Rock, Ark.:
SIR: Your patriotic response to the requisition of the President of the United States for troops to coerce the Confederate States justifies the belief that your people are prepared to unite with us in repelling the common enemy of the South. Virginia needs our aid. I therefore request you to furnish one regiment of infantry without delay, to rendezvous at Lynchburg, Va. It must consist of ten companies, of not less than sixty-four men each.

The regiment will be entitled to one colonel, one lieutenant-colonel, one major, one adjutant from the line of lieutenants, one sergeant-major from the enlisted men. Each company is entitled to one captain, one first lieutenant, two second lieutenants, fours sergeants, four corporals, and two musicians. The officers, except the staff offices, are to be appointed in the manner prescribed by the law of your State. Staff officers are appointed by the President; the term of service, not less than twelve months, unless sooner discharged. They will be mustered into the service at Lynchburg, but transportation and subsistence will be provided from the point of departure.

They will furnish their own uniform, but will receive its value in commutation. You have arms and ammunition with which to supply them. Answer and say whether you will comply with this request, and, if so, when.

L. P. WALKER.

---

50   OR,1(1):687

LITTLE ROCK, Ark.,
April 22. 1861.[51]

EXECUTIVE OFFICE,
Little Rock, Ark., April 22, 1861.

Honorable SIMON CAMERON,
Secretary of War, Washington City:
In answer to you requisition for troops [from] Arkansas to subjugate the Southern States, I have to say that none will be furnished. The demand is only adding insult to injury. The people of this commonwealth are freemen, not slaves, and will defend to the last extremity their honor, lives, and property against Northern mendacity and usurpation.

H. M. RECTOR,
Governor of Arkansas.

LITTLE ROCK, Ark.,
April 23, 1861.[52]

L. P. WALKER: Governor Rector, not being free as yet to send the regiment requested by the Secretary of War, has placed in the hands of the undersigned the dispatch. Will the President accept a regiment raised by the undersigned, complying in all other respects with the requisition of the Secretary? Further, the governor has agreed to arm and equip the regiment when rendezvoused at Little Rock Arsenal.

T. B. FLOURNOY, *Colonel.*
JNO. B. THOMPSON, *Lieutenant-Colonel.*
W. N. BROUGNAH.
JAS. B. JOHNSON.

LITTLE ROCK, Ark.,
April 23, 1861.[53]

L. P. WALKER:
You may be assured of the immediate action of Arkansas in joining the Southern Confederacy; but I have no power, I regret, to comply with your request. Our convention assembles on the 6th of May. Then we can and will aid.

H. M. RECTOR,
Governor Arkansas.

---

51   OR,1(1):687
52   OR,1(1):688
53   OR,1(1):687

FORT SMITH, Ark.,
April 24, 1861.

No. 7.[54]

Report of Major Richard C. Gatlin, Fifth U. S. Infantry, of the seizure of
Fort Smith, Ark.

COLONEL: I have the honor to report that a body of troops of the State of Arkansas, under the command of Colonel S. Borland, entered and of the First Cavalry, having evacuated it but a few hours previous. Being on a visit at the post at the time, I was made a prisoner of war by the authority of his Excellency the governor of the State, but permitted to go at large upon giving my parole not to fight against the State of Arkansas or the Southern Confederated States during the pending difficulties between the latter and the United States, unless exchanged.

In a conversation with Colonel Borland to-day I am given to understand that the governor is acting as though the State had already seceded; that last act in the drama being only a question of a few days' time.

Very respectfully, your obedient servant,
W. C. GATLIN,
Major, Fifth Infantry.

Colonel L. THOMAS,
Adjutant-General U. S. Army, Washington, D. C.

LITTLE ROCK, Ark.,
April 24, 1861. [55]

L. P. WALKER:
After the governor promised the arms, he was forced to send them to the frontier, to protect the State against invasion. There are now no arms but flint-locks. Can you furnish us arms? Answer quick. Companies are waiting your response.

T. B. FLOURNOY.

---

54   OR,1(1):650
55   OR,1(1):688

LITTLE ROCK, Ark.,
April 24, 1861.

No. 9.[56]

Report of Captain Alexander Montgomery, assistant quartermaster, U. S.
Army, of the seizure of Fort Smith, Ark.

CAPTAIN: I have the honor to report that the companies of cavalry under command of Captain Sturgis, First Cavalry, withdrew from this post yesterday evening and marched in the direction of Fort Washita. I inclose a copy of an order he issued immediately before leaving, directing the entire evacuation of the post.

About two hours after his departure a body of troops under the command of Colonel Solon Borland, aide-de-camp to his Excellency the governor of the State of Arkansas, accompanied by the adjutant-general of the State, arrived in steamers and took possession of the post, making me a prisoner of war, under authority and by direction of the governor of the State. Major R. C. Gatlin, Fifth Infantry, who happened to be in the garrison at the time of visit, was also made prisoner of war. On giving our parole that we would not fight against the State of Arkansas or the Southern Confederate States during the existing difficulties between the latter and the United States, unless exchanged, we were permitted to go at large. The force under Colonel Borland consisted of 235 men, rank and file, with battery of artillery. Colonel Borland demanded and has taken possession of all the public property at the post and in this vicinity, inventories of all the public property at the post and in its vicinity, inventories of which will be forwarded to the proper bureau.

For the information of the friends of the parties. I beg leave to state that Major Brown, paymaster, and Captain Burns, C. S., were absent from the post at the time of its evacuation. Major Brown, returning from Fort Arbuckle, received information at Scullyville that I had been made a prisoner of war, and immediately turned back and joined Captain Sturgis' command. Captain Burns had gone down the river to look after certain subsistence stores, which it was feared would be seized by the State authorities. The movement of Captain Sturgis was necessitated by the limited supply of provisions on hand and the intelligence received a short time before he left that all the public stores on the river in transit to this

---

56   OR,1(1):651

post had been detained or captured by the State authorities. He was also awarded that the governor of the State had dispatched a force, with artillery, to demand possession of the post, and possibly to capture his arms and horses. It was not expected that any orders had been given to make prisoners of war.

I have the honor to be, sir, very respectfully, your obedient servant,
A. MONTGOMERY,
Captain and Qu. M., U. S. Army.

Captain SETH WILLIAMS, Asst. Adjt. General,
Headquarters Department of the West, Saint Louis, Mo.

**LITTLE ROCK, Ark.,
April 25, 1861.**[57]

Honorable L. P. WALKER:
You will have to arm us. There are only thirteen hundred and sixty-four percussion guns; balance flint-locks. The governor has employed the percussion guns to protect the frontier, and declines now giving us any until the convention meets on the 6th May. A favorable answer desired. The men will rendezvous at once. We will inform you when ready to embark and the route.

T. B. FLOURNOY.

**LITTLE ROCK, Ark.,
April 25, 1861.**[58]

The ladies we understand have taken up the cause in earnest. They were up till one o'clock Tuesday night making uniforms for the Prairie company, who came in about twelve o'clock on Monday, on their way to Fort Smith. Fifty jackets had to be bought, cut and made; and though they were not finished in time, as they had left at eleven, yet they were sent up on the first boat.

---

57   OR,1(1):688-9
58   *Arkansas True Democrat*, April 25, 1861, Little Rock, Ark.

PULASKI COUNTY, Ark.,
April 27, 1861. [59]

We have been requested by the president of the meeting recently held in Lefevre township in this county to state, that the meeting to raise a secession pole on the 27th inst., and the barbecue intended to come off on that day, have been postponed.

LITTLE ROCK, Ark.,
April 29, 1861. [60]

Honorable L. P. WALKER, Your communication of the 17th instant is received. A battery on the Mississippi near Helena, or any other eligible point, is important as well to the Confederate States as to Arkansas, and meets my entire approval and consent.

H. M. RECTOR.

WASHINGTON, Ark.,
May 1, 1861. [61]

His Excellency JEFF. DAVIS, Montgomery, Ala.:
SIR: Arkansas will certainly secede between the 6th and 8th instant, and join as soon as may be the Southern Confederacy. As commander of the First Brigade, First Division, of the Militia, I am authorized to tender you, without limit, the whole strength of the brigade, to be used or called into active service as you may deem proper. There are, as present constituted, eight regiments in the brigade, all officered and ready for action except in arms and munitions of war. Please communicate with me immediately.

Very respectfully,
BENJ. P. JETT,
Brigadier General, First Brigadier, First Div., Arkansas Militia

---

59   *Arkansas True Democrat*, April 25, 1861, Little Rock, Ark.
60   OR,1(1):689
61   OR,1(1):689

CAIRO, Ill.,
May 4, 1861.

Query.[62]

If four dogs, with sixteen legs, can catch forty-nine rabbits, with eighty-seven legs in forty-four minutes, how many legs must the same rabbits have to get away from eight dogs with thirty two legs, in seventeen minutes and a half?
Solution. Add together the legs of the rabbits and the tails of the dogs, and divide the amount by three big dogs; this leaves four bushels of barks, and thirteen pounds of hair. Take the fractions of the rabbits, add six inches of snow, multiply by a dog fight. Then divide by a man with a double barreled shot gun, and add a side of fresh beef. Multiply by half as many legs as three times a less number of rabbits would have had, and divide by one-third of the time it would take for the rabbits to get away from the dogs, less 17½ minutes. The result depends upon the size of the dogs.

-Cairo Gazette.

LITTLE ROCK, Ark.
May 6, 1861.[63]

Hon. DAVID WALKER, President of the Arkansas State Convention:
SIR- During my absence, I was chosen by the convention, of which you are president, as one of the five delegates from Arkansas to a border states convention, proposed by Virginia, to be held this spring at Frankfort, Kentucky. I avail myself of the occasion, to express to the members of your body, through you, my grateful thanks for this unsolicited mark of confidence, and the honor thus conferred, for so it ought to be considered. And surely, if I could be of any use to Arkansas, in the position, I would most cheerfully and zealously devote whatever ability I possess to her service. For Arkansas is my own, and the home of my family; I neither look to, have, nor desire any other. A continuous residence here of twenty-five years duration, has indissolubly attached

---

62   *Weekly Arkansas Gazette*, May 4, 1861, Little Rock, Ark.
63   *Journal of the Called Session of the Convention of Arkansas. Begun and Held at Little Rock on Monday, the Sixth Day of May, A.D. 1861.* pp. 117-120

me to her soil, and taught me to appreciate and admire the worth, patriotism, hospitality and chivalry of her people. Arkansas is endeared to me by affection towards the living, and regretful memories for the dead; some of whom, near and dear to me, sleep peacefully in her soil. All my interests, hopes and feelings are, from voluntary choice, inseparably identified with Arkansas and wherever she may lead, I will follow cheerfully, contentedly and with no grudging or measured loyalty. I sincerely say of her: may she always be right, but right or wrong, I am for her, and with her. Recent and startling events, occurring since my election, render it proper, in my opinion, that I should yield back to the convention the trust with which I was honored. I do not stop to speculate upon the probabilities of border states convention being held; but if I understand the original purpose of it, it would now fail to accomplish it; recent events having entirely changed the position of the border states, and of Arkansas also.

When I was chosen, I was a Union man, and opposed to a disruption of the Federal Union, as long as there remained a hope or prospect of preserving it, and of securing our just rights, and privileges, and of maintaining our honor under, and in it. And I fondly believed that prudence, patriotism, peace, justice and concession prevailing, that result might ultimately be accomplished. But that hope has now vanished. The war cloud has risen, and is fast spreading over our country north and south, east and west. Preparations for civil war, are witnessed everywhere, and hostile squadrons are ready to meet each other in deadly conflict. President Lincoln, the nominal head, and urged on and sustained by at least the most violent of the black republican party, has, without authority and without necessity, committed himself to the criminal folly of prosecuting a coercive and warlike policy towards the seceded states, and the people thereof. In point of authority, it is a palpable violation of the constitution he professes to respect. In point of policy, it is unwise and short-sighted; because, if preserved in, must eventually result in forcing every border state out of the Union; and pitiless and cruel, because it must inevitably bring an unnatural civil war upon the country - the most dreadful and desolating of all wars, recorded in history. And it is contrary to the implied, if not express, pledges, repeatedly and solemnly given to the American people, to the effect that his administration would be peaceful and conciliatory towards the seceded states. It is a fatal error, on his part, if he supposes that he can coerce or subdue the southern states, or find men in them to aid him, or sympathize with him, in such a criminal and unholy work. The very hills and valleys will swarm with multiplied thousands of brave hearts and valiant arms, eager to resist him, and his marshalled hosts, in the defense of their own and their sister states.

It was only under a peaceful, prudent and conciliatory course towards the seceded states - the policy of leaving them undisturbed and unmolested - avoiding the use of force - that Arkansas was willing to remain in the Union; and this, with the hope that, in due time, there might be a reconstruction of the Union on fair, just and honorable terms; or that the present difficulties and troubles - perhaps not just now, but at no distant period - might be satisfactorily and honorably adjusted. And such, in my opinion - might be satisfactorily and honorably adjusted. And such, in my opinion, would have been the result of a peaceful policy, and of just and statesmanlike measures on the part of the administration. But unfortunately the war policy - the coercive policy has prevailed; and on the heads of the black republicans be the bloody consequences. Being in the possession of the government, and all its departments, the Supreme Court excepted - they held the power to save the Union, but would not do it. They had the power to prevent the effusion of blood but would not do it; and now the responsibility rests with them. By such means the Union sentiment in Arkansas has been completely changed. The honest differences of opinion that have existed among us, in reference to immediate secession - arising from expediency rather than principle, have passed away. As to become a unit; all of us standing pledged to resist force; well knowing that no free government can live if force is required to keep it together. I am a southerner by choice and by adoption. I have lived in a slave state nearly all my life. All my interests and feelings and hopes are bound with the South. For weal or for woe, I am with her, and for her. Not having been heretofore, I never expect to be, unmindful of her rights, true interests, or honor.

The black republican policy of war being now clearly indicated, Arkansas cannot see it with unconcern, nor submit to it without resistance. Everyone must now take sides for or against coercion. There can be but one voice in our state on the proposition. We shall all stand by the South; nor do I believe there are any who would think of acting at all times, to defend the people of the South, their homes, firesides, property and rights to the last extremity, if need be, and against all foes.

Respectfully, your ob't serv't,
S.H. HEMPSTEAD.

LITTLE ROCK, Ark.,
May 6, 1861.[64]

3 O'CLOCK, P.M.

Convention met. Roll called.

PRESENT: Messrs. Adams of Izard, Adams of Phillips, Austin, Baber, Batson, Bolinger, Bradley, Bush, Bussey, Campbell, Carrigan, Claingman, Crenshaw, Cryer, Cypert, Cochran, Desha, Dinsmore, Dodson, Dollarhide, Echols, Fishback, Flanagin, Floyd, Fort, Fuller, Garland of Hempstead, Garland of Pulaski, Gould, Grace, Griffith, Gunter, Hanly, Hawkins of Ashley, Hawkins of Sevier, Hill, Hilliard, Hobbs, Hobson, Johnson, Kelley, Kennard, Lanier, Laughinghouse, Mansfield, Mayo, Murphy, Parks, Patterson of Jackson, Ray, Rhodes, Robinson, Shelton, Slemons, Smith, Smoote, Spivey, Stallings, Stillwell, Stout, Tatum, Thomason, Totten of Arkansas, Totten of Prairie, Turner, Walker, Wallace, Yell and Mr. President- 70.

Mr. Grace, from the committee on ordinances and resolutions, made the following

REPORT:

Mr. PRESIDENT-

Your committee, in obedience to the instructions of this convention, have directed me to report the accompanying preamble and ordinance, and recommend their adoption.

Respectfully,
W.P. GRACE, *Chairman.*

ORDINANCE No. 2

AN ORDINANCE *to dissolve the Union now existing between the State of Arkansas and the other states united with her under the compact entitled "The Constitution of the United States of America."*

WHEREAS, In addition to the well-founded causes of complaint set forth by this convention, in resolutions adopted on the 11th March, A.D., 1861, against the sectional party now in power at Washington City, headed by Abraham Lincoln, he has, in the face of resolutions passed by this convention, pledging the State of Arkansas, to resist to the last extremity, any attempt on the part of such power to coerce any state that

---

[64]   *Journal of the Called Session of the Convention of Arkansas. Begun and Held at Little Rock on Monday, the Sixth Day of May, A.D. 1861.* pp. 121-124.

had seceded from the old Union, proclaimed to the world that war should be waged against such states, until they should be compelled to submit to their rule, and large forces to accomplish this have by this same power, been called out, and are now being marshalled to carry out this inhuman design; and to longer submit to such rule, or remain in the old Union of the United States, would be disgraceful and ruinous to the State of Arkansas.

Therefore, we the people of the State of Arkansas, in convention assembled, do hereby declare and ordain, and it is hereby declared and ordained, that the "ordinance and acceptance of compact," passed and approved by the General Assembly of the State of Arkansas, on the 18th day of October, A.D. 1846, whereby it was, by said General Assembly, ordained that, by virtue of authority vested in said General Assembly, by the provisions of an ordinance adopted by the convention of delegates assembled at Little Rock, for the purpose of forming a constitution and system of government of said state, the propositions set forth in "an act supplementary to an act entitled *an act for the admission of the State of Arkansas into the Union, and to provide for the due execution of the laws of the United States within the same, and for other purposes*, were freely accepted, ratified and irrevocably confirmed articles of compact and union between the State of Arkansas and the United States," and all other laws, and every other law and ordinance, whereby the State of Arkansas became a member of the federal union, be, and the same are hereby, in all respects, and for every purpose herewith consistent, repealed, abrogated and fully, set aside; and the union now subsisting between the State of Arkansas and the other states, under the name of the United States of America, is hereby forever dissolved.

And we do further hereby declare and ordain, that the State of Arkansas hereby resumes to herself all rights and powers heretofore delegated to the government of the United States of America - that her citizens are absolved from all allegiance to said government of the United States, and that she is in full possession and exercise of all the rights and sovereignty which appertain to a free and independent state.

We do further ordain and declare, that all rights acquired and vested under the constitution of the United States of America, or of any act or acts of Congress, or treaty, or under any law of this state, and not incompatible with this ordinance, shall remain in full force and effect, in no wise altered or impaired, and have the same effect as if this ordinance had not been passed.

Which report was received; and Mr. Yell moved that the ordinance be adopted.

Mr. Dinsmore offered the following amendment:

"And that the above ordinance be submitted to the citizens of the State of Arkansas for their acceptance or rejection, by a writ of election, issued by the president of this convention, to be held on the 1st Monday of June next."

Mr. Patterson of Jackson moved to lay the amendment of Mr. Dinsmore on the table.

On which Mr. Totten, of Arkansas, called for the yeas and neas, which call being sustained, was ordered and had with the following result:

YEAS- Messrs. Adams of Izard, Adams of Phillips, Austin, Baber, Batson, Bradley, Bush, Bussey, Carrigan, Claingman, Crenshaw, Cryer, Cypert, Cochran, Dollarhide, Echols, Flannagin, Floyd, Fort, Fuller, Garland of Hempstead, Garland of Pulaski, Gould, Grace, Hanly, Hawkins of Ashley, Hawkins of Sevier, Hill, Hilliard, Hobbs, Hobson, Johnson, Kennard, Lanier, Laughinghouse, Mansfield, Mayo, Patterson of Jackson, Ray, Rhodes, Robinson, Shelton, Slemons, Smith, Smoote, Spivey, Stillwell, Stout, Tatum, Totten of Arkansas, Totten of Prairie, Walker, Wallace, Watkins, and Yell- 55.

NAYS- Messrs. Bolinger, Campbell, Desha, Dinsmore, Dodson, Fishback, Griffin, Gunter, Kelley, Murphy, Parks, Stallings, Thomason, Turner and Mr. President- 15.

So the amendment was lost.

The question was then stated to be on the adoption of the ordinance, upon which Mr. Cryer called for the yeas and nays, which being sustained, was ordered and had with the following result:

YEAS- Messrs. Adams of Izard, Adams of Phillips, Austin, Baber, Batson, Bradley, Bush, Bussey, Carrigan, Claingman, Crenshaw, Cryer, Cypert, Cochran, Desha, Dinsmore, Dodson, Dollarhide, Echols. Fishback. Flanagin, Floyd, Fort, Fuller, Garland of Hempstead, Garland of Pulaski, Gould, Grace, Griffith, Hanly, Hawkins of Ashley, Hawkins of Sevier, Hill, Hilliard, Hobbs, Hobson, Johnson, Kennard, Lanier, Laughinghouse, Mansfield, Mayo, Parks, Patterson of Jackson, Ray, Rhodes, Robinson, Shelton, Slemons, Smith, Smoote, Spivey, Stallings, Stillwell, Stout, Tatum, Thomason, Totten of Arkansas, Totten of Prairie, Turner, Walker, Wallace, Watkins, Yell and Mr. President- 65.

NAYS- Messrs. Bolinger, Campbell, Gunter, Kelley and Murphy- 5.

At the call of Mr. President, Mr. President addressed the convention, urging unanimity; whereupon Mr. Bolinger, who had voted in the negative, arose and stated in substance, that,

"I voted against the ordinance declaring the independence of the state, in accordance with my pledges to my people, but to secure unanimity, I ask to change my vote to the affirmative, at the same time denying the right of secession."

Mr. Bolinger also asked that the explanation be spread upon the journals; which was so ordered, and his vote changed from "nay" to "aye."

Mr. Campbell, with a similar explanation, also changed his vote from "nay" to "aye."

Mr. Kelley, with an explanation in substance that, "he was in favor of revolution, but ignored the right of secession," also changed his vote from "nay" to "aye."

Mr. Gunter, with a similar explanation, also changed his vote from "nay" to "aye."

Mr. Fishback explained his vote.

So the ordinance dissolving the union hereunto existing between the State of Arkansas and the other states under the compact known as the "Constitution of the United States of America," was, at 10 minutes past 4 o'clock, declared adopted and passed by a vote of 69 in the affirmative, to 1 in the negative. Upon motion of Mr. Grace, the convention adjourned until to-morrow morning 10 of the clock.

DAVID WALKER,
President.

LITTLE ROCK, Ark.,
May 7, 1861.[65]

Dear Martha,

I have concluded to devote a portion of this morning in chatting with you. On Wednesday morning I received your letter sent by Mr. Jn Conway. I was very glad to hear that all was well. I can make as yet to Say when the Convention will adjourn. Soon I wish for I am getting tired of this place. The weather is quite warm. My health is still improving and

---

[65]   Letter written from Billy to Martha. Original Letter is in the personal archives of the author.

could enjoy myself much better if you were down here with me. I am getting really anxious to see you and the dear little ones. I am unable to tell you anything that we have done; the veil of Secrecy is on all that we do. You ask my opinion concerning the public affairs. I must say everything looks dark and gloomy at this time and no prospect for an improvement in the future.

The latest news from Washington City is that Lincoln Government is making extensive preparations to wage a war of extermination. I see no hope for the future of our country. No one can estimate the amount of Suffering we are doomed to. Provisions of every kind are very high and a good prospect of getting higher. Business of every kind has nearly stopped. Confidence seems to have been lost between men. I fear nothing but [this] will be the last of our country.

I cannot tell you when I shall be at home but as soon as possible. I deem it useless to advise you what to do at home as I am Satisfied. You are as a better farmer as I am or a little better. Enclosed you will find a copy of *Dixie* written by Albert Pike of this place. I will write again in a few days. My hands are still nervous. Give my love to all, kiss to the children for me and tell them with you for me as was a thousand times.

Your own,
Billy.

FORT SMITH, Ark.,
May 8, 1861.[66]

HEADQUARTERS EIGHTH BRIGADE, FIRST DIVISION,
ARKANSAS MILITIA,

Fort Smith, Ark., May 8, 1861.
Gov. C. HARRIS: To-day we have information that Arkansas, in Convention, has seceded, by a vote 69 to 1. Tennessee has also seceded, and made large appropriations and ordered an army of 50,000 men.

Arkansas has for several days past been in arms on this frontier for the protection [of] citizens, and the neighboring Indian nations whose interests are identical with her own. I have news through my scout that the U. S. troops have abandoned the forts in the Chickasaw country. Under my orders from the commander-in-chief and governor of

---

66   OR,1(1):691

Arkansas, I feel authorized to extend to you such military aid as will be required in the present juncture of affairs to occupy and hold the forts.

I have appointed Colonel A. H. Word, one of the State senators, and Captain Sparks, attached to this command, commissioners to treat and confer with you on this subject. These gentlemen are fully apprised of the nature of the powers intrusted to myself by the governor of this State, and are authorized to express to you my vies of the subject under consideration. I ask, therefore, that you express to them your own wishes in the premises, and believe, my dear sir, that Arkansas cherishes the kindest regards for your people.

> I have the honor to subscribe myself, with sentiments of regard,
> your Excellency's friend and servant,
> B. BURROUGHS,
> *Brigadier-General, Commanding.*

FORT SMITH, Ark.,
May 10, 1861.

From Fort Washita.[67]

We learn from Mr. Hester, who arrived last evening, direct from Boggy Depot, that the federal troops at Fort Washita, are making preparations to evacuate that post. A gentleman arrived at Boggy Depot on Saturday evening from Fort Washita, informed Mr. Hester, that the commander there had advertised for one hundred wagons, for transportation to Fort Leavenworth, Kansas Territory, but the people were unwilling to go at any price. They were offering five dollars per day, but no one could be had. It is supposed that, as soon as they can procure transportation they will evacuate the post immediately.

Mr. H., says, Capt. Sturgiss has taken a road for Fort Leavenworth, and has not gone to Fort Washita. He left the main road about 70 miles from this place. He was informed that two of Capt. S's men refused to go North with him, one was killed and the other severely wounded with a sabre.

Ft. Smith Herald, 1st.

---

67   *Weekly Arkansas Gazette*, May 11, 1861, Little Rock, Ark.

LITTLE ROCK, Ark.,
May 11, 1861.

Advice to Volunteers.[68]

How to prepare for the Campaign.

A writer, who signs himself "An Old Soldier," gives the following advice to young soldiers:

1. Remember that in a campaign more men die from sickness than by the bullet.
2. Line your blanket with one thickness of brown drilling. This adds but four ounces in weight, and doubles the warmth.
3. Buy a small India rubber blanket (only $1 50) to lay on the ground or to throw over your soldiers when on guard duty during a rain storm. Most of the eastern troops are provided with these. Straw to lie on is not always to be had.
4. The best military hat in use is the light colored soft felt; the crown being sufficiently high to allow space for air over the brain. You can fasten it up as a continental in fair weather, or turn it down when it is wet or very sunny.
5. Let your beard grow, so as to protect the throat and lungs.
6. Keep your entire person clean; this prevents fevers and bowel complaints in warm climates. Wash your body each day, if possible. Avoid strong coffee and oily meat. Gen. Scott said that the too free use of these (together with neglect in keeping the skin clean,) cost many a soldier his life in Mexico.
7. A sudden check of perspiration by chilly or night air often causes fever and death. When thus exposed, do not forget your blanket.

MOUND CITY, Ark.,
May 15, 1861.

Flag Presentation.[69]

A splendid flag was yesterday presented to the Pine Bluff Jefferson Guards, lying at Mound City, by Miss Hattie Bocage, on behalf of the ladies of Pine Bluff. The well-chosen words of the lady were responded to on behalf of the company by Capt. Carleton.

---

68 *Weekly Arkansas Gazette*, May 11, 1861, Little Rock, Ark.
69 *Memphis Daily Appeal*, May 16, 1861, Memphis, Tenn.

MOUND CITY, Ark.,
May 15, 1861.

Flag Presentation at Camp Rector.[70]

We learn that the Jefferson Guards, Captain Carlton, now encamped at Camp Rector, will be to-day the recipients of a magnificent banner from some of the fair daughters of Arkansas. The presentation address will be delivered by Miss Etta Bocage, and the ceremonies will come off at 11 o'clock, A. M. Persons from the city wishing to witness the affair can take the ferry boat *Mark R. Cheek.*

MOUND CITY, Ark.,
May 15, 1861.

Another Flag Presentation at Camp Rector.[71]

The Jefferson Guards, from Pine Bluff, Ark., who are now encamped at Mound City, and who were presented with a flag yesterday, will be honored in the same manner again to-day, by the ladies of their city. Miss Lilian T. Rozell will make the presentation speech. The ceremonies will be interesting and the ladies and gentlemen of Memphis are invited to be present. The boat will leave the wharf at the foot of Adams Street at 10 o'clock this morning.

CAMP ON WALNUT CREEK, Kans.,
May 21, 1861.

No. 8.[72]

Report of Major Samuel D. Sturgis, Fourth U. S. Cavalry, of the seizure
of Fort Smith, Ark.

CAMP ON WALNUT CREEK, KANS., May 21, 1861.

SIR: I avail myself of the first opportunity which has occurred since leaving Fort Smith, Ark., to inform you that I evacuated that post at 9 o'clock p.m. on the 23rd ultimo, and marched with my command for Fort Washita, where we arrived on the 30th ultimo, and reported for duty to

---

70   *Memphis Daily Appeal*, May 15, 1861, Memphis, Tenn.
71   *Memphis Daily Appeal*, May 16, 1861, Memphis, Tenn.
72   OR,1(1):650

Colonel W. H. Emory, First Cavalry. All the available transportation at the post, amounting to some twenty wagons and teams, was taken along.

The ordnance sergeant, hospital steward, chief bugler, sick, and laundresses were left at the post, to be shipped to Jefferson Barracks by Captain A. Montgomery, A. Q. M.

The causes which induce me to evacuate the post I presume are known to the department commander from general notoriety. After the supplies were cut off by the State of Arkansas the post, of course, became untenable, and we could have occupied it in any case but a few more days.

One hour after we left, two boats arrived with three hundred men and ten pieces of artillery. To have contended against this force with two companies of cavalry, and that, too, while the entire population of the surrounding country were ready at a moment's warning to take up arms against us, could only have resulted eventually in our being taken prisoners and the loss to the Government of all the arms, horses, means of transportation, &c., at the post.

I have the honor to be, sir,
Very respectfully, your obedient servant,
S. D. STURGIS,
Captain, First Cavalry.

Captain S. WILLIAMS, Asst. Adjt. General,
Headquarters Department of the West, Saint Louis, Mo.

LEWISBURG, Ark.,
May 25, 1861.
From Conway County.[73]

Messrs. Editors: Our old and esteemed fellow citizen, the Hon. Geo. W. Lemoyne, of Dardanelle, addressed the Conway Mounted Rifles today at the Masonic Hall. A large assembly of ladies and gentlemen were present. His effort was enthusiastic, eloquent and intensely southern - few dry lids were to be found in the assembly. The women of '61 in Lewisburg and vicinity have been at work night and day making up the uniforms for the volunteers. Three cheers for the ladies - always true, always patriotic. At the conclusion of the address, the "soldier's response

---

73 *Arkansas True Democrat,* May 30, 1861, Little Rock, Ark.

to *Dixie,*" by Lemoyne was sung with telling effect. The Conway Rifles camped Monday at Lewisburg, and will be in readiness to join Col. Churchill on his way to Ft. Smith. May the God of Battles prosper them.

W. L. M.
J. M. H.

MEMPHIS, Tenn.,
May 28, 1861.

Reported Invasion.[74]

Reports have been circulated of the advance of Jim Lane and his men into Arkansas from the State of Kansas, but little attention was paid to them until yesterday, when some fifty women, many of them with children, entirely without protectors of the other sex, arrived in this city by way of the Little Rock railroad and ferry-boat. They were generally from Madison and adjoining parts of St. Francis county. One of the gentlemen on the same train stated that information had been received of the presence of Lane on Black river, between Pocahontas and Jacksonport. He said he was one of a committee appointed at a meeting of the citizens of Madison to request Gen. Bradley, and also Gen. Pillow, to send troops and arms to their defense. He also stated that Gov. Rector had telegraphed Gen. Bradley to hasten with what troops could be spared from his command, and meet the invading enemy. John D. Adams, of the steamboat *Notrebe,* yesterday received a dispatch from George Morrison, of Little Rock, informing him that great excitement existed there in consequence of the prevalence of a report of the same tenor as given above. We were informed that dispatches had been received from Mr. Morrill, editor of the *Des Arc Citizen,* which stated that the steamboat *Mary Patterson* had arrived at that place, and her people informed them that the story of Lane and his men being on Black river was false; also that a thousand Arkansas troops were on the watch on the Missouri line to prevent invasion. This dispatch came in last evening. The *Mary Patterson* had twelve tons of lead on board, brought overland to a point on the river, from Iron Mountain, Mo.; there was more to come. It was also confidently stated that Gen. Harney with Lincoln troops was at Ironton, the termination of the St. Louis and Iron Mountain railroad.

---

74   *Memphis Daily Appeal,* May 29, 1861, Memphis, Tenn.

LITTLE ROCK, Ark.,
May 28, 1861.

Letter from Little Rock.[75]

Eds. *Appeal*: Your paper, as you know, has an extensive circulation among the people of this State. It is highly esteemed by us as a medium of general information, and is in much request as a rumor of passing events in Arkansas, identified with you, so intimately, in common interests and kindred impulses. A few days ago - three days after the passage of the ordinance of secession by the Arkansas convention, we organized, and sent to share in the earliest conflicts, in behalf of southern independence, a regiment of one thousand men, beneath whose rude garb of southern "homespun," burned spirits as gallant, cultivated and proud as ever animated southern breasts. . .

LITTLE ROCK, Ark.,
May 30, 1861.[76]

Those of our people who are compelled to stay at home and look after their crops and other business should organize themselves into guerilla bands. An invading army cannot stand a guerilla warfare. Let us prepare to attack them from every hillside and mountain fastness; from every thicket and hiding place, and we can decimate the greatest army the enemy can march against us.

LITTLE ROCK, Ark.,
June 1, 1860.

Flag Presentation.[77]

On Thursday after noon there was quite a display of beauty and gallantry on St. John's College grounds. The occasion was the presentation of a flag by the ladies of Little Rock to Capt. Churchill's Regiment. The Louisiana Regiment was present by invitation. The grounds were crowded by citizens. The flag was presented by Miss Mattie Faulkner with a handsome speech, and received by Capt. Matlock who also made an appropriate address. A part of Col. Churchill's regiment left yesterday for Fort Smith - the remainder will depart within a day or two.

---

75   *Memphis Daily Appeal*, May 31, 1861, Memphis, Tenn.
76   *Arkansas True Democrat*, May 30, 1861, Little Rock, Ark.
77   *Weekly Arkansas Gazette*, June 1, 1861, Little Rock, Ark.

MOUND CITY, Ark.,
June 1, 1861.

Presentation of Banners to the Jefferson Guards-
Patriotic Compliments from abroad.[78]

The patriotic ladies of Pine Bluff, to manifest their esteem for that noble band - the "Jefferson Guards" - from this city, and now stationed at Mound City, above Memphis, proceeded to that place, and presented the Company with two beautiful flags to fight under in the glorious struggle for Southern independence. The Memphis papers are filled up with extended and glowing accounts of the two occasions, which attracted large crowds of ladies and gentlemen of Memphis, and the surrounding vicinity. We have only time for making short extracts of complimentary notices from people abroad toward the fair ones from Pine Bluff who had the honor of presenting the banners, also the compliments paid to the popular and brave Captain of the Company.

Miss Etta Bocage presented a beautiful banner, the work of her own hands, on Wednesday the 15th inst. The *Memphis Evening Argus* pays the following handsome compliment to the fair donor, and Capt. Carlton:

The fair donor of the flag, Miss Bocage, daughter of Judge Bocage, of Pine Bluff, is one of the loveliest women upon whom it has been the good fortune of those present to gaze for a time whereof the mind runneth not to the contrary. Tall, dark eyed and dark haired, graceful in every movement, it was not surprising that the soldiery greeted her with so much joy and enthusiasm. The flag was of fine blue silk, most elegantly wrought and decorated, containing the name of the company for whom it was designed, and other inscriptions not visible from the portion of Arkansas upon which we were standing. The presentation speech was appropriate, eloquent and brief, and every word seemed accompanied by that correctness which bespoke that the fair speaker was only expressing the patriotic emotions of the heart in the words which fell from her lips.

Capt. Carlton, as brave and handsome a soldier as can be found in any corps, received the beautiful gift in behalf of his company, and responded in a few words, which, at once earnest, and most eloquent, were well received. Judge Bocage stepped forward and presented, as the

---

78   *Weekly Arkansas Gazette*, June 1, 1861, Little Rock, Ark.

gift of Mr. Dubois, an absent member of the guard, an ensign's belt for the flag. Nine hearty cheers were then given - three for Miss Bocage, three for the absent member, and three for Capt. Carlton.

On Thursday the 16th inst., Miss Lillian T. Rozelle, in the name of the ladies of Pine Bluff, presented a Confederate flag to the Jefferson Guards, to be presented to the Arkansas Regiment at Mound city, commanded by Col. Cleburne. The *Avalanche* thus speaks of the occasion, giving Miss Rozelle's speech:

"About 8 o'clock the entire battalion was put in motion for the purpose of participating in the ceremonies. They marched to the hotel in all "the pomp and circumstance of glorious war." The bristling bayonets and the general paraphernalia presented an imposing appearance. Each company was composed of stalwart men - soldiers strong in bone and muscle and nerve, and still stronger in hope and faith. The troops were drawn up in front of the stand erected for the occasion. So soon as the Jefferson Guards marched up, Miss Lillian T. Rozelle, of Pine Bluff, arose and delivered the following beautiful address:

Address to the Jefferson Guards - Our beloved Countrymen: We greet you to-day to present your brave band with this banner, arranged by the ladies of Pine Bluff - those dear to your hearts and firesides.

With souls ripe in loyal patriotism we strive with happy willingness, sparing no toil or labor in endeavoring to make the offering, this flag, to wave o'er the glorious and gifted sons of Jefferson, and that with every breeze may be wafted endless chimes of your honor, valor and glory. Our hands have made it; your hearts must defend it.

You go, brave ones, to struggle in the dearest cause an American heart has at stake - the rights of this hallowed land of the South! Remember "it was liberty, not Union, for which our forefathers fought." And now that your own cherished State has bared her bosom to breast the storm, struggle for her! Retain her a bright constellation in the brilliant galaxy of Southern States.

Not the aggressors, but the *wronged*, you secure the smiles of an all-wise and just God, who will extend his eternal arm for your protection. Let the sacred motto be inscribed on every heart, "*Honi soit qui maly pense,*" or "Evil be to him who evil thinks of it." This banner we consign to your care, with prayers and tears sent up to Heaven's throne in your behalf, by them who daily cry, "Our hearts are with you." Accept our farewell and last injunction:

Oh! Shield the bright South! This beautiful land,
Sacred and dear to your own loyal land;
Her winds sang your cradle hymns gently and low,
And tuned were your hearts to her brooklets and flow.
And now that the foe with despotic sway,
Seeks to tear all her glory and wealth away,
Nerve you strong hearts! To the rescue go on,
'Till silenced the storm and bright battles won.
There, too, the heart of true woman will go
To smile in your joy and soothe in your woe.
When laurels the brightest your brows shall entwine,
Her soul's hymns for you shall witchingly chime;
Then, on brave ones, ever on in the right,
God your defender will save you from blight.

The graceful and modest demeanor with which Miss Rozelle
discharged the duties imposed upon her won all hearts. Her address is
short, but in exquisite taste. Her articulation was clear and distinct; and
her emphasis and intonation showed that she felt while an actor on the
occasion. As we listened to her inspiring words, the lines of a noble bard
flashed across our memory:

"The light of love, the purity of grace,
The mind, the music breathing from her face."

At the close of the beautiful address, three cheers were proposed for
Miss Rozelle, which were given with an enthusiasm and stentorian voice
that showed how much each soldier was inspired. Capt. Carlton, a gallant
soldier and true gentleman as ever flashed a sword, receiving the flag in a
neat and appropriate speech, and, after receiving it, he presented it to the
1st Regiment.

Col. P. R. Cleburne received it [with] an able and eloquent speech
of some length, in which he promised that it should never be dishonored.
The speech of Col. Cleburne was appropriate and well delivered. He was
loudly cheered by his fellow soldiers."

MEMPHIS, Tenn.,
June 11, 1861.

Arkansas Volunteers.[79]

Col. Hindman's company of Arkansas volunteers, six hundred in number, with Col. Hindman in command, arrived in this city on the *Morrison* on Sunday. They will remain here until the whole regiment is collected together, when they will proceed to Virginia. The Arkansas volunteers have a splendid silk flag, presented by President Davis' Lady. The volunteers are a fine looking spirited body of men, and where they are called to action they will make their mark.

LITTLE ROCK, Ark.,
June 13, 1861.

Fast Day.[80]

In compliance with the proclamation of President Davis, there will be religious services in all the churches to-day (Thursday,) at 10½ or 11 o'clock. Every business house, and every grocery in the place have agreed to close up and suspend business for the day. It will be one of the most quiet days Little Rock has witnessed for many a year.

LITTLE ROCK, Ark.,
June 13, 1861.

Soldiers' Health.[81]
Interesting Suggestions and Recommendations.

The following article, on "Soldiers' Health," is from *Hall's New York Journal of Health*. It contains much valuable information for both soldiers and civilians:

1. In an ordinary campaign sickness disables or destroys three times as many as the sword.

---

79   *Memphis Daily Appeal*, June 11, 1861, Memphis, Tenn.
80   *Arkansas True Democrat*, June 13, 1861, Little Rock, Ark.
81   *Arkansas True Democrat*, June 13, 1861, Little Rock, Ark

2. On a march, from April to November, the entire clothing should be a colored flannel shirt, with a loosely-buttoned collar, cotton drawers, woolen pantaloons, shoes and stockings, and a light colored felt hat, with broad brim to protect the eyes and face from the glare of the sun and from the rain, and a substantial but not heavy coat when off duty.

3. Sun-stroke is most effectually prevented by wearing a silk handkerchief in the crown of the hat.

4. Colored blankets are best, and if lined with brown drilling the warmth and durability are doubled, while the protection against dampness from lying on the ground is almost complete.

5. Never lie or sit down on the grass or bare earth for a moment, rather use your hat- a handkerchief, even, is a great protection. The warmer you are the greater need for this protection, as a damp vapor is immediately generated, to be absorbed by the clothing, and to cool you off too rapidly.

6. While marching, or on other duty, the more thirsty you are the more essential is it to safety of life itself, to rinse out the mouth two or three times, and *then* take a swallow of water at a time, with short intervals. A brave French general, on a forced march, fell dead on the instant, by drinking largely of cold water, when snow was on the ground.

7. Abundant sleep is essential to bodily efficiency, and to that alertness of mind, which is all important to an engagement; and few things more certainly and more effectually prevent sound sleep than eating heartily after sun-down, especially after a heavy march or desperate battle.

8. Nothing is more certain to secure endurance and capability of long-continued effort, than the avoidance of everything as a drink except cold water, NOT excluding coffee at breakfast. Drink as little as possible of even cold water.

9. After any sort of exhausting effort, a cup of coffee, hot or cold, is an admirable sustainer of the strength, until nature begins to recover herself.

10. Never eat heartily just before a great undertaking; because the nervous power is irresistibly drawn to the stomach to manage the food eaten, thus drawing off that supply which the brain and muscles so much need.

11. If persons will drink brandy, it is incomparably safer to do so *after* an effort than before; for it can give only a transient strength, lasting but a few minutes; but as it can never be known how long any

given effort is to be kept in continuance, and if longer than the few minutes, the body becomes more feeble than it would have been without the stimulus, it is clear that its use *before* an effort is always hazardous, and is always unwise.

12. Never go to sleep, especially after a great effort, even in hot weather, without some covering over you.

13. Under all circumstances, rather than lie down on the ground, lie in the hollow of two logs placed together, or across several smaller pieces of wood, laid side by side; or sit on your hat, leaning against a tree. A nap of ten or fifteen minutes in that position will refresh you more than an hour on the bare earth; with the additional advantage of perfect safety.

14. A *cut* is less dangerous than a bullet wound, and heals more rapidly.

15. If from any wound the blood spurts out in jets, instead of a steady stream, you will die in a few minutes, unless it is remedied; because an artery has been divided, and that takes the blood direct from the fountain of life. To stop this instantly, tie a handkerchief or other cloth very loosely BETWEEN the wound and the heart; put a stick, bayonet, or ramrod *between* the skin and the handkerchief, and twist it around until the bleeding ceases, and keep it thus till the surgeon arrives.

16. If the blood flows in a slow, regular stream, a vein has been pierced, and the handkerchief must be on the other side of the wound from the heart; that is, *below* the wound.

17. A bullet through the abdomen (belly or stomach) is more certainly fatal than if aimed at the head or heart; for in the latter cases the ball is often glanced off by the bone, or follows around it under the skin; but when it enters the stomach or bowels, from any direction, death is inevitable under all conceivable circumstances, but in scarcely ever instantaneous. Generally the person lives a day or two with perfect clearness of intellect, often not suffering greatly. The practical bearing of this statement in reference to the great future is clear.

18. Let the whole beard grow, but no longer than some three inches. This strengthens and thickens its growth, and thus makes a more perfect protection for the lungs against dust, and of the throat against winds and cold in winter, while in summer a great perspiration of the skin is induced, with the increase of evaporation; hence, greater coolness of the parts on the outside, while the throat is less feverish, thirsty and dry.

19. Avoid fats and fat meat in summer and in all warm days.

20. Whenever possible take a plunge into any lake or running stream every morning as soon as you get up; if none at hand, endeavor to wash the body all over as soon as you leave your bed, for personal cleanliness acts like a charm against all diseases, always either warding them off altogether or greatly mitigating their severity and shortening their duration.

21. Keep the hair of the head closely cut, say within an inch and a half of the scalp in every part, repeated on the first of each month, and wash the whole scalp plentifully in cold water every morning.

22. Wear woolen stockings and moderately loose shoes, keeping the toe and finger nails always cut close.

23. It is more important to wash the feet well every night than to wash the face and hands of mornings, because it aids in keeping the skin and nails soft, and to prevent chaffings, blisters, and corns, all of which greatly interfere with a soldier's duty.

24. The most universally safe position after all stunnings, hurts and wounds, is that of being placed on the back, the head being elevated three or four inches only, aiding more than any one thing else can do, to equalize and restore the proper circulation of the blood.

25. The more weary you are after a march or other work, the more easily will you take cold, if you remain still after it is over, unless, the moment you cease motion, you throw a coat or blanket over your shoulders. This precaution should be taken in the warmest weather, especially if there is even a slight air stirring.

26. The greatest physical kindness you can show a severely wounded comrade is first to place him on his back, and then run with all your might for some water to drink; not a second ought to be lost. If no vessel is at hand, take your hat; if no hat, off with your shirt, wring it out once, tie the arms in a knot, as also the lower end, thus making a bag, open at the neck only. A fleet person can convey a bucketful half a mile in this way. I've seen a dying man clutch at a single drop of water from the fingers' end, with the voraciousness of a famished tiger.

27. If wet to the skin by rain or by swimming rivers, keep in motion until the clothes are dried, no harm will result.

28. Whenever it is possible, do, by all means when you have to use water for cooking or drinking from ponds or sluggish streams, boil it well, and when cool, shake it, or stir it, so that the oxygen of the air shall get to it, which greatly improves it for drinking. This boiling arrests the process of fermentation which arises from the presence of organic and

inorganic impurities, thus tending to prevent cholera and all bowel diseases. If there is no time for boiling, at least strain it through a cloth, even if you have to use a shirt or trouser leg.

29. Twelve men are hit in battle dressed in red where there are only five dressed in a bluish gray- a difference of more than two to one; green, seven; brown, six.

30. Water can be made almost ice cool in the hottest weather by closely enveloping a filled canteen, or other vessel, with woolen cloth, kept plentifully wetted and exposed.

31. While on a march lie down the moment you halt for a rest. Every minute spent in that position refreshes more than five minutes standing or loitering about.

32. A daily evacuation of the bowels is indispensable to bodily health, vigor and endurance; this is promoted in many cases by stirring a teaspoonful of corn (Indian) meal in a glass of water, and drinking it on rising in the morning.

33. Loose bowels, namely, acting more than once a day, with a feeling of debility afterwards, is the first step towards cholera. The best remedy is instant and perfect quietude of body, eating nothing but boiled rice, with or without boiled milk; in more decided cases a woolen flannel, with two thicknesses in front, should be bound tightly around the abdomen, especially if marching is a necessity.

34. To "have been to the wars" is a life-long honor, increasing with advancing years, while to have died in defence of your country will be the boast and the glory of your children's children.

POCAHONTAS, Ark.,
June 13, 1861.

An Arkansas Heroine.[82]

The *Pocahontas Herald* details the following:

Miss Williams, a daughter of Isaac Williams, living in Black river swamp, about seven miles from this place, heard the report of the approach of troops to this place on Sunday evening. Her father was not at home, but she immediately caught a horse, and was soon off in search of him. She found him at a neighbor's, and told him to hurry on home and

---

82   *Memphis Daily Appeal*, June 13, 1861, Memphis, Tenn.

get his gun and come here and help to drive back the enemy. She then returned home, got down her father's rifle, moulded his lead all into bullets, took the gun, powder and bullets and hid them under the house, and again got on the horse and rode to several houses and spread the alarm, returning home in time to give the old man his gun and ammunition, and started him, with a crowd of ten men whom she had collected for the scene of action. All of this she done in less than two hours. Such acts of heroism should not be passed by without notice.

LITTLE ROCK, Ark., June 22, 1861.

A Card.[83]

Feeling the deepest sense of obligation to the ladies of Little Rock, for their many and repeated kindnesses, and particularly for the large amount of labor performed by them in making the entire uniform for our company, it is by the "Dixie Grays" unanimously

"*Resolved*, That the thanks of each and every member of this Company is most heartily tendered to the noble and patriotic ladies of Little Rock: the industry and self-sacrificing spirit displayed by them shall serve as an example to each soldier, and nerve him to bear with patience the unavoidable ills of the ensuing campaign; and the remembrance that fairest fingers have aided in equipping him for the field, will lend double force to the blow dealt in defence of the homes of those whose place shall ever be nearest the soldier's heart.

Resolved, That this card be presented for publication at the office of the "*Gazette*."

Dixie Grays.

LITTLE ROCK, Ark., June 22, 1861.[84]

Some days before the departure of the Sixth Regiment, Miss Pleasants presented a flag to the "Dixie Grays." We subjoin her remarks on the occasion:

---

83   *Weekly Arkansas Gazette*, June 22, 1861, Little Rock, Ark.
84   *Weekly Arkansas Gazette*, June 22, 1861, Little Rock, Ark.

Countrymen and Soldiers: Conflicting feelings agitate my heart as I survey this assemblage. Here are the strength and valor of our own "sunny South," willing, anxious, to move at her bidding.

A war has commenced, where it will end, God only knows! But there is one thing of which we are heartily glad- money-bought patriotism has fled our ranks.

No doubt Northern pomposity has thriven on fancied conquest. Sweet, sweet honey, the bees are in it, and they are not idle. They know that to will is easier than to accomplish, and while they pity the poor deluded honey-eaters, they are busily and silently sharpening their stings, and weaving their beautiful flag, the South, with a keen insight, made keener by the aroused spirit of proud resentment, and holy love for their wronged country, deliberately scans the question from every stand-point, and marks with unnerving judgment, the most accessible points.

Has the North taken this precaution: Have they looked at home and abroad? They talk enthusiastically of help from our slaves. They will fight us hand to hand, and hilt to hilt, until a path of desolation is made through our fertile valleys, and then they will give a victorious shout, and the whole race of precious darkeys will rush to their protecting arms, and fight their battles. Magic! Magic! Was a darkey ever charmed by gun or lance, when presented to his own heart? Had he not rather hoe corn and cotton, and feat on pork and potatoes? It is not hard to answer, and Yankeedom will find it so. But what will become of the poor starving wretches they leave at home, while they are exterminating us? Form a home guard? No! They will arise and lay that now prosperous land in ruins...

Lincoln says he fights for the Union and Flag, *you* fight for neither, but for Liberty! The God of Liberty will be with you - your cause is just and honorable, and victory will be your reward. Ere you go we will consign *this* flag to your charge. Friends, in the hour of conflict look on it and be chased [sic], for it emblems many hearts united in one for the well-wishing of the South and her cause. Bear it proudly! In victory unfurl it - in death fold it close to your hearts as the shield of honor, and the zeal of glory.

To which Capt. Sam. Smith of the *Grays*, replied:

"Fair lady and fellow-soldiers: When a soldier is on the eve of departure from his home- when he is about to break asunder, perhaps forever, all the social ties that make life dear, there is no occasion which is better calculated to fill his heart with patriotism and which can awaken in his soul a firmer determination to meet in deadly conflict on the battle field, the foe of his country, than one like the present.

To know that woman smiles upon us, to hear her charming voice inciting us on to deeds of valor; to feel that we have her warmest sympathies, is enough to penetrate the inmost recesses of the coldest hearth, and stir up feelings that perhaps were never aroused before. Her influence is supreme. We have seen her following the army to the ice-clad regions of Russia, administering to every want of the soldier as he presses his dying pillow, and as his soul takes its flight to the regions of eternity, she mutters a faint prayer that it may there find that rest, that it never knew here below. We have already experienced their kindness since our short sojourn here, and I know I can speak for every volunteer, when I say that they will long remember with gratitude, the ladies of the Capital of our State.

Soldiers: remember when you leave here it is for no trip of pleasure. Many of you will never more meet the approving smile of a mother, a father, a wife, a brother, a sister. You go as sacrifices upon the altar of your country. You go with the expectation, and I hope with a heartfelt willingness, to lay down your lives, if necessary, to sustain the honor and reputation of our glorious newly formed Confederacy.

And if the Northern hordes persist in the reckless course they have already begun, it will not be long before the wailing voice of the orphan and widow will be heard through the hills and valleys of the sunny South. Let every sword leap from its scabbard, and let them not be sheathed until the enemy will have been driven back into the heart of their own country, and forced to admit the superiority of Southern chivalry.

Color bearer take this flag and defend it, remember her who places it in your charge. Suffer it not to be brought back trailing in the dust, but rather, if it should ever return, may they behold victory perched upon its standard. Let everyone be inspired with the determination to take a stand, either to live or die in Dixie.

MEMPHIS, Tenn.,
June 23, 1861.

Grateful Acknowledgements.[85]

A letter from one of the Arkansas volunteers, makes acknowledgements to the patriotic ladies of our city as follows:

The ladies of the Southern Mother's Home have laid us under lasting obligations. When we reached Memphis there were many sick amongst us. Through the kindness of Gen. Pillow our sick were received by the ladies of the Southern Mother's Home, where our boys are kindly cared for. Mrs. Law, who so nobly leads in this association, and her assistants, have our heartfelt thanks for their untiring attention to the sick. The heart of the soldier can never forget such disinterested patriotism. They are the mothers of the second war of independence, worthy descendants of the women of '76. And when the day of battle comes, we will endeavor to prove ourselves not unworthy descendants of our sires. Such recollections will nerve our hands and strengthen our hearts, to

Strike for our altars and our fires;
Strike for the green graves of our sires,
God and our native land.

Many of the citizens have been kind enough to furnish us vegetables and other delicacies, chief among whom I may mention Captain McManus, who shows himself a true man by his appreciation of the soldier in this the trying hour of our country's history.

A Sick Private.

LITTLE ROCK, Ark.,
June 27, 1861.

Address to the Ashley Volunteers.[86]

'Tis with a mingled feeling of pleasure and regret that I address this brilliant array of Ashley's gallant sons. A feeling of joy and pride awakes in our hearts a just appreciation of the bravery and nobleness, by which you have been actuated in enrolling your names as candidates for the battle field, since you march thither, to defend the sunny South against the oppression and fanaticism of the North. But a feeling of sadness

---

85 *Memphis Daily Appeal*, June 23, 1861, Memphis, Tenn.
86 *Arkansas True Democrat*, June 27, 1861, Little Rock, Ark.

pervades the soul, because many of our highly esteemed friends will soon cease to gladden our little town with their presence - the community will miss you - in vain will the mother watch for the return of her darling boy - the wife shed tears for her absent husband - and the sister sigh for the companionship of her brother; for you will be gone from our midst.

Ashley volunteers, what has prompted you to forego life's sweetest pleasures? What has induced you to exchange the consecrated fireside, around which the brightest associations cluster - for the field of battle, where you will encounter so many hardships, and perchance, yield your lives in the struggle? Duty calls, freedom leads the way, and patriotism, that same great passion which fired the bosom of your ancient prototypes lures you on!

The proclamation of war has startled the nation, and 'tis now time for every old man to think profoundly - for every young man to act with a determined and patriotic spirit! We sincerely hope that the South holds not, in all her broad domain, a man who would have the face to live in a country, "enjoy its immunities and privileges," and then refuse to fight its battles. Notwithstanding the discouragements interwoven with the contemplation of your undertaking, and the great perils that must attend its completion - heed not the voice that would charm you from it; but go forth in defence of your liberty! The eye will soon learn to kindle at the sight of Lincoln's deluded minions, and the heart will bound with delight, as the roar of the cannon and the sound of the drum fall upon your ear.

The presence of the ladies plainly indicate that woman is not indifferent to the glorious cause in which you are determined to engage - although she does not brave the cannon's deadly fire, and win the laurels of the conqueror. No! She is *proud* to know that there are hearts in the land *patriotic* enough to embark in it, and *heroic* enough to face its mighty terrors without fainting. Many such prayers as mingled with our infant liberties, will ascend in your behalf, from the *anxious*, though *hopeful* hearts of faithful mothers, devoted wives and affectionate sisters.

Their pure and sympathetic spirits will follow you to the field where the battle is wildly raging; and what can better arm the heart to endure, and cause it to be cheerful in the midst of danger and death!

Captain Manning, in behalf of the ladies of Hamburg, I present to you and your gallant company, this silken flag. 'Tis a token of the confidence, with which we contemplate your energy and lofty patriotism. Long may it wave! Shield it from the accursed hand of tyranny, until the ruthless weapon of the enemy shall sever the arm which bears it, from the body! Though some may fall in the contest, the South must finally conquer; for right and justice will prevail. Remember that your liberty, your prosperity, "your social relations, your future glory," and even your existence as a free and independent race are endangered:

"God and our rights, it was their cry,
When your fathers of old went forth to die;
They conquered in death, and so shall we,
Men of the South, ne'er bend the knee!"

Stand by that flag; 'tis the flag of the Confederate States of America! May it bear the glad tidings of triumph and liberty, when it floats over the nation in war! Then, when peace again sheds o'er our country her genial dews - when you shall have returned as conquerors - the friends whom you now leave in sadness, will greet you with tears of delight; your State will encircle you with her praise - her sons will bring their tribute of honor - her daughters will meet you with smiles of approval - and you will be hailed as energetic and patriotic men! Your deeds will remain as bright as "the stars in the dark vaulted heavens at night," and when the dust falls on your shroud, you will have living monuments in grateful hearts that will not crumble to decay.

Annie E. Watson.

MEMPHIS, Tenn.,
July 3, 1861.

Report.[87]

To the Executive Committee of the Southern Mothers:

Having been elected by you on the 7th of June, as surgeon of the institution under your charge, I immediately entered upon the discharge of my duties, and herewith have the honor to submit to you this, my first monthly report:

Number discharged 52, sent to private houses 25, in the wards 27, died 2. total 106.

Diseases- Diarrhea 11, dysentery 6, neuralgia 3, constipation 1, contusion 3, fatigue and exposure 9, measles 2, gun shot 3, opthalmia 1, pneumonia 19, intermittent 42, ptyalism 2, congestive chill 2, abscess 1,

---

87 *Memphis Daily Appeal*, July 3, 1861, Memphis, Tenn.

cut with bowie-knife 1. Total 106.

Of these there were from army of Tennessee 14, Missouri troops 1, 2d Arkansas regiment 91. Total 106.

In examining the above list of diseases, it will be seen that nearly twenty per cent. have been pneumonia. The causes of this are readily explained by the facts attending the trip of the 2d Arkansas regiment, Colonel T. C. Hindman, commanding, to Knoxville and back. These troops, fresh from the back woods of Arkansas, unaccustomed to excitements, and actuated by the loftiest patriotism, thought it incumbent upon them to cheer at each flag station, village and town upon the road, both going and coming, until their bronchias became inflamed in the highest degree.

In addition to this, the dust and cinders, the open scars, the heat of the days, the cold nights, the sudden change of the weather while in East Tennessee, insufficient clothing, the want of blankets, and sleeping on the damp earth, rendered their trip everything but one of pleasure. Hence our rooms were filled on their return with fully developed cases of pneumonia. None are so classified that did not present several of the characteristic symptoms and phenomena of the disease. In addition to there, nearly all the cases of intermittent were more or less accompanied with congestion and pleuritic affections of the lungs.

In view of the number of patients and the character of the disease, it affords me pleasure to state that only two have so far proved fatal, and that there is only one man whose case may be regarded as critical. Mr. Gallagher, of the Crocket Rangers, died on the 15th ult., having come under my charge after he had been abandoned by his physician. I immediately called Dr. Hopson in consultation with me, but he had become so prostrated and diseased that our efforts were unavailing to restore him. He died in consequence of secondary hemorrhage. The other, Mr. S. L. Poston, of Capt. Harvey's company, 2d Arkansas regiment, was attacked with pneumonia in Knoxville on the 14th ult., and arrived here on the 17th. His case was complicated with phthisis pulmonalis, and was in the third stage on his arrival here. He died June 23d.

In my attendance upon the sick soldiers under my charge I have been nobly aided by the excellent council and advice of Drs. Allen, Shanks, Holliday, Erskine, Cypert, Wilson, Irwin, and others of the city, and Surgeons Bartlett and Darling of 2d Arkansas regiment. They have visited our rooms as friends and as physicians, and I earnestly hope that each member of the profession will consider himself at all times a welcome visitor to our rooms.

The druggist and military board of Memphis have aided us by contributions of valuable drugs and medicines, and to them we should return our sincere thanks. I have endeavored to use the strictest economy in the administration of medicines by having them compounded at my rooms, saving valuable time.

It is a source of pleasure to me to bear testimony to the patriotic, self-sacrificing devotion of the different members of the association, who have been engaged in nursing the sick during the last two weeks. Assiduous in their daily vigils, they have accomplished as much, or more, by the tender care of the patients confided to them, than could have been done by any other means. It could not be otherwise. Actuated by the holiest and noblest patriotism they left their splendid palaces to administer to the wants at the bedside of the humble soldier. They have watched over their patients with a devotion and interest that excites the liveliest admiration. Mothers have left the cares and charms of home, to bathe the fevered brow and cool the parched tongue of those who were sons and brothers in the holy cause of defending our sunny South. The zeal and devotion of the "Southern Mothers" displayed at the rooms has extended to the fireside, and they have thrown open their doors, and taken the convalescing to their homes. So far, the demand for them to be thus provided for, has exceeded the supply.

Our thanks are due to Capt. A. B. Jewell, for many acts of kindness, especially in providing us, on several occasions, with good barbers; thereby aiding materially the comfort and appearance of the patients...

No "southern mother" shall ever blush at the recollection of ever having crossed the threshold of our rooms. No invalid soldier will ever regret that he was nursed by a "southern mother."

I will close by saying to the commanding officers and to the patriotic soldiers of the South that the rooms of the "southern mothers" in Memphis are always open, that they are ready and willing to receive their sick and wounded, and that they will be provided with everything to render them comfortable; that they will be watched over and nursed with the tenderest care by the members of the order, without fee or reward.

Respectfully yours, etc.,
G. W. Curry.

123

ULTIMATHULE, Ark.,
July 3, 1861.[88]

Messrs. Editors: The Sevier County Star company, after several ineffectual efforts to get into service, left this place on yesterday for Fort Smith. . . They are armed with the Minnie Muskets that were sent to this county in accordance with an act of the last legislature - they are a most excellent weapon, and are in the hands of good and true men; and should an opportunity present itself, you will hear a good *report* from these boys. . . The company is uniformed with a light blue suit, and when on parade or the battle field will compare favorably with any in the State. Annexed you will find a list of the officers and privates of the "Star Company."

Camillus.

John G. McKean, Captain, John P. Stroud, 1st Lieutenant, James H. Hopson, 2d "Felix McKean, 3d ". . .

MEMPHIS, Tenn.,
July 3, 1861.

Harry Macarty.[89]

The Arkansas Comedian, Vocalist, Banjoist, Dancer, the Author and the Man of Many Parts, will give his Personation Concerts
Every Night This Week, At Odd-Fellows' Hall.
Admission 50 cents. Servants and Children 25 cents.

LITTLE ROCK, Ark.,
July 4, 1861.[90]

Mr. Editor: I have been permitted to see and copy the constitution of the gallant and glorious company of the "Stay at Home Guards." It is not entirely original, being copied, in part, from one of a like organization in Texas. After you shall have read the constitution I think you will let us put your name down for one scholar.

H. A.

---

88 *Arkansas True Democrat*, July 18, 1861, Little Rock, Ark.
89 *Memphis Daily Appeal*, July 3, 1861, Memphis, Tenn.
90 *Arkansas True Democrat*, August 1, 1861, Little Rock, Ark.

Constitution of the Stay at Home Guards.

Adopted July 4, 1861. Motto: *Euge!* which, being translated, meaneth O.K.

Art. 1. This company shall bear the name of the "Stay at Home Guards."

Art. 2. The number of the Stay at Home Guards shall be from ten or less, to five hundred, or more.

Art. 3. The entire company shall consist of officers - each member being entitled to select his own office.

Art. 4. This company shall repudiate all military rules and usages. Every member shall arm himself in his own way, for active service, and hold himself in readiness to do as he pleases at an hour's notice from his commander.

Art. 5. The Stay at Home Guards shall be commanded by each member in rotation, but it is left entirely at the option of members to obey the orders of the acting commander or not as they may please.

Art. 6. The Guards will parade semi-occasionally, or oftener, provided they have nothing else to do.

Art. 7. Each member of the Stay at Home Guards shall, while in actual service, draw the following daily rations: One bottle of claret, one bottle of champagne, three fingers of cognac, six fingers of bourbon, one dozen segars, one broiled chicken, one boiled turkey, oysters in season, and one basket full of knicknacks, assorted.

Art. 8. When on marching orders, each member of the guards shall be allowed one boot boy, one barber, one laundress, one carriage with two horses, one set of fishing tackle, one pack of dogs, (at option,) two double-barrel shot guns, one portable two story dwelling house, one library of select novels, one dozen selected periodicals, one traveling billiard table, a backgammon board and three decks or packs of cards.

Art. 9. Members are expressly forbidden to perform any duty contrary to their wishes, and any order which shall be given by an acting officer without its having previously been discussed by the entire corps, in debating society assembled, shall subject the officer giving it to be fined as much as he is willing to pay.

Art. 10. Members who have musical instruments are required to bring them into the field, but no two members shall play at the same time unless they please to do so.

Art. 11. The active duty especially assigned to this corps by their own direction shall be to treat and retreat...

CARROLL COUNTY, Ark.,[91]
July 4, 1861.

Capt. Smith - 'Tis with feelings deep and thrilling that I come to-day to present to you and your valiant company, a band of Arkansas' bravest best, the flag (made by Miss Baily and myself) of the Southern Confederacy:

"The flag of the South, aye fling its folds
Upon the kindred breeze,
Emblem of dread to tyrant holds
Of freedom on the seas;
Forever may its stars and stripes,
In cloudless glory wave,
Red, white and blue, eternal types
Of nations true and brave."

Although Arkansas has lacked the agility of some of her southern sisters in defying the norther foe, she is none the less true to our fair land. Not until "forbearance ceased to be a virtue," did she, proud, liberty loving Arkansas, too true to herself to *think* of submission - *too loyal* to crouch to oppression, rise in all her majesty and strength, sever the chain which bound her to the tyrant's sway, and clamor for admission in the Southern Confederacy. Gladly, gladly, methinks did they welcome the "Young Cotton State" with her noble and fearless heart, as another bright gem in the southern galaxy. What, though the demagogues and fanatics of the North, exultingly and unfeelingly talk of our *subjugation* - of conquering a people who *never knew* subjection, (but who do know how to "die in duty's line,") to us 'tis but as "sounding brass and tinkling cymbal." Have they forgotten the brilliant display of southern valor and courage on the gory battle fields of Buena Vista, Monterey and others? Or think they southern chivalry tarnished by the lapse of years? If so, I fancy their spirits will *cower*, when like Assyria's guilty monarch they read the "hand writing on the wall" - valor, purity and truth; and while they read will believe, and while believing, "fear and tremble." Should the proud bird of liberty ere cease to nestle amid our hills that lift their

---

91   *Arkansas True Democrat*, July 4, 1861, Little Rock, Ark.

blue ridges up to the "storm king's home," or cease to flap triumphantly its broad wings o'er our lovely valleys, smiling in perpetual beauty? 'Twill be after the graceful folds of this beautiful banner have mingled with the dust. I feel assured that when it waves no longer in proud defiance, the last of this gallant number shall have fallen, nobly fallen, on the "bosom of our Sunny South."

> "If there is on this earthly sphere,
> A boon, an offering heaven bolds dear,
> 'Tis the last libation liberty draws
> From the heart that bleeds and dies in her cause."

Strong are the ties which bind you to home and friends - dear are the associations which cluster around you, and those associations how intractably they are woven with every fibre of your souls, then fain would you linger, but your country calls and you go to "fight till the last armed foe expires." Go, and on this banner which I now present you may victory perch e're you return—take for your motto: "*Aut vincere aut mori.*" May the "God of the South" protect you, and may you all live to see the dark clouds of the present disappear and that bow of golden promise which rose upon our revolutionary sires, once more span the Heavens. May you live, not only to enjoy the blessings of a prosperous Confederacy, but may wreaths, immortal wreaths, be woven with Fame's bright garlands "to tell the world your worth."

Joe Wright.

Capt. Smith's Response.

Miss Wright - Permit me in behalf of the company that I represent and myself, to receive at your hands this banner—this patriotic testimonial of the generous impulses that prompted the heart and hands that gave beauty and grace to the folds of this emblem of our glorious country. Whenever and wherever the interest of my country shall demand me and my men, there shall its beautiful folds wave in testimony of the patriotism of her who gave it and of the loyalty of the fair daughters of Arkansas. And as you, Miss Wright, said in your address to me and my brave volunteers, Arkansas, though among the last to give up the (once glorious) Union, is none the less true to the Confederate States. And allow me further, in behalf of the brave and noble sons of our "young cotton State," to assure you that not until the last man of this company is writing in the dust from the stroke of our enemy, shall this emblem of your respect for me and my brave fellows be trailed to the ground. Accept the gratitude of this company for this token of respect and esteem, and when the toils of war shall have ended, may we be permitted to enjoy a peaceful and happy country, one *thoroughly purged of abolitionism* and tyranny. May we be allowed not only to return to a happy country, but may we return to you this beautiful banner without a single taint of a dishonorable act.

John Smith.
Searcy Eagle copy.

PULASKI COUNTY, Ark., July 4, 1861.[92]

The Sheriff of Pulaski county having been notified of a vacancy in the House of Representatives, caused by the resignation of Hon. J.T. Trigg, the undersigned *reluctantly* yields to the urgent solicitation of friends, and is accordingly a candidate for said vacancy at the election to be held on the *earliest possible* day that may be fixed by the proper authority.

JOHN C. PEAY
July 4, 1861

LITTLE ROCK, Ark., July 4, 1861.

Hempstead County Davis Blues.[93]

Resolved, That we tender a grateful acknowledgement of our gratitude to our fellow citizens of Nashville and vicinity, for the well provided barbecue they gave us on the occasions of our departure.

Resolved, That we will cherish an unfading regard and warm esteem for the gentle ladies, mothers and daughters, for the assiduity with which they labored to clothe the Davis Blues with uniforms and other articles of clothing, thus setting a praiseworthy example to succeeding generations,

---

92   *Arkansas True Democrat*, August 22, 1861, Little Rock, Ark.
93   *Arkansas True Democrat*, July 4, 1861, Little Rock, Ark.

as did the mothers and daughters of the old revolutionary age.

Resolved, That the patriotic banner, with its inspiring inscription, "our rights or death," given us by the hands of lovely beauty, will be cherished, and under its stars and bars and colors we will meet our country's foes and by the grace of God conquer or die.

Resolved, That we tender our thanks to Hon. C. B. Mitchel for his appropriate and eloquent address on the above occasion and that we solicit its publication.

Resolved, That an acknowledgment of our thanks are due and are hereby publicly tendered to many of the citizens of Pike, Hot Spring, and Saline counties, who appreciating our motives, offered without money or price whatever was necessary for the comfort of man or beast.

Resolved, That we unanimously tender our thanks to Dr. J. H. Delaney for the careful, diligent and successful treatment he has generously given the sick of our company.

Resolved, That we return our thanks to the wagoners for the kind and self-sacrificing spirit they have manifested in bringing us to this place without cost.

Resolved, That the above resolutions be published in the Little Rock and Washington papers.

Joseph Neal, Capt.
D. M. Cochran, Sec'y.
Arsenal Grounds, Little Rock, June 26, '61.

LITTLE ROCK, Ark.,
July 4, 1863.

Our paper.[94]

Newspapers, as well as other institutions, North and South, are constantly succumbing to the storm, but the *True Democrat* still weathers it bravely and securely. No matter at what sacrifice to ourselves pecuniarily, we intend the *True Democrat* shall live and issue regularly during the war; but while we so intend, it is our purpose to furnish it to no one who will not contribute his mite, at least to the amount of his subscription. We may have to decrease the size of our paper - we expect to be compelled to do so - but as our advertising will be small during the

---

94   *Arkansas True Democrat*, July 4, 1861, Little Rock, Ark.

prevalence of the war - we shall always be enabled to furnish as much reading matter as we do with our present proportions.

Since the commencement of the troubles between the North and the South, the increase of our subscription list, with the subscription price always in advance, has been unprecedented. In north-eastern Texas alone we have received over two or three hundred subscribers within the last six or eight weeks.

LITTLE ROCK, Ark.,
July 4, 1861.

A Song for the Arkansaw Boys.[95]
By Lillian Montecalm.

On! On, in haste brave volunteers!
And fearless take your stand
Within the rear, and 'till you die
Fight for the South'rn Land.
The stars and stripes still wave aloft
O'er heads of warriors brave,
An emblem of the love they bear
The land they'd die to save.
Jeff. Davis *stands* to give commands,
Win ne'er expiring breath-
Delights to see the flashing sword,
Nor fears the monster death.
Oh, God in mercy help the South,
And give to her her rights,
To whip old Abe, the north'rn king,
And hellish Lincolnites,
Who thought to bring 'neath their control,
Our glorious southern band,
To subjugate or starve us out,
And desecrate our land;
And hear him noble *boys*, nor bear
While health your lives illume,
His threaten'd, old inebriate,

---

95   *Arkansas True Democrat*, July 4, 1861, Little Rock, Ark.

To rob our father's tomb.
Then Davis on with musket, sword,
Until the day you've won,
And honor, fame shall crown they name,
A second Washington.

SEARCY, Ark.,
July 4, 1861.

Searcy Girls.[96]

Many are the vicissitudes connected with the life of a soldier; but occasionally in the midnight of his misfortunes, a ray from the sun of pleasure illumes and cheers his heart - a ray, bright and brilliant from this sun shot athwart my pathway at the hospitable little village of Searcy. It was caused by the school girls of said village, and I have no language adequate to express my heart-felt thanks to Miss E., who, in behalf of the school, presented me with a beautiful flag with the very appropriate inscription: "No Backing Out." Glorious motto; and I can safely say that it expresses the sentiments of every member of the "Yellow Jacket Company," (of which I am a member.) Fair Flowers of Searcy, I in behalf of the Yellow Jackets, thank you for the flag, and will pray even amid the din of battle, that each of your path-ways through life may be strewn with flowers culled from the sweet fields of unbroken peace and love, and when length of days shall have made you tired of earth, may you find a sweet resting place in the Paradise of God.

S. M. Black.

LITTLE ROCK, Ark.,
July 4, 1861.

The Ladies of Little Rock.[97]

When the tocsin of war was sounded throughout the land none were more prompt to respond to their country's call than Arkansians, and none in the State more prompt than the citizens of Little Rock and Pulaski county. Pulaski county has furnished and sent to the seat of war eight full companies, and the ladies of Little Rock have worked night and day for months making uniforms, not only for the soldiers of their own county,

---

96   *Arkansas True Democrat*, July 4, 1861, Little Rock, Ark.
97   *Arkansas True Democrat*, July 4, 1861, Little Rock, Ark.

but for soldiers from all portions of the State.

It is not our purpose to speak in praise of one section of our State over another - we believe all are alike devoted in this struggle for liberty and sanctity of our hearthstones - but since an unjust and malicious report has been circulated to the prejudice of the Little Rock ladies, it becomes us not only to correct it, but to accord to the ladies their full merit. It has been reported of them that they were paid for their work out of the State treasury.

The report is false, and the originator of it a malicious slanderer. What the ladies did, and they did much, as thousands of soldiers will attest, was a free-will offering to the State and its gallant defenders. They labored night and day - spent their time and their money - in equipping the many soldiers that passed through our city on their way to the war, but they neither charged or received one cent of remuneration for any service. The report to the contrary was a cruel slander, and should be accordingly denounced.

LITTLE ROCK, Ark., July 6, 1861.

Military Barbecue & Flag Presentation.[98]

Messrs. Editors *True Democrat*: Knowing that you are ever fond of hearing of the patriotism of your country, send you for publication an account of the militia barbecue [sic] of Gray township.

The barbecue to the militia of Gray Township came off on the 6th inst., at the residence of Dr. Craft. This was a brilliant affair. There were quite a number of persons present, not only from the adjoining townships, but from the adjoining counties.

The patriotic mothers and daughters who had come forth to lend their smiles and their approbations composed about one-third of the assembled multitude. Capt. Bennett's company of militia was called on parade at ten o'clock; and after a short time spent in drilling, were discharged, when the Home Guard of Gray township was paraded, and after a very short exercise, were marched in single file, encircling the stand, where they received in silence a beautiful flag of the Southern confederacy, also encircled by eleven of old Gray's fair daughters representing the eleven southern States in the following order:

---

98   *Arkansas True Democrat*, July 18, 1861, Little Rock, Ark.

Miss S. E. Ferguson, represented South Carolina.
" Frances Malone, " Georgia.
" Henrietta Nicholas" Alabama.
" Laura Ferguson, " Florida.
" Panina Maggart, " Texas.
" Cloe Beall, " Arkansas.
" M. C. Thrailkill, " Mississippi.
" Mary Martin, " Virginia,
" S. Dodson, " Tennessee,
" H. Killingsworth, " Louisiana.

Miss Cloe Beall was next introduced as the representative of the State of Arkansas, who in an appropriate manner, and in the name of Gray Township, presented to the Guards of said township, a beautiful flag. Miss Beall said:

"We give this to you, untouched but by the delicate fingers of your mothers, your wives, and your sisters - unfurled but by the gentle zephyrs of your own sunny clime. We give it to you with confidence, for we know, that its ample folds will ever shadow as true hearts as ever throbbed in the breast of mortals," etc. etc.

It was a well-timed and appropriate address for the occasion. At the close of the address she presented the flag to Mr. James M. Stovall, who received it in behalf of the Gray Township Guards. Mr. Stovall delivered quite an interesting address. After returning his thanks to the fair daughters of Gray Township for their patriotism, he spoke fluently and eloquently on the present crisis of our country, briefly stating the causes and reasons, justifying the southern States in "withdrawing themselves from a compact wholly disregarded, wherein corruption and fraud reigned triumphant over reason, truth and justice." He closed with an appeal to the young men, which was beautiful and eloquent; giving undoubted testimony that true patriotic blood flowed in his own veins.

Col. T. F. Murff being called on, addressed the audience in a few brief remarks. Dinner was then announced as being ready; the ladies were first marched to the table, followed by the gentlemen, where was found a neat barbecued dinner, together with various kinds of vegetables, etc. I say in honor to old Gray, that this affair was one hardly to be surpassed. I had forgotten to say that Capt. Geal's company of cavalry were present. The exercises ended in peace and quietude.

Yours truly,
One Present.

**QUITMAN, Ark.,
July 9, 1861.**[99]

Mr. Editor - On Tuesday, the 9th inst., the people of Quitman and vicinity made a dinner in honor of the Quitman Rifle Company, commanded by Capt. A. R. Witt, consisting of 95 men, 11 of which are from Conway county. On the occasion Miss Rachel P. Billings presented the company a flag, with a very patriotic address, which was received by the captain, who made a very appropriate response. After which we had the pleasure of listening to the patriotic strains of eloquence, delivered by Rev. P. W. Stark. On the day following the company took up their line of march for Fayetteville.

A Citizen.

**BENTON, Ark.,
July 11, 1861.**

Address of Miss Frank J. Pack,
Delivered in presenting a flag to the "Saline Rifle
Rangers," at Benton, Ark., July 11th, 1861.[100]

Captain Henderson and Company,

Soldiers, defenders of your country's liberties. The ladies of Benton, appreciating the gallant motives that actuate you in preparing to fight the battles of your country, have contributed their small mite, by preparing for and presenting you with a flag, the *flag of our Southern Confederacy*.

You are now called upon to assist in repelling the advances of the abolitionists on our own soil. We feel assured that you will nobly and bravely do your duty, and that in responding to your country's call, you feel that

"No fetters, no tyrants, your souls shall enslave,
While the ocean shall roll, or the harvest shall wave."

We wish you to preserve it unsullied, never permit it to be trampled upon, or trailed in the dust, by Northern abolitionists or those of whatever name that would ruthlessly destroy your homes, devastate your fields and gardens, as they say, "exterminate us from the face of God's bright and beautiful earth."

---

99 *Arkansas True Democrat*, July 25, 1861, Little Rock, Ark.
100 *Arkansas True Democrat*, September 5, 1861, Little Rock, Ark.

134

When this flag is unfurled to the breeze and waves above your heads, may each breath of Heaven remind you of those near and dear ties, that are common to all human beings, your wives, mothers, children, sisters and friends. There are none in your company I trust who have not some such ties existing, and may the remembrance of those dear ties serve to nerve your arms to do their utmost in the day and hour of need. We trust in your patriotism, we feel convinced the love of your country is too deeply imbued in each and every heart that may have to do battle beneath the folds of this flag of our Southern Confederacy, ever to do aught that may reflect upon the honor of our cause. We expect you to fight for our rights as southrons, we feel convinced that ours is the right cause; we are not the aggressors, we only wish to defend the rights and liberties our maker has given us and we trust in God, the giver of all good, that he will defend the right.

Let each heart throb with such sentiments as those the poet has so nobly expressed.

"No fearing, no doubting, our soldier shall know,
When here stands his country and yonder his foe;
One look at the bright sun, one prayer to the sky,
One glance where our banner floats gloriously on high,
Then on as the young lion bounds on his prey;
Let the sword flash on high, fling the scabbard away;
Roll on, like the thunder bolt over the plain,
We come back in glory, or come not again."

We now commit this flag to your care and you to the care and protection of Almighty God; our hearts beat simultaneous in the hope that you may prove victorious and that ere long we may hear the welcome tidings that we have gained the victory and that soon you may be permitted to return to your homes and firesides and to gladden the hearts of the ladies of Benton.

The flag was received by Capt. M. J. Henderson, in a brief but appropriate and patriotic speech, when the "Rangers" took up the line of march for Missouri.

MEMPHIS, Tenn.,
July 11, 1861.

Southern Mothers' Association.[101]

The southern mothers desire gratefully to acknowledge the reception of a large and timely donation of chickens from the ladies five miles east of Cold Water depot, Mississippi, through the hands of W. Powers; also, of $52 from friends in Panola county, Miss.; of $24 from city schools, Nos. 6 and 24, through Dr. A. P. Merrill, and of $22.60 collected on the steamer *Hartford City*, during a fourth of July pleasure excursion, and presented to the society by Mrs. Halstead. During the five days ending Friday night, when the change of the time of meeting made a report from the surgeon necessary, there had been sixty in the rooms; of these one had died, making two since the opening of the rooms, twenty-two had been discharged, and fourteen removed by order of Col. Hindman, of the 2d Arkansas regiment, leaving twenty-three in the rooms from different regiments, but mostly of the 1st Arkansas regiment, Col. Clabourne [sic].The illness of the secretary has prevented an earlier publication. Some of the soldiers are extremely ill, though better than when they entered the rooms; some have been in a most critical condition.

Mary E. Pope,
Secretary.

LITTLE ROCK, Ark.,
July 11, 1861.

Presentation of a Flag to Hot Springs Rifle Company.[102]
By Miss Ann Bennet, on behalf of the Ladies of Ouachita and surrounding townships.

Messrs. Editors - Saturday, June 22d, was one of the days long to be remembered in the traditionary legends of our hitherto quiet ridge, viz: Dividing Ridge. Some time since, it was supposed that the ladies here would present a flag to our volunteers, on the above day. At an early hour a large number of our citizens were collected at the Primitive Baptist Church, (Macedonia) around which an extensive arbor was erected for the ladies.

---

101 *Memphis Daily Appeal*, July 11, 1861, Memphis, Tenn.
102 *Arkansas True Democrat*, July 11, 1861, Little Rock, Ark.

The volunteers being formed into line, the fair oratoress advanced, bearing the flag of the Confederate States, and on behalf of the ladies, who surrounded her, delivered one of those soul stirring and animating addresses, which reminded us of the female courage of our revolutionary times, and like the men of that time, we *determined in our souls*, and with our fair oratoress, that with our honor, and our last drop of blood, we would defend that flag, as the ensign of our liberty and our rights. I have rarely, indeed, never have I seen more enthusiasm displayed by our citizens; nor do I wonder at it, everything around tended to that result. The young lady who addressed us, is one of those captivating angels of earth - her beautifully proportioned figure, a charming and bewitching face and highly cultivated mind - her voice and style of delivery, soft, easy and impressive.

The address of Miss Bennet was responded to on behalf of the volunteers, by our own gifted orator, Col. Gantt. After complimenting the fair one who preceded him, he addressed the crowd of beauty and fashion, which surrounded her, assuring them on the part of the volunteers, that their lives and their honor were freely pledged to protect their sex from violence and suffering, as well as to defend their country's rights - that every volunteer was a cavalier in that particular; at this stage of his remarks, he was interrupted by a shower of boquettes from the ladies, to which he replied in those touching, softening expressions, so peculiar to himself, and so sensitively felt by the female heart.

Our talented orator next entered on the absorbing subject of the day, viz: our present difficulties as a nation. He ranged over volume after volume of the histories of nations, which had risen, fallen and passed away; traced the basis on which society was formed, applying his views and arguments with a master mind. He traced the construction of our once happy government, as to its compacts, social and political, and the inroads made by a corrupt class of politicians, up to the present time. His metaphors, his train of reasoning and argument were so eloquent and convincing, and so powerful was the effect upon those present that few of either sex could refrain from shedding tears.

Messrs. Editors, Col. Gantt is a young man, you doubtless know him better than I do; a few of our gamblers in politics may try to crush his rising greatness, but we, the people, who alone make great men greater, will yet place him where his talents, as an orator and a statesman, will be a blessing to the nation. Often during his discourse did I wish that old Abe Lincoln and Seward were present, that they might be convinced and return to their corrupt coadjutors, to inform them that the eloquent Gantt was our orator, that his convincing eloquence was too clear and powerful to withstand any longer. They would also see in the determined countenance of her brave volunteers, that they are men determined to do battle to the death for the cause of our country, and that nothing short of victory can satisfy them. They could tell the old warrior, Gen. Scott, sir, they are just such brave fellows as fought under you at Chepultapec, and under Taylor at Buena Vista. During the proceedings, at proper intervals, volleys were fired by the volunteers by platoons, and our anvil artillery made the hills and valleys resound with its thunder.

K.

MEMPHIS, Tenn.,
July 17, 1861.

To the Ladies of the Society of Southern Mothers.[103]

Allow me to return to you my heartfelt thanks for your kind and unremitting attentions to the unfortunate men under my charge, who have been confined to your rooms by sickness, several of whom were snatched as it were from the very jaws of death, by their opportune arrival in this city, when another day in camp would, in all probability, have placed them beyond the reach of medicine or kind treatment; and I can assure you, now that they are about to depart, that they will ever remember your kindness; and although they may never see you again, nor be able to return to you or yours the compensation their grateful hearts would willingly offer, the moral influences will still be impressed upon them, and they will extend to such other unfortunates as may come in their way, the same kindnesses that they received from you.

And thus, fair ladies, the germ planted and nourished by the Southern Mothers will grow into a vigorous plant, its branches reaching into the remotest parts of our beloved South, and thousands who never knew you will feel the blessings of this great work of charity, and the merited prayers of its many recipients will ascend to heaven and there be registered to the credit of you and yours for all time. I would also return to Dr. G. W. Curry the sincere thanks of all the soldiers in my charge for his kindness, and I congratulate you in being so fortunate in securing the

---

103   *Memphis Daily Appeal*, July 19, 1861, Memphis, Tenn.

services of one so thoroughly versed in medical science, and so well adapted to the difficult position he how holds.

Respectfully,
G.A. Hanson,

1st Regiment Arkansas volunteers,
Col. Claiborne commanding, C. S. A.

UNION COUNTY, Ark.,
July 18, 1861.

County Script Called In. [104]

IT IS Ordered by the court that all persons who hold County Script issued, or that may be hereafter issued against the county treasury of Union county, between this and the 3rd day of our next January term hereof, be and they are hereby required to file the same in the clerk's office on the 1st Monday in January, A.D., 1862, for the purpose of canceling or re-issuing the same. It is further ordered by the court that all persons who fail to comply with the requisitions of this order shall be forever bared from collecting any script that they may hold in violation of this order.

Nevertheless, this order shall not be so construed as to prevent any person from using any Script that they may have or hereafter have, between this time and the time of said canceling, in paying their taxes. And that notice issue hereof to the Sheriff of Union county.
A true copy of the record.

Attest, W.E. Morgan, Clerk.

I hereby certify that the above is a true copy of the original.
JOHN D. HOLLOWAY, Sheriff.

By Wm. CHANDLER, *Deputy*
Thursday, July 18, A.D. 1861.

---

104   *Arkansas True Democrat*, August 22, 1861, Little Rock, Ark.

SULPHUR ROCK (INDEPENDENCE COUNTY), Ark., July 18, 1861.

Flag Presentation.[105]

My Gallant Countrymen-

With deep and soul-felt pride I behold the brave and self-sacrificing spirit displayed by you who are among the first to march from our beloved home to the battle field, in defence of southern independence. In behalf of the ladies of Sulphur Rock, I present to you this proudly waving banner of our southern land. Will it not return to us with a halo of liberty gleaming from its sacred folds, to float once more proudly and unmolested in the balmy breezes of the south, bearing the history of many a gallant deed of those who fight beneath it? Hope whispers, it will.

I believe this flag waves over not a timid heart, and that ere it goes down on the field of battle to trail in the dust, the last of the brave "Pike Guards" will rest in death from the fierce struggle for liberty. The cause of justice and truth is ours, and the great Ruler of events will exert his omnipotent arm in our defense if we will but trust Him. We cheerfully yield up our patriotic brothers and sons to stand by the side of others of the south, to fight bravely for the homes and liberties of our native land.

To offer up so precious a sacrifice upon our country's altar, is a privilege rather than a bereavement; and instead of repining and lamenting your absence, or deploring the hardships of your campaign, we will rather rejoice that the fire of liberty burns brightly in your bosoms, that you are willing to sacrifice your lives for your country's welfare and glory.

We feel assured that you will not for one moment be known to quail or falter; that you will ever be the same bold and unflinching heroes. Hard, indeed, will it be to nerve the heart for the last farewell, to obey duty's stern decree; gladly would we linger near you forever; but this cannot be. Go, then, bravely in discharge of your duty to your country, wives, mothers, and sisters, and when in battle's trying hour, remember that there are loving friends daily offering up prayers for your safety and success.

---

105 *Arkansas True Democrat*, July 18, 1861, Little Rock, Ark.

May the God of love be with you, to protect you from danger, to nerve your gallant heart for the stern conflict, and crown your efforts with liberty and peace, while loving and anxious friends await to welcome your joyous and happy return.

Response of Capt. John H. Dye...

Miss Mollie T. Jernigan, and Ladies of Sulphur Rock and Vicinity - Permit me, in behalf of the "Pike Guards, to acknowledge the receipt of your beautiful, and by us, long-to-be-remembered banner - and whilst it has never been my happy lot to witness the presentation, much less acknowledge the reception of one, yet the assemblage of the intelligent and vast audience convinces me that they too, as well as myself, feel that this is no ordinary occasion. This universal out-turn of feeble matrons and aged sires, leaning upon their staffs, associated with and surrounded, as they are, by all the youth and beauty of the land, and in whose every countenance was depicted an intense anxiety to hear your feeling charge and eloquent address to us, in behalf of an injured and outraged people, has conjointly, I must confess, overwhelmed me with emotions, both of feeling and duty, which the language of this feeble heart and faltering tongue is inadequate to express. And in attempting a feeble response, my mind is necessarily driven back to the early history of our country; to the scenes and incidents with which, perhaps, many of this audience are more familiar than myself. . .

LITTLE ROCK, Ark.,
July 20, 1861.

Socks for the Soldiers.[106]

As the cold weather approaches it is the part of wisdom to provide for it - especially should we provide for the comfort of the brave soldiers who are in the field in our defence. They are now, with some exceptions well clothed and provided.

Their comfort and health in the winter will be greatly increased by keeping their feet warm - hence we suggest the propriety of every lady in the country knitting at least one good pair of woolen socks for our

---

106 *Weekly Arkansas Gazette*, July 20, 1861, Little Rock, Ark.

soldiers. And if any of the ladies in the country have a surplus of yarn, they can serve the cause by forwarding it to town, that it may be knit by the ladies here.

Mr. S. H. Tucker will receive contributions from the country in this part of the State, and see that they are properly forwarded to their destination. Let the people of every county take this matter in hand, and a great good can be achieved by a comparatively small effort on the part of all.

LITTLE ROCK, Ark.,
July 20, 1861.

Col. Cleburne's Regiment.[107]

Though, as a general thing, our army is admirably clothed, Col. Cleburne's regiment have been in the field until their clothes are somewhat the worse for the wear. We would suggest the propriety of a complete new suit being made and forwarded to every soldier in that regiment.

It can be done by a few counties, and the burden not felt. Even if more clothes were sent than this regiment need, they can, doubtless, be distributed advantageously among some of the soldiers of the other commands.

Who will move in this matter?

LITTLE ROCK, Ark.,
July 25, 1861.

An Arkansas Farewell.[108]

"Persimmons, jr." in the Spirit of the Times, gives an account of the parting of Old Ben Winnie, of Arkansas, with his son Joe, who was leaving home for business in Texas. The old man was accustomed to deal in eucherism, and his discourse is enlivened by similes that the smoking car passengers on some of our longest local railway trains will

---

107   *Weekly Arkansas Gazette*, July 20, 1861, Little Rock, Ark.
108   *Arkansas True Democrat*, July 25, 1861, Little Rock, Ark.

understand. Thus the story runs.

In course of time Uncle Winnie's eldest son, a boy of some eighteen years of age, was most unexpectedly invited to what was then the new country of Texas. A distant relative, who desired an assistant, offered great inducement, and Winnie, jr., a chip of the old block, and a real honor to Arkansas, made his preparation for the first time to leave home. His mother treated the thing a good deal as mothers do, and filled up the time before his departure with crying, packing up a trunk, and making "cake fixins."

Old Winnie took a most grasping and philosophical view of the matter. He remarked that life was a pack of cards, and that your success depended upon how they were dealt out. He said he knew fellows who never could get above a four spot, and never enough of them to make more than a pair. He'd knowed others, again, who always had their hand full of queens and aces; and even if the deal runs low, they would get two pairs, or three deuces, and war even better in this case than pictures. In short, Uncle Winnie said some men had luck; play as they would, they could not in fact, help winning, whether they sot down with green ones or took a shot at the tiger.

At last the "boy" was about to take his departure; his mother gave him her last kiss, and her most fervent blessing, and Uncle Winnie accompanied him to the wagon that was to take him to the steamboat landing. The moment of leaving came; he had held up wonderfully all through the preliminaries, but now his heart was too full, and he broke out as follows:

"Bob you are about to leave home for strange parts. You're going to throw me out of the game and go it alone. The odds is agin you, Bob; but remember always that industry and perseverance are the winning cards; they are the 'bowers.'

"Book learning and all that sort of thing will do to fill up with, like small trumps, but you must have the bowers to back 'em, else they ain't worth shucks. If luck runs agin you pretty strong, don't cave in and look like a sick chicken on a rainy day, but hold your head up and make 'em believe you're flush of trumps; then they won't play so hard agin you.

"I've lived and traveled around some, Bob, and I've found out that as soon as folks thought you held a weak hand, they'd buck agin you strong. So when you're sorter weak, keep on a bold front, but play cautious; be satisfied with a pint. Many's the hand I've seen euchered 'cause they played for too much.

"Keep your eyes well skinned, Bob; don't let 'em 'nig on you; recollect the game lays as much with the head as with the hands. Be temperate - never get drunk, for then, no matter how good your hand, you won't know how to play it - both bowers and the ace won't save you, for there's sartin to be a 'misdeal,' or something wrong. And another thing, Bob," (this was spoken in a low tone, and in Bob's ear,) "don't go too much on the women; queens is kinder poor cards; the more you have of 'em the worse for you; you might have three, and nary trump. I don't say discard 'em all; if you get hold of one that's a trump, its all good, and thar's sartin to be *one* out of the four.

"And above all, Bob, be honest; never take a man's trick wot don't belong to you; nor 'slip cards' nor 'nig,' for then you can't look your man in the face; and when that's the case there's no fun in the game; 'it's a regular cut throat.' So now, Bob, farewell; remember what I tell you, and you'll be sure to win, and if you don't, serves you right to get skunked!"

Old Winnie's feelings now overcame him, and, with tears in his eyes he concluded:

"Good-bye agin, Bob, and God bless you! Be a man, and do honor to your native State, and never be so mean as to run for the legislature, or try to get into Congress; to do either is worse than keeping a sweat-cloth at a mule race, or thimble-rigger at a negro camp-meeting." Here the old man fell upon Bob's neck, and the two wept together and parted.

SPRINGFIELD, Ark.,
July 30, 1861.

Our Correspondents.[109]

Our table is literally full of letters and communications, the most of which we would cheerfully publish had we room. The telegraphic items take up much space; we have to make room for our letters from Virginia and for the current news of the day. Very likely we offend a great many by not publishing the articles sent to us, but it is impossible. Were we to publish all sent, it would be to the exclusion of everything else.

We have been favored with a letter from a gentleman in Kentucky to a citizen of the State. He says the first congressional district has a majority for secession. Much of the matter in his letter has been

---

109   *Arkansas True Democrat*, August 15, 1861, Little Rock, Ark.

corroborated by the recent election in that State. He says that a great many who really favored the Southern Confederacy voted for Union candidates, being falsely persuaded that such a course would maintain peace. We give an extract from this letter:

> "We have had fears of Ky., yet within 120 days she will be in revolution, and that when her money and blood have to go they will go for the South emphatically, though with some division. No violence has been done in this part of the State, except driving out one or two abolitionists, and we are not expecting any fight here until the dance commences in Ky., which will be soon in our opinion as above stated. Two companies from Calloway have left for the Southern Confederacy and some from every county in the purchase, and many other counties in this State.
>
> We once ardently desired a compromise, and to avoid bloodshed and ruin, and still would if there was any hope, but as no chance exists, we are for the South, but we will scarcely be able to vote out but will have to fight out, and may be in as bad or worse condition than Missouri."

We would still publish the communication of Bosin, but it can do no good now. Such men as he refers to are callous, and not to be reached in that way. If the war continues and they pursue the same course, other means must be resorted to.

"A Volunteer" from one of the Montgomery county companies, writes us an interesting letter. The two companies from Montgomery, two from Hempstead and one each from Lafayette, Pike and Polk counties were organized on the 2nd inst. They are styled the South Arkansas Regiment and elected McNair, of Hempstead, Col.; B. Williams, of the same county, Lieut. Col., and J.H. May, of Montgomery county, Major. We regret to learn that there have been several deserters from the Mt. Ida company. We give the following extract from the letter:

"Dr. C.B. Mitchel from Hempstead county, U.S. Senator, is with us. He has just returned from McCulloch's camp. He made us one of his stirring patriotic speeches. He tells he claims no position, nor does he want any in the regiment, but the privilege of shouldering his musket and marching with us to share our fate, our triumphs, and if need be, our sorrows."

"Soldier" sends us a communication which is interesting but too long for our columns. He praises the hospitality of the people in Drew county, who would receive no pay from soldiers. Says he: "Old Drew has nobly demonstrated her patriotism, for from a voting population of twelve hundred she has sent a full regiment to the field." He complains that in the wealthy county of Chicot, the charges were exorbitant. The M.O. & R.R. railroad, he tells us carried the soldiers free of charge, which should be remembered to the credit of the company. He pays a high compliment to Mr. Nelson Blanchard and his patriotic wife, who keep a hotel at Carson's landing, and has on his cards "free for soldiers." "Soldier" proposes several things in his letter, among which are a general test oath for all citizens and the reduction of the pay of the officers. The first is unnecessary, for a traitor would as soon commit perjury as not. As to the latter, it is useless now, as the control has passed from the State, except that an attempt will be made to keep two or three dozen Dowbs in various offices, but that will be a matter for future thought.

The publication of the following is earnestly requested by some twenty or more volunteers, whose names are signed to the note which accompany it:

Camp Wilson, Springfield, ARK.,
July 30, 1861

EDITOR *TRUE DEMOCRAT*: It is with pleasure we state the fact, that our company arrived at quarters on Saturday previous, in time to participate in the elections for superior officers, and are satisfied with the selections. Our camp is situated near the village in a grove; we have an excellent spring which affords us an abundant supply of good water. And the boys enjoy camp life, for cheerfulness and good humor pervade the entire camp, and we have but little sickness and none of serious character, only such as we might expect from change of habits, diet, etc. The regiment is generally healthy and anxious for a fight, provided they had arms. But there is a great deficiency in our regiment - some companies having no guns, others only a few common guns. The companies are improving rapidly in drill and will be ready for service in a few weeks.

Our commissary department is badly supplied and managed...They supply us with beef daily, and the commissary store is so badly kept that it has become a nuisance to the town and regiment.

A number of the companies are not yet full, but are rapidly filling up. Our company will be full this week when they all get in unless they desert, as some did that participated in the election of company officers. It is important that the community know how a number of individuals are that joined the company. We will only specify a few instances which will show the nature of their excuses. After finding that the company was determined to go, one man it is said, promised his wife a dress to induce her to withhold her consent, and unfortunately her patriotism vanished, and I might mention many other names, but think it is unnecessary. Their true excuses may be said in a few words, a want of patriotism and courage.

One township when called on to send men to defend their country, replied that they were not interested in the war and afterwards joined an independent cavalry company which they knew would not be received, to prevent public odium. And it is a lamentable fact that many men were opposed to the formation of a company, because they were too cowardly to volunteer and go themselves..."

CALHOUN COUNTY, Ark., August 1, 1861.

Presentation Address of the Flag to the Moro Grays, Calhoun County, Ark .By Miss Lucy Lorraine Adams.[110]

Officers and privates of the Moro Greys - I appear before you as the representative of the ladies of Moro township, as the bestower of a gift wrought by their own fair hands, as the reflex of hearts beating hopefully, prayerfully, tearfully in your behalf; hopefully, as they have unwavering confidence in the integrity of the cause in which you have thus voluntarily enlisted; prayerfully, as they believe in God, and that He is the disposer of all human events and protects in the hollow of an omnipotent hand, *the children of the brave*; tearfully, as the taper of joy will flicker but fitfully in the hearts if the night-lamps of their hopes should go out on the field of battle - if the eyes that beam so brightly to-day should never throw their softened radiance again on scenes made lovely by their luster!

Thus honored with this pleasing, yet painful position, I congratulate you for the invincible spirit that animates your daring souls, that prompts the mighty purpose to make our land,

---

110 *Arkansas True Democrat*, August 1, 1861, Little Rock, Ark.

The home of the good, the brave, the wise,
Where all may climb fame's dizzy steep;
Or where, like magic, the valley lies,
Life's humbler sheaves, contented heap!

Through the broken arches of our *once* glorious Union, methinks, from the spirit land, there comes the voice of Vernon's slumbering hero, rallying its dismembered dust, to lead with Davis, his chosen South *again* to victory! The chambers of Heaven that rolled back through their resounding mansions the glad tidings of 76, *still* reverberate with peans [sic] of glory to his undying name, and resound with pleas to the ear of the God of Battles, to prosper our efforts against a fratricidal foe - to bow the knee of oppression in the dust at our feet, and compel the Goliath of the North to fold the menacing arm of power in *inglorious defeat!*

Our country calls! A sacrifice is demanded. Like the Patriarch of old, the ready South, strong in faith, binds her beloved Isaac on the altar, but, may the uplifted sword of war reek with the blood of different victims...

JACKSON COUNTY, Ark.,
August 1, 1861.

Speech of Miss Elizabeth Higginbotham.[111]

Officers and Privates of the Jackson Minute Men:

I am selected by the ladies of this vicinity to express to you their sympathy with the cause to which you have so gallantly offered your services.

Now is the day, now is the hour, spoken by the clock of Time, for the South to speed onward as swiftly as an eagle, in the path which her energies, interest and safety demands. Now is the hour of her greatest peril. The mistaken idea of the proud enemies of our land and institutions cannot be corrected, except by meeting their invading hosts on the battle field. A band of noble hearted men are marshalled to conquer them or to fall. Go, assist these defenders of our cause. Let the retreat never be beaten. Though our numbers be inferior, let every freeman be a host - let

---

111   *Arkansas True Democrat*, August 1, 1861, Little Rock, Ark.

him feel as if on his sole arm depended victory.

We believe you have girded on the sword in defence of our homes. Heaven is smiling on the men who are prompted by such motives as yours to take the sword. Providence will overrule all circumstances that those who shield us from the violation of our most sacred interests, may attain their object. March on then, and may the star of Freedom lead you to the place where our fond hope shall be realized. Onward! To the place where our new born Confederacy is to be acknowledged as a power before the nations of the earth! Hasten to the place where patriots inaugurate peace on a firmer foundation than it has existed between the North and South heretofore.

Gallant Ensign, if you are worthy of the honor of bearing this flag which I present, as you stand beneath its folds you will remember the people of eleven States are anxious for the honor of it. Remember that our hands have made it, and we would not have it dishonored. I know that each heart and hand will feel pledged to bring it unsullied from the field. With anxiety my vision follows it to the scenes of death and danger to which you are hastening. Shall a mercenary enemy claim it as a trophy?

Shall it trail in the dust? We trust it will not. We believe that every form will first be bleeding beneath its folds. We imagine it floating aloft as you cry victory, the strain rolled back, and reechoed with rapture, and our bosoms stirred with gratitude that you are successful. What a glorious future is opening to the South! How many glorious deeds and great sacrifices are to be recorded of southern patriots of the revolution of 1861? How many sons of Washington who were worthy of their great sire, will have their names annexed to the scroll of history for the instruction and love of the men of the distant future. Though your perishing ranks be heaped together like weeds, look proudly to heaven from that death bed, if untainted by cowardice, your face is to the foe. Our spirits shall bend over you as mourners, and exult that you were true. In your fall we are lost, but you will conquer. In your breast dwells a fire that shall consume your enemies, fed by remembrance of injuries, love of country and desire of independence. On this day, the glorious Fourth of July, the tree of freedom sent out new roots. Let that glorious tree be expanded by a new growth upward. In your victory we live...

**LITTLE ROCK, Ark.,
August 8, 1861.**

STATE OF ARKANSAS.[112]

Proclamation by the Governor

Whereas, the President of the Confederate States of America deems it proper to organize a reserved army corps from the different States in the Confederacy.

AND WHEREAS, The quota of 3,000 men is apportioned to the State of Arkansas, and a requisition having been made by the Secretary of War, upon the Governor of the State for 3,000 men to serve during the war. Authorizing and empowering him to receive the said number, by independent companies, and to establish camps of instruction at suitable and accessible points.

NOW Therefore, I, HENRY M. RECTOR, Governor of the State of Arkansas, by virtue of the authority in me vested by law, and in accordance with the requisition made upon me as Governor aforesaid, do hereby make known, that I will receive for the war, for Confederate State service, in independent companies, 3,000 men, each company to be composed of one Captain, one 1st Lieutenant, two second Lieutenants, four Sergeants, four Corporals, two musicians, and from sixty-four to one hundred privates.

Fifteen hundred of which will rendezvous at Clarksville, Johnson county, and the like number at Batesville, Independence county, Ark's., there to be formed into battalions and regiments, at the pleasure of the President, and to be armed, equipped and officered by the Confederate Government. Organized companies reporting to me from the respective points of rendezvous, will be received and provided for until the requisite number is supplied.

IN TESTIMONY WHEREOF, I have hereunto set my hand, and caused the seal of the State to be affixed at Little Rock, on the 8th day of August, A.D. 1861.

H.M. RECTOR,
By the Governor:

JOHN I. STIRMAN, Sec'y of State
Aug. 8, 1861

---

112 *Arkansas True Democrat*, August 15, 1861, Little Rock, Ark.

LITTLE ROCK, Ark.,
August 8, 1861.

A Chance for the Girls - Gold Medals for the Most Industrious.[113]

The press of this State has been urging upon the women the importance and necessity of making jeans and linseys. In a conversation with Gen. Wm. E. Ashley, president of the state agricultural society, he gave us permission to say that he will give a large gold medal, with suitable inscriptions, to a lady, married or single, who shall weave the most woolen cloth, quantity and quality both being considered, during the three months of September, October and November. The cloth will bring a full price and the fair worker will get the medal as an award and reward for industry.

Other gentlemen tell us that the next most industrious shall also have a gold medal. In determining this, the number of yards woven, will be considered in connection with the fineness of the cloth, and it will be left to competent persons at the place where the cloth is sent to be examined or sold, to decide.

Our Washington county friends, and other places where they have agricultural societies, may also take the matter in hand and award premiums to the most industrious. As for the gold medals offered above, we pledge ourselves they shall be forthcoming. Start fair young ladies and see who can win in this race.

LITTLE ROCK, Ark.,
August 8, 1861.
Development of the Resources of Arkansas.[114]

There are three or four cotton factories in this State, but we do not know of the number of spindles driven, or their capacity for turning out thread and cloth. If not now in operation, we hope to hear soon that they are under full headway. If they would be profitable at any time, it will be now and during the continuance of the war. We will be glad to receive information concerning this and other branches of industry in this State.

---

113 *Arkansas True Democrat*, August 8, 1861, Little Rock, Ark.
114 *Arkansas True Democrat*, August 8, 1861, Little Rock, Ark.

As a great deal of coal was floated down the Mississippi river, which is now closed above, and none can be brought up to New Orleans and other points, it appears to us that the coal beds of Arkansas can now be profitably worked. Those on the Ouachita river will, probably, be managed by a company from New Orleans. There is excellent coal up the Arkansas and plenty of it; that at Spadra being on the bank of the river and easily obtained.

Salt will become scarce and valuable unless we avail ourselves of the many salt springs in our State. Some of these salines are worked now. Others give a strong brine which would yield sufficient salt to pay for the erection of pumps, boilers, etc. And it should be remembered that the invariable rule is "the deeper the well, the stronger the brine."

Every man who has a good tannery now, has a little fortune. We are afraid that there will be a great scarcity of leather and shoes next winter, unless more tanneries are established and better care taken by our farmers of the hides or skins of animals. We must economize in this respect, not only from patriotism, but from necessity. We have within ourselves a full supply for all our wants, and only need a development of our resources to make us independent. Let any man count up the amount paid by Arkansas to the North, in a year for the single articles of boots and shoes. At three dollars to each person, it would largely exceed a million of dollars.

Now is the time to set about these things, and by cold weather we can be prepared to supply those wants heretofore supplied by importations. We urge upon the farmers to be careful of the furs and skins of all wild and tame animals, and have them properly tanned. Let none be thrown away or nailed to barn doors and suffered to dry up and become worthless. A large tannery has been, or will be, established in the eastern part of the State. There is room for such a one in the west, as large numbers of hides can be procured from our Indian neighbors.

As regards salines and coal beds, those desiring information on that point will find it in the reports of the geological survey. The second report, though printed and delivered, has not been distributed, but, no doubt, any gentleman seeking information of that kind, can procure one by applying to the Governor, or Secretary of State.

LITTLE ROCK, Ark.,
August 12, 1861.

TO THE VOTERS OF THE

5th Judicial District of the State of Arkansas, composed of the counties of Conway, Prairie, Dallas, Hot Spring, Saline and Pulaski:[115]

GENTLEMEN- A vacancy having occurred in the office of Prosecuting Attorney in your district, by the resignation of J.L. Hollowell, esq., I present my name as a candidate before you. My engagements on the circuit as Prosecuting Attorney pro tem., and want of time will prevent me from calling on you before the election. For my qualifications to discharge the duties of the office, I can therefore only refer you to my past conduct in 1855 and '56 when I held the same office.

The election will be held on the 26th inst. I trust my friends will give publically of the time, and promptly attend at the polls and vote.

Very respectfully, your ob't serv't,
PLEASANT JORDAN
Little Rock, ARK., Aug. 12, 1861

SPRINGFIELD, Mo.,
August 12, 1861.[116]

Numbers 19.

Report of Major General Sterling Price, commanding Missouri
State Guard, of operations from July 25 to August 11.

HEADQUARTERS MISSOURI STATE GUARD,
Springfield, Mo., August 12, 1861.

SIR: I have the honor to submit to your Excellency the following report of the operations of the army under my command at and immediately preceding the Battle of Springfield:

I began to move my command from its encampment on Cowskin Prairie, in McDonald County, on July 25, towards Cassville, in Barry County, at which it had been agreed upon between Generals McCulloch,

---

115   *Arkansas True Democrat*, August 22, 1861, Little Rock, Ark.
116   OR,1(1):98-102

Pearce, and myself that our respective forces, together with those of Brigadier-General McBride, should be concentrated, preparatory to a forward movement.

We reached Cassville on Sunday, July 28, and on the next day effected a junction with the armies of Generals McCulloch and Pearce. The combined armies were then put under marching orders, and the First Division, General McCulloch commanding, left Cassville on August 1 upon the road to this city. The Second Division, under General Pearce, of Arkansas, left on August 1; and the Third Division, Brigadier-General Steele, of this State, commanding, left on August 2. I went forward with the Second Division, which embraced the greater portion of my infantry, and encamped with it some 12 miles northwest of Cassville.

The next morning a messenger from General McCulloch informed me that he had reason to believe that the enemy were in force on the road to Springfield, and that he should remain at this then encampment, on Crane Creek, until the Second and Third Divisions of the army had come up. The Second Division consequently moved forward to Crane Creek, and I ordered the Third Division to a position within 3 miles of the same place. An advance guard of the army, consisting of six companies of mounted Missourians, under command of Brigadier-General Rains, was at this time (Friday, August 2) encamped on the Springfield road, about 5 miles beyond Crane Creek.

About 9 a. m. of that day General Rains' pickets reported to him that they had been driven in by the enemy's advance guard, and that officer immediately led forward is whole force, amounting to nearly 400 men, until he found the enemy in position some 3 miles on the road. He sent back at once to General McCulloch for re-enforcements, and Colonel McIntosh, C. S. Army, was sent forward with 150 men, but a reconnaissance of the ground having satisfied the latter that the enemy did not have more than 150 men on the ground, he withdrew his men and returned to Crane Cree. General Rains soon discovered, however, that he was in presence of the main body of the enemy, numbering, according to his estimate, more than 5,000 men, with eight pieces of artillery, and supported by a considerable body of cavalry. A severe skirmish ensued, which lasted several hours, until the enemy opened their batteries and compelled our troops to retire. In this engagement the greater portion of General Rains' command, and especially that part which acted as infantry, behaved with great gallantry, as the result demonstrates, for our loss was only 1 killed (Lieutenant Northcut) and 5 wounded, while 5 of

154

the enemy's dead were buried on the field, and a large number are known to have been wounded.

Our whole forces were concentrated the next day near Crane Creek, and during the same night the Texas regiment, under Colonel Greer, came up within a few miles of the same place.

Reasons which will be hereafter assigned induced me on Sunday, the 4th instant, to put the Missouri forces under the direction, for the time being, of General McCulloch, who accordingly assumed the command [of] armies.

A little after midnight we took up the line of march, leaving our baggage trains, and expected to find the enemy near the scene of the late skirmish, but we found as we advanced that they were retreating rapidly towards Springfield. We followed them hastily about 17 miles to a place known as Moody's Spring, where we were compelled to halt our forces, who were already nearly exhausted by the intense heat of the weather and the dustiness of the roads.

Early the next morning we moved forward to Wilson's Creek, 10 miles southwest of Springfield, where we encamped. Our forces were here put in readiness to meet the enemy, who were posted at Springfield to the number of about 10,000. It was finally decided to march against them in four separate columns at 9 o'clock that night, so as to surround the city and begin a simultaneous attack at daybreak. The darkness of the night and a threatened storm caused General McCulloch, just as the army was about to march, to countermand this order, and to direct that the troops should hold themselves in readiness to move whenever ordered.

Our men were consequently kept under arms till towards daybreak, expecting momentarily an order to march.

The morning of Saturday, August 10, found them still encamped at Wilson's Creek, fatigued by a night's watching and loss of rest.

About 6 o'clock I received a messenger from General Rains that the enemy were advancing in great force from the direction of Springfield, and were already within 200 or 300 yards of the position, where he was encamped with the Second Brigade of his division, consisting of about 1,200 mounted men, under Colonel Cawthorn. A second messenger came immediately afterwards from General Rains to announce that the main body of the enemy was upon him, but that he would endeavor to hold him in check until he could receive re-enforcements. General McCulloch was with me [when] these messengers came, and left at once for his own headquarters to make the necessary disposition of our forces.

I rode forward instantly towards General Rains' position, at the same time ordering Generals Slack, McBride, Clark, and Parsons to move their infantry and artillery rapidly forward. I had ridden but a few hundred yards when I came suddenly upon the main body of the enemy, commanded by General Lyon in person. The enemy and artillery, which I had ordered to follow me, came up immediately, to the number of 2,036 men, and engaged the enemy.

A severe and bloody conflict ensued, my officers and men behaving with the greatest bravery, and with the assistance of a portion of the Confederate forces successfully holding the enemy in check. Meanwhile, and almost simultaneously with the opening of the enemy's batteries in this quarter, a heavy cannonading was opened upon the rear of our position, where a large body of the enemy, under Colonel Sigel, had taken position in close proximity to Colonel Churchill's regiment, Colonel Greer's Texan Rangers, and 679 mounted Missourians, under command of Colonel Brown and Lieutenant-Colonel Major. The action now became general, and was conducted with the greatest gallantry and vigor on both sides for more than five hours, when the enemy retreated in great confusion, leaving their commander-in-chief, General Lyon, dead upon the battle-field, over 500 killed, and a great number wounded.

The forces under my command have possession of three 12-pounder howitzers, two brass 6-pounders, and a great quantity of small-arms and ammunition taken from the enemy; also the standard of Sigel's regiment, captured by Captain Staples. They have also a large number of prisoners. The brilliant victory thus achieved upon this hard-fought field was won only by the most determined bravery and distinguished gallantry of the combined armies, which fought nobly side by side in defense of their common rights and liberties with as much courage and constancy as were ever exhibited upon any battle-field.

Where all behaved so well it is invidious to make any distinction, but I cannot refrain from expressing my sense of the splendid services rendered under my own eyes by the Arkansas infantry, under General Pearce; the Louisiana regiment of Colonel Hebert, and Colonel Churchill's regiment of mounted riflemen. These gallant officers and their brave soldiers won upon that day the lasting gratitude of every true Missourian.

This great victory was dearly brought by the blood of many a skillful officer and brave man.

Others will report the losses sustained by the Confederate forces. I shall willingly confine myself to the losses within my own army.

Among those who fell mortally wounded upon the battle-field none deserve a dearer place in the memory of Missourians than Richard Hanson Weightman, colonel, commanding the First Brigade of the Second Division of the army. Taking up arms at the very beginning of this unhappy contest, he had already done distinguished services at the battle of Rock Creek, of the lamented Holloway [sic], and at Carthage, where he won unfading laurels by the display of extraordinary coolness, courage, and skill. He fell at the head of his brigade, wounded in three places, and died just as the victorious shout of our army began to rise upon the air. Here, too, died in the discharge of his duty Colonel Ben. Brown, of Ray County, president of the senate, a good man and true.

Brigadier-General Slack's division suffered severely. He himself fell dangerously wounded at the head of his column. Of his regiment of infantry, under Colonel John T. Hughes, consisting of about 650 men, 36 were killed, 76 wounded, many of them mortally, and 30 are missing. Among the killed were C. H. Bennett, adjutant of the regiment; Captain Blackburn, and Lieutenant Hughes.

Colonel Rives' squadron of cavalry, dismounted, some 234 men, lost 4 killed and 8 wounded. Among the former were Lieutenant-Colonel Austin and Captain Engart.

Brigadier-General Clark was also wounded. His infantry, 200 men, lost in killed 17, and wounded, 71. Colonel Burnbridge was severely wounded; Captain Farris and Halleck and Lieutenant Haskins were killed.

General Clark's cavalry, together with the Windsor Guards, were under the command of Lieutenant-Colonel Major, who did good service. They lost 6 killed and 5 wounded.

Brigadier-General McBridge's division, 605 men, lost 22 killed, 67 severely wounded, and 57 slightly wounded. Colonel Foster and Captains Nichols, Dougherty, Armstrong, and Mings were wounded while gallantly leading their respective commands.

General Parson's brigade, 256 infantry and artillery, under command, respectively, of Colonel Kelley and Captain Guibor, and 406 cavalry, under Colonel Brown, lost, the artillery, 3 killed and 7 wounded; the infantry, 9 killed and 38 wounded; and the cavalry, 3 killed and 2 wounded. Colonel Kelley was wounded in the hand. Captain Coleman was mortally wounded, and has since died.

General Rains' division was composed of two brigades. The first, under Colonel Weightman, embracing infantry and artillery, 1,306 strong, lost not only their commander, but 34 others killed and 111 wounded. The Second Brigade, mounted men, Colonel Cawthorn commanding, about 1,200 strong, lost 21 killed and 75 wounded.

Colonel Cawthorn was himself wounded, and Major Charles Rogers, of Saint Loius, adjutant of the brigade, was mortally wounded, and died the day after the battle. He was a gallant officer, and at all times vigilant and attentive to his duties, and fearless upon the field of battle.

Your Excellency will perceive that our State forces consisted of only 5,221 officers and men; that of those no less than 156 died upon the field, while 517 were wounded. These facts attest more powerfully than words can the severity of the conflict and the dauntless courage of our brave soldiers.

It is also my painful duty to announce the death of one of my aides, Lieutenant Colonel George W. Allen, of Saline County. He was shot down whole communicating an order, and we left him buried on the field. I have appointed to the position thus sadly vacated Captain James T. Cearnel, in recognition of his gallant conduct and valuable services throughout the battle as a volunteer aide.

Another of my staff, Colonel Horace H. Brand, was made prisoner by the enemy, but has since been released.

My thanks are due to three of your staff-Colonel William M. Cook, Richard Gaines, and Thomas L. Snead-for the services which they rendered me as volunteer aides, and also to my aide-de-camp, Colonel A. W. Jones.

In conclusion, I beg leave to say to your Excellency that the army under my command, both officers and men, did their duty nobly, as became men fighting in defense of their homes and their honor, and that they deserve well of their State.

I have the honor to be, with the greatest respect,
your Excellency's obedient servant,
STERLING PRICE,
Major-General, Commanding Missouri State Guard.

HELENA, Ark.,
August 14, 1861.

Shoemakers Wanted Immediately.[117]

The undersigned wish to employ twenty-five or thirty good Shoemakers, at their Boot and Shoe Factory, in Helena, Arkansas, and are prepared to give them permanent employment and the highest prices for work. Those wishing a good situation in that line of business, will do well to apply immediately. All work paid for at the end of each week.

Porter, Richardson & Co.,
Helena, Ark.

LITTLE ROCK, Ark.,
August 15, 1861.

Direct Taxation.[118]

It was said all over the North and by many in the South, last Winter, that the Confederate States would have to resort to direct taxation to support its government. This we denied, and the result so far has proved our assertions. It is the United States that have to resort to direct taxation. The Confederate States government will be the wealthiest on earth. Its custom under the lowest possible tariff will be more than sufficient to defray its expenses and pay off its war debt.

The following from the *New York Tribune* shows the amount to be raised in each State by direct taxation. The amount apportioned to Arkansas is nearly $400,000, besides a special tax on stills, liquors and carriages. Old Able will have a lively time collecting it in the southern seceded States. Before his "assessors and collectors" get through there is very apt to be "somebody hurt." The Washington correspondent of the *New York Tribune* writes under date of the 18th:

"In accordance with the recommendation of the secretary of the treasury, the committee of ways and means will introduce a bill to provide for levying a direct tax. This bill will be entitled 'an act to provide additional revenues for defraying the expenses of the government and maintaining the public credit, by the assessment and collection of a direct tax, and internal duties.' By the provisions of this

---

117   *Memphis Daily Appeal*, August 14, 1861, Memphis, Tenn.
118   *Arkansas True Democrat*, August 15, 1861, Little Rock, Ark.

159

act a direct tax, probably of the amount of $30,000,000 annually, will be laid, and distributed in the following proportions among the respective states:

Maine	$331,329.00	Indiana	$1,375,313.00
New Hamp	$327,610.00	Illinois	$1,719,827.00
Vermont	$396,602.00	Missouri	$1,141,691.00
Massachusetts	$1,236,372.00	Kansas	$107,615.00
Rhode Island	$175,445.00	Arkansas	$392,829.00
Connecticut	$462,321.00	Michigan	$751,645.00
New York	$3,905,378.00	Florida	$116,284.00
New Jersey	$675,201.00	Texas	$532,660.00
Pennsylvania	$2,920,079.00	Iowa	$678,132.00
Delaware	$112,025.00	Wisconsin	$779,539.00
Maryland	$655,235.00	California	$462,321.00
Virginia	$1,406,326.00	Minnesota	$152,786.00
North Carolina	$864,292.00	Oregon	$52,711.00
South Carolina	$545,356.00	New Mexico	$93,973.00
Georgia	$876,551.00	Utah	$40,473.00
Alabama	$700,820.00	Washington	$11,633.00
Mississippi	$619,627.00	Nebraska	$23,918.00
Louisiana	$578,803.00	Nevada	$6,889.00
Ohio	$2,350,625.00	Colorado	$4,358.00
Kentucky	$1,070,543.00	Dakota	$4,862.00
Tennessee	$1,004,247.00	D.C.	$74,155.00

In order to connect this it is further provided that the President shall divide the State and territories into convenient districts, and shall nominate by and with the advice of the Senate an assessor and collector for each district. If this appointment or any of them are not made during the present session of Congress, the President may make them during the recess, the commissions so issued to expire at the end of the next session.

The collectors are to execute a bond for such amount as the secretary of the treasury shall direct, with surities to be approved as sufficient by the solicitor of the treasurer. The principal assessor of each district is to appoint assistants, and all are to be governed by regulations to be prescribed by the secretary of the treasury in carrying out the provisions of the bill.

The tax is to be laid on all lands and lots of ground, with their improvements, dwelling houses, chattels and slaves. The bill provides that any person who shall give a fraudulent list of property under his charge, or owned by him, shall be fined in a sum not exceeding five hundred dollars and pay all costs and charges of prosecution. From the valuation of the board of assessors there is to be no appeal, but they are in any case when it is demanded to give a careful hearing to the parties claiming reduction of valuation.

It is proposed to tax all stills, boilers, and other utensils employed in the distillation of spirituous liquors 15 cents on every gallon of capacity; and to lay a tax of five cents per gallon on all fermented and malted liquors. In order to furnish the proper data for assessing such a tax, distillers will be obliged to keep a correct record of the amount distilled from day of date.

It is further proposed to lay a tax upon carriages; the amount of tax to be proportioned to the value of the carriage. From this all vehicles need exclusively for the transportation of merchandise are to be exempted. On all others not exceeding in value $50, it is proposed to lay a tax of $1, exceeding $50 in value, but not over $150, a tax of $4; above $200, but not exceeding $400, a tax of $16; above $500 but not exceeding $600, a tax of $22; above $600, but not exceeding $800, a tax of $30; above $800, but not exceeding $1,000, a tax of $40; above $1,000 in value, a tax of $50.

This bill will be submitted at the earliest possible day. Though in some unimportant features it may differ from the synopsis given, will in the main correspond with the indications here made."

LITTLE ROCK, Ark.,
August 15, 1861.

Lead.[119]

Some of our exchanges in the Confederate States have expressed an anxiety concerning a supply of lead during the war. We have excellent lead mines in Arkansas, and some so rich that hunters had moulded bullets directly from the ore. We have lead mines in the vicinity capable of yielding enough lead to supply the Confederacy. Will not some enterprising person or persons take this matter into consideration and have these mines worked?

---

119   *Arkansas True Democrat*, August 15, 1861, Little Rock, Ark.

FORT SMITH, Ark.,
August 15, 1861.

GEN. N.B. Pearce.[120]

We were led by a paragraph in the *Ft.Smith Times* to state that a misunderstanding existed between this officer and Gen. McCulloch. By a published letter from the latter officer to the Military Board, we find this was an error and that unanimity has ever existed between them.

LONG VIEW, Ark.,
August 15, 1861.[121]

EDITOR *TRUE DEMOCRAT-*
DEAR SIR: I am this morning in receipt of the No. of your paper in which "Many Citizens" of Union county complain of the ferrymen at Moro and at this place for a want of patriotism which they evinced by charging the Three Greeks company with ferriage, when on their way to Virginia. Believing as I do, that you prefer publishing truth to false-hood, and knowing that your correspondent either willfully or ignorantly has caused you to publish an untruth in regard to this matter, which may injure me in the estimation of some. I wish to give you a true statement of the facts as they occurred here and have you correct the error. The Captain asked me what I would charge him for crossing his company with their wagons, etc., I replied that I had not charged other companies anything and would cross him free; he said that he did not expect me to do it for nothing - that he had paid full fare at Moro and expected to do so here. I then told him that I paid a rent of $450 for the ferry and that if he saw fit to pay me $5 (less than one third the regular rates) I would take it and be obliged to him. He paid me that amount and nothing more was said about it. As to our patriotism in Ashley, we don't boast much, but have already equipped and sent to the battle field, over one-half of our men who are able to bear arms, and the rest of us are ready to go when needed.

Truly yours,
R.J. Withers

---

120   *Arkansas True Democrat*, August 15, 1861, Little Rock, Ark.
121   *Arkansas True Democrat*, September 5, 1861, Little Rock, Ark.

LITTLE ROCK, Ark.,
August 20, 1861.

Clothing for the Soldiers
Circular Letter from the Military Board.[122]

Office Military Board,
Little Rock, August 20, 1861.

A large number of our fellow-citizens having gone forth to the field of battle for the defense of their country, and being destitute of those articles of clothing made indispensable by the rigors of the approaching winter, it is necessary that some effort should be made to supply these articles and to provide for their comfort. The enemy trusts to the depression of trade and the blockade of our ports to prevent sufficient supplies from reaching our army, and the Military Board deems it their duty to appeal to the patriotism of the country to aid them in their winter preparations.

None will be forgetful of the wants of their friends and kindred in the army. For the purpose of systematizing this appeal to the country, the Military Board has appointed the county judge, the county clerk, the sheriff, or in his absence the deputy sheriff of each county, a central committee for the purpose of collecting such clothing as may be procured in the county. This committee again (two being a quorum) shall invite the ladies of each township in the county to form soldiers aid societies and shall assist in their organization. The animating patriotism of the ladies is especially invoked in furtherance of this effort to supply the volunteers with clothing. The ladies of this State have already done much, and their efforts are held in the highest appreciation. Similar appeals to the one we make have been made to the patriotism and devotion of the ladies in other States, and they have been nobly responded to. We feel assured that the ladies of Arkansas are not deficient in patriotism; that they will not lag behind their sisters in other States, but will act in concert with the State authorities in providing for our citizens soldiers who have gone forth to defend them.

We have no misgivings or doubts as to the result of this appeal. The patriotism of the people is equal to any emergency or any occasion, and it is only necessary that it be systematized and directed in such channels as to render it available and useful. For this purpose the central

---

122 *Arkansas True Democrat*, August 22, 1861, Little Rock, Ark.

committee already indicated, will establish clothing depots at such point in their respective counties as they may deem the most advisable. At this place they will receipt for everything in the clothing line suitable for the army that may be placed there, which they will place in the care of safe and reliable persons. And the Military Board will pay in Arkansas or Confederate Bonds, for all goods of the description herein indicated that the patriotism of the country may place at their disposal. That price will be paid which is reasonable in the county where the articles are purchased. As fast as the garments accumulate the central committee will report them to the Military Board so that the immediate and pressing wants of the soldiers may be relieved at as early a period as practicable.

Blankets are greatly needed and are indispensable to the comfort of our soldiers. In many instances domestic blankets may be manufactured. In others they may be supplied by a division of the articles of that kind which families have provided for themselves. There is scarcely a house in the State in which there is not an excess of bed-clothing. It is not making too great a call on the patriotism of the county, at a time like this, to ask that the soldiers be supplied from this surplus and abundance. Where blankets cannot be supplied comforts may be substituted; but blankets are much preferred. All the other articles of soldiers clothing such as woolen uniforms, flannel shirts, drawers, socks, etc., are equally needed. Whenever shoes can be supplied they will also be received and paid for in the manner and in the currency already indicated.

The central committee will keep a book in which they will register the names of those who furnish clothing - the number and character of the goods and the price to be paid for them. In order to facilitate and systematize this, blank forms will be sent with this circular letter to the various central committees. The individuals comprising the central committee have already been selected by the people for responsible positions; this selection will be a sufficient guarantee that their exertion will be active and that they will place the goods at the different depots for clothing in the care of gentlemen responsible in character and in property.

Thus the people will entertain no doubt that the goods delivered will reach the destination for which they were intended. The rapid approach of winter renders it necessary that our efforts should be prompt and energetic, and our inability to procure clothing in the usual market, leaves us no other course but to appeal to the patriotism and domestic resources of the country. Our soldiers are already in need of clothing.

They will need them still more as the winter approaches. Is it right that they should be permitted to suffer while fighting our battles for us? We feel confident that the people will not permit this.

H. M. Rector,
Benj. C. Totten,

Aug. 22, 1861.
Military Board.

POND SPRINGS, Mo.,
August 21, 1861.

Extract of a Letter from Capt. Galloway.[123]

We are getting along tolerably; our men are suffering for want of *tents, blankets* and *clothing*; we are also running short of provisions, have only flour, beef and bacon; no sugar or coffee. This state of things cannot last long - if we cannot get provisions here, we will have to move into Arkansas. I told Lieut. King to see Vaughan, Ashley, Keatts and others, and try and get them to send us 80 or 100 suits of clothes. Try and do all you can for us. If there is any probability of getting them, have the blouse or sack coat made of some gray color - could get along without the pants if we can't get them. I must close, nothing more at present.

M. G. G.

LITTLE ROCK, Ark.,
August 22, 1861.

Address of Mrs. W. M. Aikin to the Izard Volunteers.[124]

It gives me much pleasure to address the gallant volunteers of our State and county, our noble defenders of southern rights and independence; and I am proud of the occasion which justifies me to do so. A second time you have been called upon to test your courage and valor, and thank God in either case you have not been found wanting. Truly our sunny South ought to be proud of her sons, when she knows how eagerly they have responded to their country's call, how promptly they have gone to the battle field to avenge our wrongs and to drive the invaders from our homes and firesides. All honor to the brave and true.

---

123 *Arkansas True Democrat,* September 5, 1861, Little Rock, Ark.
124 *Arkansas True Democrat*, August 22, 1861, Little Rock, Ark.

I take pleasure in presenting this flag to your gallant company; well knowing I could commit it to no better hands. Eleven stars now deck its blue field, and I feel assured at least, and hope I can soon place the other three there. How happy I will be to do so you all well know. When you look upon its waving folds, think, is it not an emblem of liberty? of freedom? Yes my friends the liberty our noble forefathers shed their best blood for, that they might transmit it to their children.

"Oh liberty can man resign thee,
Once having felt thy generous flame;
Can dungeons bolts or bars confine thee,
Or whips thy noble spirit tame?"

Men of '61, will you not emulate those heroes of '76? Will you not prove that the same generous blood flows through your veins, the same heroic fire animated your hearts and nerves your arms? I feel assured you will. Liberty is dear as ever; and it now remains with *you* to decide our future fate. Oh, what a responsibility - what a privilege. Yet it is a glorious one, and the God of battles who has mysteriously protected us so far will, I trust, not desert us now. Then when you unfurl this banner in the battle field, let it ever be "a beacon light to glory, and a guide to victory."

Mothers, though it may be hard to part with your sons, do not dissuade them from going to battle; rather be proud that you have sons to offer. I have a little son whom I dearly love, yet, oh it would wring my heart, should he grow up and then prove to be a coward or a traitor to his country.

A brave man is ever entitled to woman's respect and admiration; but a *coward* - forbid it heaven that *such* should ever disgrace the soil of Arkansas. Wives our men were never more entitled to respect than they are now, and should they return victorious from the battle field, our hearts will throb with pride and pleasure, we will welcome our heroes home, and know that we have men who have truly proved that they are both able and willing to defend us when danger is near. Sisters your influence is greater over your brother than you may imagine; then never be the ones to discourage them, bid them go and prove themselves worthy of the name of men. Let us tell them that though the bitter tears may flow, we will bless them, and prayers warm from loving hearts will ascend to the Most High for their safety and welfare. Then brave

166

volunteers, go forth, let not those ruthless and insolent minions of the North pollute our sacred soil, step by step drive them back, and let them feel that they have men, *iron hearted men*, and not *pet lambs* to deal with.

"Then take our flag, let it stream on the air,
Tho' our fathers are cold in their graves,
They had hands that could strike, they had hearts that could dare;
And their sons were not born to be slaves.
Up, up with our banners where 'er it may call,
Our millions shall rally around,
A nation of freemen that moment shall fall,
When its stars shall be trailed on the ground."

Volunteers, your cause is a noble one, it is just and holy, may success crown your efforts, and may God bless you.

LITTLE ROCK, Ark.,
August 22, 1861.

Clothing for the Soldiers.[125]

We direct attention to the circular letter of the military board, in regard to this subject. We have repeatedly directed the attention of our readers to the necessity of making some effort among the people to supply our soldiers with clothing. We are glad to see that the board has determined to avail themselves of the domestic resources of the country. Our soldiers must be clothed, let the cost be what it may. We are satisfied that it cannot be secured in the usual markets of the country. The secretary of war, we understand, has addressed a circular letter to the executives of the various states, in which he urges the impossibility of securing clothing in the usual markets, and suggests some such plan as that adopted by the board. The people, we are satisfied, will respond to the call upon their liberality and patriotism in a proper spirit. It only needs that their efforts should be directed in a systematic channel, to make them efficient and valuable. It addresses itself particularly and especially to the ladies. It relates to a department with which they are familiar, and their active and systematic aid in this matter, will do much to relieve the wants of their brothers, their husbands and their fathers.

---

125   *Arkansas True Democrat*, August 22, 1861, Little Rock, Ark.

LITTLE ROCK, Ark.,
August 22, 1861. [126]

Lieut. Lockman, of the "Capital Guards," arrived here a few days since, and will leave for his company about Sunday next, the 25th inst. He comes home for the purpose of getting recruits for his company.

FORT SMITH, Ark.,
August 22, 1861. [127]

Just as we are about going to press the western mail is in. A letter from the postmaster at Ft. Smith says, "The news from Missouri is better and better all the time, the federalists have scattered to the woods and are completely routed." The State troops under command of Gen. Pierce left Springfield for Camp Walker on the 16th ins. Gen. McCulloch with his forces has gone to Ft. Scott. The bodies of Capt. Brown and Lieuts. Weaver and Walton were to have arrived at Ft. Smith to-day.

LITTLE ROCK, Ark.,
August 22, 1861.

The Call for More Troops. [128]

We call the attention of our readers to the proclamation of the governor calling for three thousand troops to serve for theree years or during the war. Arkansas has already sent to the field a large number of volunteers. In this respect, she has won the appellation of the "volunteer state." These volunteers, however, have enlisted but for twelve months. While this is all right, and while the country will and ought to avail itself of the patriotism of these citizen soldiers, whose circumstances will not permit a larger enlistment, yet the good of the service and our ultimate success requires that a portion of our soldiers should enlist for a longer period. The contest in which we are engaged will be a high exhibition of rival will and opposing power, and will require a prudent husbandry of

---

126   *Arkansas True Democrat*, August 22, 1861, Little Rock, Ark.
127   *Arkansas True Democrat*, August 22, 1861, Little Rock, Ark.
128   *Arkansas True Democrat*, August 22, 1861, Little Rock, Ark.

all the resources of which we can avail ourselves, for success. It will be necessary that our soldiers should be trained and disciplined in the school of the camp, and in the art of war. They cannot acquire in the brief space of twelve months that trained discipline, that familiarity with a soldiers life and duty, and that high capacity for physical endurance which will fit and prepare them for the stern conflict of actual war. It is the experience of our best military men that volunteers who enlist but for twelve months, do not acquire the necessary discipline to enable the country to repose security upon their efforts before the expiration of their term of service. The quota assigned by the President to Arkansas is reasonable and can be easily filled. Arkansas has yet to furnish but two regiments for the war. In this respect, she lags in the rear of her sister States. This should not be the case. The term of service ought not to be objected to; for we will have to give exclusive attention to the war till it is over, and during its whole continuance, it will require the exertions of all our people to bring it to a successful termination.

We hope the press throughout the state will call attention to the proclamation, and urge upon the people the necessity of filling the new levy at as early a period as possible.

LITTLE ROCK, Ark.,
August 22, 1861.

EXECUTIVE OFFICE[129]

The continued absence of a large number of State officials, most of whom are connected with the Confederate army - members of the General Assembly, sheriffs, judges and agents, attorneys, etc., etc. - renders it almost impossible that the machinery of government can be kept in motion, and the laws executed.

These gentlemen, though prompted by patriotic impulses, seem to be mindful of the embarrassment and confusion induced by their absence.

One-half of the offices in the State, from this cause, are now practically vacant. Nor is there authority in law to supply the deficiency.

The public interests, meanwhile, are suffering materially, the rights and liberties of the people postponed and illy protected - and the reins of

---

129   *Arkansas True Democrat*, September 9, 1861, Little Rock, Ark.

government hang loosely, for the want of proper officers to hold and guide them!

It may be necessary that the legislature should be assembled. If so, it is altogether uncertain whether a quorum could be obtained for the transaction of business.

In many counties there are neither sheriffs, judges, coroners nor justices of the peace, to administer the laws or enforce justice.

The constitution of the State of Arkansas provides: That "no person holding an office of trust or profit under the Confederate States, (except post masters) shall be eligible to any office of trust or profit, belonging together of the three departments of this State."

Upon which it is insisted, in many instances, that the offices held by those who have accepted service in the Confederate army, have thereby vacated their offices.

The troops from Arkansas, now in Confederate service, have been organized, and hold their commissions from State authority.

Hence, they are State officials in Confederate service, and are not holding office of trust and profit under the Confederate government.

In my view of the law, therefore, vacancies do not exist in the cases cited. The executive, consequently, has no power to order new elections, and I know of no better mode by which to remove the difficulty, than to appeal to the good sense and patriotism of absent officials, and conjure them to resign or return to their posts of duty. For it may be well to remember that they have a government at home, whose internal organization and efficiency they must chiefly rely on in the future, for the manifold blessings, dispensed to a free and prosperous people - the principle now being practically vindicated, that the States are sovereign and independent powers, inferior to none, but the equals of any on earth. Let the structure be preserved in all its parts. Let everyone holding a public trust, discharge with decision and promptness the duties assigned to him or resign his place to someone who can.

It is made my duty as the executive of the State, "to see the laws faithfully executed." This I shall sedulously labor to accomplish, but must fall far short of the task, if left with the mere skeleton of a government, having neither sinews nor muscle to operate it.

HENRY M. RECTOR.
Governor of Arkansas.

LITTLE ROCK, Ark.,
August 24, 1861.

Clothing for the Soldiers.[130]

The Military Board has sent circular letters to the different counties, and published an advertisement in the *True Democrat*, calling on the citizens to furnish clothing for our soldiers now in the field.

The county Judge, the Clerk and the Sheriff of each county have been appointed, by the Military Board, a central committee in each county, for the purpose of collecting such clothing as may be procured. These committees are requested to urge the ladies to form societies for the purpose of furnishing soldiers clothes.

The central committees are directed to form clothing depots at such points in their respective counties as they may deem advisable. At these depots they will receive and receipt for everything suitable for the army that may be placed there. The Military Board proposes paying in Arkansas or Confederate Bonds for the clothing so received. As blankets are necessary to our soldiers in camp, all who have extra numbers of them are asked to divide with the soldiers. All shoes which may be supplied will be paid for. As winter approaches the committees are urged to be diligent and prompt in the discharge of the duties assigned them.

HUMBOLDT, Tenn.,
August 24, 1861.

Death of a Soldier.[131]

Mr. JOHN P. HOWARD, a member of the "Lisbon Invincibles," from Union county, Ark., died of typhoid fever, at Pocahontas, Ark., on the 25th of July, 1861. Mr. Howard was a young man of unblemished reputation, and possessing many noble qualities both social and moral, and earing [sic] to his numerous friends. He left the home of his childhood to vindicate his country's rights, and was eager to meet and engage the foe. Providence, however, willed otherwise, and the young soldier has fallen by disease and not by the sword. He was interred by his companions in arms, in the burying ground near Pocahontas, with the

---

130   *Weekly Arkansas Gazette*, August 24, 1861, Little Rock, Ark.
131   *Arkansas True Democrat*, September 5, 1861,Little Rock, Ark.

honors of war, and there his manly form sleeps in peace beneath the soil of his native South, to defend which he risked and lost his life. *Resquiat in pace.*

A.M.S.

Humboldt, Tenn., Aug. 24, 1861

* * *

Died - At Birnam Wood, in Lafayette county, Ark., August 3d, 1861, EMILY ORNE, wife of Judge D.W. Harris. The idol of a fond husband - the loved one of an extensive circle of acquaintances and relations.

On board steamer Dan'l B. Miller, at the mouth of Delaware Creek, Arkansas river, Aug. 27th 1861, of dysentery, GEO. O'Brien, aged about 35 years.

At Clarksville, Ark., on the 26th of Aug., 1861, LOUISA ELIZABETH, infant child of Henry A. and Sarah Ann Powers, aged 1 year and 19 days.

VAN BUREN, Ark.,
August 28, 1861.[132]

From the *Van Buren Press.*

Camp - Crawford Artillery.

Camp Frank Rector, Aug. 28, 1861: Friend Dunham: We arrived at this place, about seven miles below Bentonville, on Sunday, and are here awaiting the arrival of Paymaster Duval and our discharges to be off for "Home, Sweet Home." . . .Many of the soldiers and officers are entirely destitute of clothing, hundreds being barefoot and clothes so torn and tattered as to scarcely cover their nakedness. These brave and patriotic men are perfectly content, if necessary, to go home without a cent of pay, but they will not be trifled with by the officers placed over them by that universally obnoxious Military Board. Brigadier General Napoleon Bonaparte Burrow made a narrow escape at our camp near Springfield, and a few days longer only will be necessary to place Paymaster General Ben. T. Duval in a delicate and precarious situation.Col. Thos. C. Hindman will address us in a day or two upon the importance of remaining in the service, and allowing ourselves to be transferred, like so

---

132   *Arkansas True Democrat*, September 12, 1861, Little Rock, Ark.

much livestock, to the service of the Confederate States. He will be very eloquent, no doubt, and appeal to every sentiment and feeling of our natures, but we all understand the nature of the case very well, and instead of getting a regiment, as he expects, to go away from our western frontier, and join Hardee's force at Pittman's Ford, he will do well if he gets a full company out of the four regiments. We intend going home, just now, and in the course of a month or two the most of us, no doubt, will be ready and anxious to go out again. . .

Yours, in a hurry,
Private.
Brigadier-General Commanding

LITTLE ROCK, Ark.,
August 29, 1861.
Clothing for the Soldiers Again.[133]

We again direct attention to the effort to supply our brave volunteers with the clothing necessary for the winter. The change of the weather and the time of the year admonish us that winter will soon be upon us and that we must be active and vigilant to meet the necessities of our winter preparations. The general and universal suspension of trade and commerce render it impossible to procure clothing in the ordinary markets of the country. We *must* rely upon the patriotism and liberality of the people to supply such comforts as will be necessary to keep our brave and patriotic little army in the field, during the coming winter months. It is a high necessity that addresses itself to every citizen who feels an interest in the cause in which we are all alike embarked. Then let the different agents of the State in the various counties proceed at once to the establishment of depots of clothing, and the procurement of subscriptions to it. Let the blankets and all supplies needed for clothing, or for shelter and comfort be forwarded immediately. At home, if need be, we can dispense with blankets, and substitute comforts, quilts and other coverlets. In the camp and in the field nothing will supply the place of the blanket. Let our lady friends also bring up the thick winter flannels in comfortable styles and let them not waste time in fancy uniforms and other knicknacks. The women of the revolution were ready and willing to

---

133   *Arkansas True Democrat*, August 29, 1861, Little Rock, Ark.

sacrifice a window curtain, a table cover, or a Jupon of the finest and costliest texture for the use of a patriotic soldier - when William Washington asked for an ensign, a noble matron ripped the rich damask from one of her finest chairs, and gave the red ensign which floated at Cowpen and Eutaw, and which still waves over arms and hearts as stout as those of '76. The women of the South have preserved and emulated and imitated the spirit of '76, even more generally and effectually than the men. The soldiers of the South need supplies of clothing for bed and body. We feel assured that they will get it if the ladies of the South can supply. Never was there a period or a cause which more imperatively called for self-sacrificing devotion upon the part of all classes, than the present. The success of our cause requires that all should sacrifice something of personal ease and comfort. We are engaged in a struggle which will try the virtue, the patriotism and endurance of every one. It will require all our energies and all our resources to keep our soldiers clothed and fed. Let the sacrifice be what it may, there must be no uncertainty about this. Indeed, liberality to our soldiers has become a great necessity to every property holder in the Confederacy. Let no more men think of making money until every battle field is whitened with the bones of our sensual, depraved and brutal invaders. Every thought about gain and self must now yield to the necessities of our brave soldiery. If through our neglect and indifference our armies become disorganized, then will lands, slaves, mules, horses, cattle, bonds and stocks become worthless except to the rapacious Yankee invaders. Every feeling of patriotism and every consideration, alike, requires us to devote money, labor - indeed, everything - to the comfort of our soldiers.

LITTLE ROCK, Ark.,
August 29, 1861.
THE WAR- WHEN WILL IT CEASE?[134]

Throughout the northern cities there are unmistakable indications of a desire for peace. The conservative press is becoming bolder and more outspoken, and we hear of peace petitions in Philadelphia, and an imposing call for a peace demonstration in New York. Similar evidences

---

134 *Arkansas True Democrat*, August 29, 1861, Little Rock, Ark.

of a re-action in the war feeling are exhibited in other northern cities. But too much importance should not be attached to these demonstrations of feeling in the cities. The cities are not fair exponents of northern feeling and opinion. "Paris" is not "France" in America, and the voice of the northern cities is not the voice of the northern people.

The interests of the cities are directly identified with peace. The war status is utterly ruinous to the business and prosperity of the northern cities. These, too, constitute an infinitely larger proportion of the aggregate wealth and money value of their respective States, than is the case in the South. Destroy the business of the northern cities and you desolate a whole region. Destroy the cities of the South and southern resources and wealth are but temporarily crippled. The South will continue as strong as ever, and her cities under the magic wand of Ceres would again spring into life and activity. There is no need for them to be many or populous. The business of an agricultural country can be prosperous and well conducted without the creation of mammoth cities, which are oftener the sources of corruption and weakness than of wholesome vigor.

But we must look beyond the cities of the North for the tone of northern sentiment and for the impulse to its political action. The cities of the North were comparatively conservative and entirely pacific up to the bombardment of Sumter. There were in hopes "the secession fever" would die out, if let alone, and that their trade and profit would after a while go on in the accustomed channel. But the rural districts have for years been fanatically anti-slavery in sentiment, and growing more intolerant and hostile to the South from year to year, until it reached the election of Lincoln, the climax of its fierce exultation. Its long baffled and long delayed vengeance upon "the slave oligarchy" seems near at hand and an "irrepressible" yell of delight went up from the universal black republican press. The metropolitan papers of that party being edited with more of ability attracted more of southern attention. But they did not exceed, or even equal, in venom the rural papers. Indeed, they were but the concentration and reflex of the rural sentiment. It is notorious that their patronage is derived more from the country than the city. Their readers were mostly among the rural population.

It is the country vote that sends black republican members to congress. It is the rural sentiment that is now chiefly heard upon its floor and speaks in its legislation. Now, the country population that tills the soil or hangs around the villages and finds employment along the lines of rivers, and canals and railroads at the North, have not yet felt, as the cities have felt, the sore pressure of war. They have no large sums gathered up in brick houses, and city lots, and wharf stocks, bank stocks, insurance stocks, in ships and steam lines and mills and factories. They have made but a hand-to-mouth living hitherto with a quarter of a dollar to spend every week to attend an abolition free-love and women's right lecture as the whim dictates, and thus far they do not feel materially worse off for the war. The sore pinch of "nothing to eat and nothing to wear" in its literal agonies has not yet visited them. They have not yet learned to direct their curses from "the slave-driving rebels" to their own abolition preachers, lecturers and teachers who are the real authors of the ruin fast coming upon their country.

Notwithstanding Bethel, and Manassas and Springfield, they still believe the rebellion can be put down, and they fill their imaginations with pictures of pendent traitors upon innumerable scaffolds to appease the shades of their canonized John Brown. They do not comprehend the real strength of southern resources and their capacity for war. They exult in the fancied power of numbers, and are truculent of northern ships and ship yards, of the wealth of their cities, and their mills, and mines, and factories and foundries, and imagine that they have only a half starved, enervated poverty stricken and divided people to conquer. They see only the bloated belly of northern wealth that has gormandized so much of southern wealth, and do not see the members that have fed it, and without whose continued labors it must shrink up and perish. The rural population of the North have much to learn, ere they realize the evils their own fanaticism has brought upon the country. At present an abundant production makes food cheap for all, while the stimulus of a government demanded for army uses, prevents a ruinous depreciation. The war, too, creates a war party of the officers, ambitious of distinction, and in the army of contractors, of mechanics and laborers in almost every branch of industry to which it gives employment and fat jobs.

These are some of the reasons why we do not look for immediate peace. There is nothing in the tine and action of the northern government indicative of peace. The national pride of the North has been aroused by their late disastrous defeats and now adds intensity to their hatred. They will make no proposals for peace until they have been thoroughly humiliated. They are still for war and there will be no peace until one has been conquered.

LITTLE ROCK, Ark.,
August 29, 1861.

Arms Wanted.[135]

The undersigned, having been appointed Agent by the Confederate States for the purchase of Arms, it is desirous of purchasing all the good Guns in the country. He will not only purchase "regulation arms," such as Muskets and rifles, both Flint and percussion made for the army, but also Double Barreled Shot Guns and Country Rifles, Percussion Locks. Every man who has a Gun of the above description, can sell it for Cash by making application to the undersigned. Apply at the Arsenal.

JOHN A. JORDAN
Little Rock, ARK., Aug. 29, 1861

LITTLE ROCK, Ark.,
August 29, 1861.

PRESIDENTIAL AND CONGRESSIONAL ELECTIONS. [136]

By an act of Congress of the Confederate States, an election for President and Vice President and for four members of Congress will take place in this State on the 6th of next November. We hope by next week to have some suggestions to offer in regard to obtaining electors for President and Vice President without resorting to a State convention of the people, which at this time, we deem would be impracticable and perhaps unnecessary. In the meantime we will be glad to obtain suggestions from our friends upon the subject.

LITTLE ROCK, Ark.,
August 29, 1861.

War Coffee.[137]

A very good coffee can be made, by costing only12½ cents, by mixing one spoonful of coffee with one spoonful of toasted corn meal; boil well and clear in the usual way. I have used it for two weeks, and several

---

135 *Arkansas True Democrat,* September 5, 1861, Little Rock, Ark.
136 *Arkansas True Democrat*, August 29, 1861, Little Rock, Ark.
137 *Arkansas True Democrat*, August 29, 1861, Little Rock, Ark.

177

friends visiting my house say they could not discover anything peculiar in the taste of my coffee, but pronounced it very good. Try it, and see if we can't get along comfortably, even while our ports are blockaded by the would-be king. I can assure you it is very pleasant, though not strong enough to make us drunk.

Exchange.

JEFFERSON COUNTY, Ark.,
September 3, 1861.

To the Ladies of Jefferson County.[138]

The undersigned committee, having been appointed by the Military Board for the purpose of obtaining winter clothing for our soldiers, now in service, will enter immediately upon the discharge of their duties, and as soon as material can be obtained will make a call upon the ladies of each township for the purpose of organizing societies to aid in the manufacturing garments for those in the service of their country. Due notice of the time and place will be given by hand-bills, and one or more of the committee will endeavor, under their instructions, to be present to assist in the organization, and to give such information as may be necessary for the expeditious accomplishment of the object in view.

We know the ladies of Jefferson - first to offer upon the shrine of liberty their patriotic devotion, and to encourage the brave soldier as he marches beneath the folds of freedom's flag, against an infatuated and insulting foe, who would "wipe us from the face of the earth" - who would ruthlessly destroy our homes - enslave and make us the associates of the negro - will come forward with that interest that has ever characterized the true, noble and generous daughters of our own dear South, and cheerfully bestow the labor of their hands and the sympathy of true and generous hearts in aiding to comfort and warm the brave men who are now fighting our battles, and must soon, *very soon*, need clothing to protect them from the chilly blasts of a more northern clime.

Remember, ladies, that this is not all - the poor soldier far away from home, weary by fatigue, famished by hunger, exhausted by the duties of the field, or, perhaps, bleeding upon the battle ground, feels half

---

138 *Arkansas True Democrat,* September 12, 1861, Little Rock, Ark.

his trouble gone to know that he is not forgotten at home, and that those he leaves have not been unmindful of his necessities, but have been prompt in adding to comfort and relieving his wants. The ladies of Vaugine township are earnestly requested to meet at the court house in this city on Saturday, the 13th inst., at 10 o'clock, A.M., for the purpose of organizing under the direction of the Military Board.

Z. Wells, Judge.
J. DeBaun, Clerk.
A. F. Kendall, Sheriff.

PITTMAN'S FERRY, Ark.,
September 3, 1861.

Clothing for the Soldiers.[139]

To the People of Arkansas:
Heretofore, whenever I have had occasion to address you, it has been as a politician, discussing questions arising from differences of opinion upon the policy of our civil government - questions of a character making such differences allowable, and admitting of delay in their settlement. But the times have changed; and I - nay, all of us - have changed with them. Our country is involved in war. I am a politician no longer - having not been since the war begun, and shall never be again; for should I survive the contest, which I do not expect, I shall, at least, be too old for the wearing toils of political life, (of which I have long since had sufficient, if not satisfactory experience) - even if "the fiery ordeal" we will have passed, shall not (as I trust it will) have purified my patriotism enough to forbid my giving up, again, to party, what belongs to our country.

I appear before you, now, in another character, and for a widely different purpose. I come as a soldier, and as the representative of soldiers - of that band of devoted volunteers - your own sons, brothers, friends and relations, who have left all the comforts and endearments of home, to stand, as they are now standing, on your northern line, to defend and protect your State from invasion by a cruel and implacable enemy, who, but for this defense, would, even now, be polluting your

---

139 *Memphis Daily Appeal*, September 18, 1861, Memphis, Tenn.

soil with the tread of mercenary legions, and desecrating your firesides and domestic altars with fire and slaughter. I come to ask your co-operation and assistance in the work of making good this, your own defense. Not that you, yourselves, should take up arms and enter the service, but that you will contribute, what you can easily and without inconvenience spare, from your supplies means, and appliances, in the way of clothing, to protect and defend your own volunteers - not against the arms of the enemy, but against the inclement weather of autumn, already upon us, and the cold of winter, now rapidly approaching - which defense and protection against the elements are indispensable to enable us to make good your defense against the enemy; for we are made of flesh, and blood, and nerves, like yourselves (a little ruder and sterner, it may be); and while we shrink from no required exposure and complain of no necessary hardships, we are so far human as to need some seasonable clothing, to shield us from the winds and rains through the day, and something to cover us when we lie down upon the cold wet ground at night - if we are to preserve our health, and keep in a condition to perform our duties with effect.

Let it be remembered that these volunteers entered the service and left home, early in the summer, and with only summer clothes - in many instances with only a single suit. This was under the promise that the government would, in due time, furnish an abundant supply of suitable and seasonable clothing. This promise has failed. Not an article of clothing has been furnished by the government (either State or Confederate,) and not a dollar of pay or commutation has been given to the soldier, wherewith to furnish himself, while his duty to defend and protect you in the safety and comfort of your homes and firesides - keeps him where nothing of the kind is to be had. We do not complain of this, nor blame the government. Doubtless, the reasons for this failure are good ones, and blame justly attaches to no one. But the facts remain - the soldiers are without clothing, or the means or opportunity for obtaining it - they are in a climate several degrees farther north than they have been accustomed to - a large portion of them (nearly one-half) have been prostrated and are still feeble from the effects of fever, measles, and other debilitating diseases - and will perish if exposed, without the protection of clothing and blankets, to the bad weather of fall and winter.

These are not questions for politicians, allowing of differences of opinion, and admitting of delay in their settlement. They are stern and solemn facts, which challenge the assent of all, and demand immediate attention. They make up business which must be done at once, for every citizen, who cherishes the sentiment of patriotism or humanity, or has a due regard for his own interest. Who will disregard - who will neglect it?

I am here, by order of Gen. Hardee, to aid, as far as may be in my power, in giving effect to the efforts which I know are already on foot, and, I doubt not, will be actively continued, for the accomplishment of the object I have set forth. The following is his letter of instructions, under which I am acting:

Headquarters Upper Dist., Arks.
Pittman's Ferry, September 3, 1861.

Colonel: You will proceed to Little Rock and concert, with the Military Board of Arkansas, measures necessary to secure clothing for the troops under my command. The men are destitute of everything - shoes, hats, shirts, socks, drawers, pantaloons and coats. Unless clothing is obtained, it will be impossible to make a campaign this winter. But, independent of this consideration, it is due to the gallant men who have volunteered in the service of their country, that they should be supplied with clothing to protect them from the inclemency of the weather, and the rigors of winter.

The patriotic citizens of Arkansas, I feel well assured, will respond promptly to the call made on them by the Military Board. But it is necessary that they should be made acquainted with the actual condition of the troops; and it is for this purpose that you have been selected to go to Little Rock.

The people who are appealed to should be informed that their aid is invoked as the only means, within our reach, by which the troops can be supplied.

By an agreement made with me, by the military board, the State of Arkansas agreed to furnish the troops of that State with clothing, and the State was to receive from the Confederate States the commutation allowed in lieu thereof. The military board, I am credibly informed, took proper measures to procure clothing, beyond the limits of the State - but failed. The failure was beyond their control. It was not their fault. They did all within their power.

The only thing now left is to aid the military board in getting the clothing within the State. Accordingly, officers have been sent by me, to the different counties from which troops have been raised, to inform the people of our wants, and to urge their co-operation and assistance. It is

181

presumed that each family in the State has something to spare, which it can give without inconvenience.The smallest offering will be acceptable; a pair of socks, a shirt, a blanket - everything and anything which would keep the soldier warm, and contribute to his health and comfort.

Very respectfully,
W. J. Hardee

Central Committee.
Pine Bluff, Sept. 3, 1861.

LEWISBURG, Ark.,
September 3, 1861.[140]

Messrs. R. S. Yerkes & Co.

Gentlemen: I thought you might like to know what we were doing up here about clothing our volunteers. We got word about the 20th ult., of our troops, under Col. Churchill of your city, getting their clothing and tents burnt, during the battle of Oak Hills, in Missouri, and in about 10 days the citizens of Cadron and Welborn townships have bought and made up some 300 garments, and on yesterday we started two 2 horse and one 4 horse wagon with them to the volunteers in Missouri. Messrs. R. W. Benedict, A. J. White, A. J. Lucas, Dr. T. W. Shore, Rev. J. Hargis Hogans and many others of Cadron township, contributed liberally towards clothing our unfortunate volunteers. The citizens of this place and Welborn township, done nobly towards rendering our brave volunteers both contented and comfortable. Up here we are all for prosecution of the war to the bitter end. Crops good - health fine.

Your friend,
A. Gordon.

MEMPHIS, Tenn.,
September 5, 1861.
A GALLANT ARKANSAS YOUTH.[141]

Benjamin S. Johnson, son of Robert W. Johnson of Arkansas, was engaged in the recent battle of Oak Hill, near Springfield, Mo., upon which occasion he served as volunteer aid-de-camp to Gen. McCullough.

---

140   *Arkansas True Democrat*, September 12, 1861, Little Rock, Ark.
141   *Arkansas True Democrat*, September 5, 1861, Little Rock, Ark.

Though less than eighteen years of age, he behaved with great gallantry and coolness, and had a horse killed under him during the action. When even the boys run away from school to take part in the war, what chance has Lincoln to "subjugate" the South? For information of the Yankees, it may be well to state that Arkansas has a "full crop" of just such boys as Ben. Johnson, growing up to take the places of those that may fall in defense of the southern cause.

-Memphis Appeal

LITTLE ROCK, Ark.,
September 5, 1861.[142]

GUNS! GUNS! It is the purpose of the Confederate Government to establish immediately an armory at this place to repair and fix up guns for the service.

Dr. John A. Jordan has it in hand, and he is prepared to buy up all the guns in the State that he can find. He wants all descriptions of barrels, shot guns, rifles and muskets, with or without stocks or locks, and it is his purpose immediately to repair them for service.

So send up your old guns. You will not only get their value, but you will be performing a patriotic duty. You will be arming the State against invasion, and enable it to carry the war into the enemy's country. All that we need to whip the Yankees at every point is a sufficiency of arms. These we must have. Anyone having guns to spare should address Dr. John A. Jordan at Little Rock.

MEMPHIS, Tenn.,
September 7, 1861.[143]

The "Camden Knights," Company B, Capt. Logan, reached Memphis last Monday as a part of Col. Smith's 11th regiment of Arkansas volunteers, and are now encamped near the Fair Grounds. They are represented to be one of the best drilled companies that has yet been raised in the State, and are armed in excellent style for a fight with the Hessians - each one

---

142   *Arkansas True Democrat*, September 5, 1861, Little Rock, Ark.
143   *Arkansas True Democrat*, September 19, 1861, Little Rock, Ark.

having a minnie musket, a navy repeater, and a ponderous "toothpick," which they have learned to use in a very expert manner. The company is the thirteenth one that has been furnished to the Confederate service by Washita county, which has a voting population of eighteen hundred.

-*Memphis Appeal*, Sept. 7.

LITTLE ROCK, Ark.,
September 12, 1861.[144]

 Mr. Editor - The officers and privates of Camden Knights Company B., desire to express through the medium of your paper, their heartfelt thanks to the ladies of Little Rock, for the numberless acts of kindness of which they have been the recipients during their stay in this city. Their messes have been supplied daily and bountifully with the luxuries of the gardens; fair hands have prepared them a uniform for the campaign, upon which they are now about to enter, and their camp has often been graced with the presence of those whose cheering smile and encouraging words go so far towards mitigating and relieving the asperities of a soldier's life. If any incentives were required (other than those presented by the holy cause in which we fight,) to nerve our arms in the coming struggle, it would surely be found in the thought that we are the guardians and defenders of the homes of those who have so generously and patriotically contributed their exertions to promote our comfort and ease; next to those who mourn our absence around our own hearthstones, thoughts of them shall furnish our most cherished recollections in the bivouac, our noblest stimulant to action, when the cloud of battle gathers around us; and may that God whose blessings are promised to the beautiful and good of earth, grant to the noble ladies of Little Rock, a higher and worthier reward than this, our poor tribute of thanks.

John L. Logan, Captain.
W. A. Thomas, 1st Lieut.
F. T. Scott, 2d "
J. K. Whitfield, 3d "
and eighty-six privates.

---

144 *Arkansas True Democrat*, September 12, 1861, Little Rock, Ark.

LITTLE ROCK, Ark.,
September 12, 1861.

Clothing for the Soldiers of the Hot Spring Rifle Company "E." 12th Regiment Arkansas Volunteers.[145]

It is earnestly requested by the captains, lieutenants and privates of said county, that all who can do so should, at the earliest possible day, make up something like the following for their friends and relatives:

Two pair of pants, of heavy brown or gray mixed jeans, lined if though proper, with domestic. One roundabout or jacket of the same material, lined throughout, with side and vest pockets, it should be long enough to come some four inches below the waistband of the pants and large enough to be worn over the vest or outside shirt. One heavy vest of jeans, linsey or kersey, one over shirt of woolen or mixed goods; one or two pair of drawers, as the case may require, two pair of socks, one good blanket is advisable, one overcoat or a loose sack coat, or a hunting shirt with a belt.

E. C. Jones, Capt.,

of Hot Spring Rifle Co., "E." 12th A. R. V.

P. S. - These goods can all be boxed up together with each man's name upon his goods and forwarded. The proper information will be given in due time how and where they will be forwarded to.

E. C. J.

LITTLE ROCK, Ark.,
September 12, 1861.

Capital Guards.[146]

The following preamble and resolutions were presented and adopted by the officers and soldiers of the Capital Guards, 1st company, 6th regiment Arkansas volunteers, at a meeting held on the company parade ground at "tattoo," on the evening of the 12th Sept., 1861, to-wit:

Whereas, The Capital Guards, company "A," 6th regiment Arkansas volunteers, having just received through the liberality of the citizens of Little Rock an entire suit of uniform clothes and other articles of good material, neat and appropriate in style, and altogether such as will be quite useful and sufficient for our comfort during the coming winter - be it

---

145   *Arkansas True Democrat*, September 26, 1861, Little Rock, Ark.
146   *Arkansas True Democrat*, October 10, 1861, Little Rock, Ark.

Resolved, That these citizens have placed the Capital Guards under renewed and lasting obligations to them by this crowning act of favor and forethought of our coming wants - that the company has not been made to feel that "friends in need are friends in deed," but that they are *doubly* our friends who will not allow us to entertain even an apprehension of need or want.

Resolved, That such acts of liberality and such ready care of the soldiers of the Confederate States by her citizens, nerve the arms of the young republic, and in this her first necessity freely supply the place of a treasury at home and credit abroad.

Resolved, That the numerous former acts of kindness from the citizens of Little Rock towards the Capital Guards have been of so munificent a nature that they cannot receive this too liberal aid as a mere gratuity, but while they thank them for a favor so timely conceived and freely given, they will hold it a privilege and claim it right to reimburse them for the outlay for this uniform at their earliest opportunity.

Resolved, That we are profoundly grateful to the ladies of Little Rock for making the uniforms and the many other useful and tasty garments which the hand of affection or friendship have provided until all have been supplied.

Resolved, That the untiring exertions and ceaseless toil of the ladies of Little Rock to prepare comfortable and appropriate clothes for the thousands of soldiers who have rendezvoused there during the last five months, have no parallel, as we believe, in the Confederate States, and that the noble characteristics of self-forgetting devotion to the welfare of our army and the success of our cause so universally exhibited by the ladies of the Confederate States has been shown by the ladies of Little Rock in so intense a manner as to excite our warmest admiration for them and a burning emulation to deeds of virtue and of valor that on our return, when

"Wild war's deathly blast has blown,

And gentle peace returning," we may in some degree meet the smiles and approbation which the fair delight to bestow upon the brave.

Resolved, That the proceedings of this meeting be signed by each officer and member of the company, and that copies be forwarded to Gen. Wm. E. Ashley and S. H. Tucker, esq., with the request that they communicate the same to the ladies and others of our friends who have placed us under obligations.

LITTLE ROCK, Ark.,
September 12, 1861.

Office Military Board.[147]

The Central Clothing Committees in the various counties are informed that it is of the highest importance that such Clothing as they have procured be sent as early as possible to the army. Hence they will send such as have accumulated on their hands with the least possible delay.

Individuals may designate for what particular company their clothing is intended, and the Central Committees will have them put up in separate boxes and labeled so as to reach the desired destination. They will be sent to the headquarters of Gen. Hardee, and on their arrival at Pocahontas or Pittman's Ferry, will be delivered to John H. Imboden, Quartermaster for the 2d Division, or directly to the Quartermaster of the Confederate States, who will distribute them in accordance with the design of those who have contributed them. In every instance boxes will be labeled for the particular company for which they are designed and directed either to the State or Confederate Quartermaster. Receipts will be given for them by either of those individuals, and transmitted to the Military Board.

The Military Board takes this opportunity of expressing its thanks to the country for the very general and patriotic response that has been made to its call, and in order to relieve the immediate and pressing wants of the soldiers would again impress upon the Central Committees the necessity of immediately sending such articles as they have on hand to the army. Where it is convenient let them be sent to the river for shipment. Where it is not, let them be sent by wagon. Their transportation will be paid on proper certification at this office.

H. M. Rector, Governor
and Ex-officio President Military Board.

Attest:
D. W. Davis,
Secretary Military Board. Sept 12, 1861.

---

147   *Arkansas True Democrat*, September 12, 1861,Little Rock, Ark.

LITTLE ROCK, Ark.,
September 12, 1861.

Clothing for the Army.[148]

Col. Solon Borland arrived on Sunday last, and is now in the city, to superintend and facilitate the supply of clothing for that portion of our army under Gen. Hardee's command. He has conferred with the Military Board, and with Dr. Jordan, the agent for the Confederate States, and is co-operating with them in the important work of protecting our soldiers against the inclement weather of the fall and winter now rapidly approaching. He is ready to confer with those of our citizens who desire to contribute to this necessary work, and give all desirable information and assistance, in the way of making the joint labors of all available for the greatest good. Col. Borland will, within the next day or so, address the people in this city, and at other places in the surrounding country, on this subject; of which notice will be given, as to particular time and place. In the meantime he may be seen and consulted at his residence on Rock street, or at the counting room of S. H. Tucker & Co.

LITTLE ROCK, Ark.,
September 12, 1861.

For the Soldiers.[149]

We publish the following schedule of such articles of clothing as our soldiers are bound to have for the winter:
One good country jeans coat or jacket.
Two pairs of pants, same material.
Two good cotton shirts, heavy.
Two " linsey " "
Two pairs of good linsey drawers, (or other heavy goods.)
Two pairs of good woolen socks.
One pair of first rate shoes.

---

148   *Arkansas True Democrat*, September 12, 1861, Little Rock, Ark.
149   *Arkansas True Democrat*, September 12, 1861, Little Rock, Ark.

LITTLE ROCK, Arks.,
September 19, 1861.

To the people of
Ashley, Desha, Drew, Dallas, Hot Spring and Union counties,
Arkansas.[150]

Pursuant to an order addressed to the commanders of regiments and battalions composing the army of the north west in Virginia, by the General commanding that division, to select each a suitable officer to return to the places in which the men composing their regiments were enrolled, to receive and convey to them such clothing and other articles as may be required during the winter, and may be furnished by their families, neighbors and friends, I have detailed Lieutenant J. M. D. Sturges for that purpose. Under the army regulations of the Confederate States, the government pays each soldier forty-two dollars per annum in lieu of clothes which are to be supplied by the soldiers themselves.

Justly appreciating the patriotism and devotedness of the people of Arkansas, which seems only to increase with the new demands their country is compelled to make upon them, I deem it only necessary to tell them that the soldiers under my command are operating in the mountains of Virginia, where more and warmer clothing is necessary to their comfort and health, than anywhere else in the Confederate States, to insure a liberal supply of flannel shirts, drawers, yarn socks, heavy pants, a warm coat for each, and two pairs of heavy shoes. I would suggest that the counties of Union, Ashley, Drew and Desha, make Monticello their depot, and the citizens of Hot Spring and Dallas forward the articles for the soldiers from those counties to the quarter master of the Confederate States at Memphis, there to await the order of Lieut. Sturges. Each parcel should be marked with the name of the person for whom it is designed, and each box addressed to the Captain of the company for whom it contains clothing, to my care. After the goods are delivered into the possession of Lieut. Sturges, he is on no account to become separated from them until they reach their destination.

A. Rust, Colonel
Com'd'g 3d Ark. Reg.
Brigade Headqu'rs, North-west, Va.
September, 1861.

---

150 *Arkansas True Democrat*, September 19, 1861, Little Rock, Ark.

MEMPHIS, Tenn.,
September 19, 1861.[151]

There will be a flag presentation to the Ninth Arkansas Regiment, at 10 o'clock this morning, near the Fair Grounds.

LITTLE ROCK, Ark.,
September 21, 1861.[152]

From the Little Rock *Gazette*, of the 21st, we learn that Col. S. C. Faulkner, military store keeper at the Little Rock arsenal, in obedience to orders received from the War Department, will proceed immediately to establish an armory, with ample machinery for the making and repairing of all kinds of arms. Col. F. is instructed to purchase all the good arms which can be procured, either infantry, cavalry, or ordnance. It is to be hoped that every man in the State who has any arms of the kind wanted, will bring them forward promptly.The same paper states that the whole of the lady population of Arkansas seemed to be engaged in making clothing for our soldiers. Regiments of ladies are at work. Thimbles and needles are kept moving. Spinning wheels which had lain by as useless for years are again strung, and the houses in the country cheered, night and day, by their music. The looms are kept busy. No lady is now prepared to receive her friends without her knitting work in her hands.

LITTLE ROCK, Ark.,
September 26, 1861.
The Preacher's Regiment.[153]

A regiment of troops, from the southern part of the State, passed up last Sunday, en route for the seat of war, that should properly be styled the Preacher's regiment. The colonel Bradley, from Pine Bluff, is a Methodist minister, and besides him there are no less than eight preachers in the regiment - one of whom is over seventy years of age!

-Helena Shield.

---

[151] Arkansas True Democrat, September 19, 1861, Little Rock, Ark.
152 *Memphis Daily Appeal*, September 25, 1861, Memphis, Tenn.
153 *Arkansas True Democrat*, September 26, 1861, Little Rock, Ark.

Oh no, Mr. Shield, Col. Bradley's regiment is not entitled to the name of "the Preacher's regiment." Col. McCarver's regiment, now organizing at this place has forty-two preachers in it now, and will have over fifty when organized. Hence we claim the title for Col. McCarver.

-Pocahontas Herald.

LITTLE ROCK, Ark.,
September 26, 1861.[154]

Some of the military companies raised during the present war have assumed queer names. We have "avengers," "invincibles," "fencibles," and "rangers," without number. In our State we have, or had, a company of "yellow jackets," another of "hornets" and one called the "sassafras invincibles." In Texas they have one called "the Yankee hunters." In Alabama one is styled "the rosin heels." Wild cats, tigers, rattlesnakes, and bears, have furnished names for other companies.

LITTLE ROCK, Ark.,
October 3, 1861.[155]

Edmund Hays, Esq., of Magnolia, Columbia county, Ark., arrived here on Monday last with a large lot of ready-made clothing for the volunteers from that county, in Gen. Hardee's command. The energy and self-sacrificing devotion and patriotism manifested by the ladies of Columbia county, and indeed all over the Confederacy in making up clothing, is worthy of all praise and commendation. Their great zeal for the success of the South is unlimited and the urgent necessity for the clothing to be hastened on to the quarters of the army under Gen. Hardee, caused many to labor night and day to accomplish the object in due time. We also learn from Mr. Hays, that two companies recently organized in Columbia county, for the war, are *en route* for the headquarters of Gen. Hardee, via Memphis, Tenn.

---

154 *Arkansas True Democrat*, September 26, 1861, Little Rock, Ark.
155 *Arkansas True Democrat*, October 3, 1861, Little Rock, Ark.

LITTLE ROCK, Ark.,
October 3, 1861.

Soldiers' Clothing.[156]

I am authorized to receive any clothing which may be contributed to Capt. J. B. Johnson's company, of Little Rock. They will be deposited at the *True Democrat* office, and sent on to the company at an early day. The clothing furnished them by the Confederacy were of poor material, and they need warm clothing, and are unable to purchase them.

Henry C. Ashley.
October 3, 1861.

LITTLE ROCK, Ark.,
October 3, 1861.

Soldiers Aid Society.[157]

The patriotic Ladies of Little Rock have this week organized a society, to be known as the soldiers aid society, the object of which is to provide clothing for our army. The following officers were elected: Mrs. E. H. English, President; Mrs. C. Langtree, Superintendent of the work; Miss E. Field, Secretary; Mrs. F. E. Ashley, Treasurer. More than forty ladies have already signed the constitution and became members of the society. It is hoped that many others will enlist in the good work.

-Gazette.

MEMPHIS, Tenn.,
October 5, 1861.

Arkansas Items.[158]

The Washington *Telegraph* says that Col. Gantt's regiment has been ordered to New Madrid to join Gen. Pillow's command. The same paper has the following: Lieut. Col. Williams left this place last week with four wagons, each drawn by four mules, loaded with clothing, contributed by the citizens to the volunteers from this county in McNair's regiment, and

---

156 *Arkansas True Democrat*, October 3, 1861, Little Rock, Ark.
157 *Arkansas True Democrat*, October 3, 1861, Little Rock, Ark.
158 *Memphis Daily Appeal*, October 5, 1861, Memphis, Tenn.

Capt. Gamble's company of Hempstead cavalry. In portions of the county the ladies, God bless them, are still busy weaving, sewing and knitting for the soldiers, and in a few days another wagon load or two of clothing will be started to our volunteers. The ladies of Hempstead are nobly doing their duty.

JACKSONPORT, Ark., October 9, 1861.

Arkansas Items.[159]

Our streets during the past two weeks, on several occasions, have been filled with Missouri migrants who are fleeing their native State with their movable property.

They appear to be persons of wealth, judging from the number of slaves accompanying them. What a sad spectacle to behold, when it is remembered that it is the work of one poor, besotted, ignorant and tyrannical old fool.

From the *Jacksonport Herald*.

HELENA, Ark., October 9, 1861.

Arkansas Items.[160]

The *Helena Shield* gives a statement of the number of garments made by the Sewing Society of Helena, from the 20th April to the 3d inst., which exhibits a most commendable spirit of industry on the part of the ladies composing that society.

Number of pairs of pants, 579; coats, 295; shirts, 378; drawers, 120 pairs; sheets, 60; pairs of blankets lined, 58; mosquito bars, 30; pillow cases, 20, and six dozen haversacks. In addition to this there were a large number of garments made by ladies of the town and vicinity who were not members of the society.

---

159 *Memphis Daily Appeal*, October 9, 1861, Memphis, Tenn.
160 *Memphis Daily Appeal*, October 9, 1861, Memphis, Tenn.

UNION COUNTY, Ark.,
October 10, 1861.

Socks, Clothing, etc.[161]

In the course of a business letter received from a friend in Union county, he stated, as an evidence of what the noble women of that county were doing, that Mrs. Nettie Hearin had knitted a certain number of socks and would knit more for our soldiers. This we made public in a paragraph, but it is due to the lady to say that our information was received from a gentleman not at all connected with her, and given as an item of news. There are many whom "Do good by stealth, And blush to find it fame."

All over the State the patriotic women are at work, and besides the lady above referred to, others in Union county, and all the counties in the south-west are working freely for the good cause. The call for clothing has met a noble response, and the amount is so large that great difficulty is experienced in procuring means for its transportation. Let them not weary in well doing, for a use will be found for all they can furnish.

LITTLE ROCK, Ark.,
October 10, 1861.

The Concert.[162]

A number of the patriotic ladies and gentlemen of this city got up a concert and a number of tableaux, for the benefit of the Soldiers' Aid Society. On Tuesday night the theatre was rammed, jammed and crammed with a large and delighted audience. The music, rather too artistic for the general earl, was said, by judges, to be very fine. The charade and tableaux were well selected, well represented and were received with shouts of applause. The attitudes, poses and making up were all good. The ladies and gentlemen who got up this affair deserve credit and thanks, and we hope they will give us others and the proper time. We must not close our notice without referring to the first appearance, as a public speaker, of the gentleman who was most prominent in making up the concert. His speech though short was pithy and pointed.

---

161 *Arkansas True Democrat*, October 10, 1861, Little Rock, Ark.
162 *Arkansas True Democrat*, October 10, 1861, Little Rock, Ark.

VAN BUREN, Ark.,
October 11, 1861.

Arkansas Items.[163]

We find the following notice from Maj. Clark, Quartermaster of the Arkansas forces, in the *Fort Smith Herald*, and copy for the information of our readers in that State, who should promptly respond to the call: Clothing for the Army. Capt. James H. Sparks, of Fort Smith, and Samuel Martin, of Van Buren, have been appointed agents to purchase blankets and clothing for the army. The former will conduct the agency for Fort Smith and the south side of Arkansas river, at the Army clothing depot, on Garrison avenue. The latter for the north side of the river for the present at Messrs. Ward & Southmayd's, Main street, in Van Buren. Materials for making clothing will be purchased to the extent of our ability to make them up. Employment will be given to cutters and seamstresses throughout the country. Funds are not in hand, at present, to make payments for these purchases and for this work. A short indulgence of a few weeks is asked, when prompt payments will be made. The government expects that a spirit of patriotism and fair dealing will prevent any attempts being made to raise the prices of articles and labor thus needed for our soldiers as the costs will be deducted from their pay. Payments will be made in Confederate notes, *which are receivable at par in the banks of New Orleans and other cities.* The same officer also gives notice that all packages of blankets, clothing, socks, boots and shoes, donated by the liberal citizens of Arkansas to the troops, will be received at the quartermaster's office, Fort Smith, and at the store of Messrs. Pennywit & Scott, Van Buren, and forwarded without delay to our suffering soldiers.

CAMP HARDEE- PITMAN'S FERRY, Ark.,
October 14, 1861.

Letter from Capt. Holmes.[164]

Men and Women of Dallas County: If anything could add to the pleasure and satisfaction of this hour, it would be to know that you were gazing upon the scene that greets my eyes. It would need no words of

---

163 *Memphis Daily Appeal*, October 11, 1861, Memphis, Tenn.
164 *Arkansas True Democrat*, October 24, 1861, Little Rock, Ark.

grateful and heartfelt acknowledgment from *me* for your prompt, energetic and efficient aid in behalf of the gallant and brave boys of my command, could you see them as I do, *now* neatly and comfortably clad; behold their smiling, happy faces; and hear them greet each other with the oft-repeated, "God bless the good people of Dallas county." But I have just returned from a visit among you and my heart tells me that I must thank you.

No one knows better than myself how much you have labored, nor how willingly and cheerfully you have given your money to aid in clothing these honorable, noble hearted, yet half naked soldiers. To this end, I have seen the mothers and daughters of Dallas, bending over their work, day after day, night after night; yes, week after week. I have seen mothers strip the soft, warm blankets from their beds and with their blessings send them as covering to their absent soldier husbands and sons. 'Tis true the beauties of the "elder time" gave their jewels and miserable gewgaws to grace the bloody triumphs of a Ceazar and to sustain the mighty government of imperial Rome. 'Tis true the mothers of old Sparta reared their sons only for the battle fields of their native land and those of her enemies. But you wives, mothers and daughters of Dallas have done more. Your own fair hands spun, wove and made the garments which now protect the forms of this "*my little band of braves*," who as certainly as that the sun will rise to-morrow, will not disgrace you by dying (if die they must) with their backs to the foe. Whatever of labor and suffering, of duty and danger the dark and mysterious future holds for us, shall be met and endured as becometh the husbands and sons of so generous and noble a people. With such as *you* to care for and love us, it is impossible for us either to falter or fail. No! the South will yet be free. Free from the disgraceful legislation of northern fanatical demagogues; free from the insulting tread of northern hireling soldiery; free from the *attempted* rule of Mr. Lincoln and all his miserable cormorant crew. The soldiers still ask your united prayers to the "God of battles." If the South can have this, her triumph is certain. She cannot fail! Fail, did I say? No! rather would the prairie flower fail the spring; rather the thunderbolt fail the storm. And now with my parting hand in yours, let me only add, a God bless you one and all.

From yours most truly,
Wm. T. M. Holmes,
Company A, Col. Borland's Rg't of Mt. Vol.

196

CAMDEN, Ark.,
October 18, 1861.[165]

Patriotic Ladies.

When the aged matron, who has passed her three score years, takes hold of the distaff and makes clothes and jeans for the soldiers, Abraham Lincoln may never expect to subdue the South. Here the ladies of South Arkansas are at work - some knitting socks and making jeans, and 150 have joined into a society, the Soldier's Aid Society, in Camden; that the sons and brothers of our county may never want for warm clothing or blankets. We will send them our blankets most willingly - we can make plenty of comforts for our homes.

I know of an aged matron that works ten hands and spun 30 yards of thread for her weavers, with her own hands, and as long as there is a call for cloth she will continue to make it. Another one that always bartered wool for socks has been knitting all the fall, and can knit a sock in a day, and will continue to knit all winter. My dearest aim is to work for our rights and freedom, and our sons and brethren can fight the battles, and we will work at home to preserve our young sons, that there may be new armies to fill the place, when those that are active now have passed away. I have three young boys coming on for their country's service.

LITTLE ROCK, Ark.,
October 18, 1861.

Barbecue and Flag Presentation.[166]

On the 18th of October, 1861, at the residence of Eylas Beals, there was a grand barbecue given to Capt. Murff's company. At the same time, the company was presented with a beautiful flag by Mrs. J. R. R. Adams. Mrs. Adams said in a plain, easy and graceful manner:

Captain Murff -

In respect to you and your gallant soldiers, and in behalf of the married ladies here assembled, I present to you this silken flag. It is

---

165 *Arkansas True Democrat*, October 17, 1861, Little Rock, Ark.
166 *Arkansas True Democrat*, November 21, 1861, Little Rock, Ark.

emblematic of that flag which is now struggling so hard to wave in freedom over our shores. You will perceive upon it inscribed the words, "Conquer we must, In God is our trust."

We have placed these simple, but beautiful words there, hoping that they may remind you, when you're far away, of the great necessity of placing all your trust on Him who knoweth all things, and who doeth all things well. His ever watchful eye will beam with love upon you; He will be your solace and hope in the hour of need; your light and comfort in the dark night of trouble. That God who has promised mercy to the shorn lamb will never forsake you if you will love Him, obey Him, and reverence His holy name. Ask of Him, then, to smile upon you in this most glorious undertaking; place yourselves under His heavenly protection, and then, valiant warriors, rally forth in the defence of your country, your homes and your firesides, and say with confidence, and with cheerful hearts,

"Oh, conquer we must, for our cause is just;
See, there is our motto, in God is our trust."

This was the chosen motto of your honored, illustrious Washington. Under it he led forth the gallant heroes of the revolution; under it your forefathers fought and died, and thereby purchased for us those blessings, of liberty, freedom and peace, which once were ours, and which shall be ours again.

You are now about to leave your friends, your homes and your loved ones here, for the tented field, to battle in your country's cause; and I sincerely trust that this flag may be a pillar of light by day to shield and protect you, and as a pillar of fire by night to lead you on to victory and success. Think not that you will be forgotten by those you are leaving behind. Oh, no, brave soldiers, our thoughts will follow after you, and, in spirit, we will wander with you far over the beautiful hills and pleasant valleys of our own dear sunny South, and we will bless our weary soldiers; and from our hearts will ascend to heaven a silent and a fervent prayer that the God of battles will be with you; that He will shield and comfort you, and return you all again, crowned with honors, to the homes and friends from which you are now parting.

Then take this flag, and have it carried in triumph until peace shall be restored to our beloved country, and until our independence shall be recognized by all the great nations of the earth.

(Advancing and placing the staff in Captain Murff's hand, continued,)

Our fingers have made for brothers and sons,
I give it to you now in trust,
That you never will leave it while sabers and guns
Can save it from trailing in dust.
Bright banner of beauty in glory unfurl,
On continent, ocean and sea,
To nations and kingdoms throughout the wide world;
Go, flag of the brave and the free.
May laurel on laurel around thee entwine,
And still they dominion be peace,
Whilst the stars in thy circle forever shall shine,
And God's blessings on thee increase.

Capt. Murff's Reply.

Mrs. Adams: In accepting at your hands, in behalf of the "Bayou Metre Hornets," this beautiful banner, wrought by the fair hands of a lady of this vicinity, I feel my utter inability to respond in that strain of fervid eloquence which swells up from my heart, but fails to find utterance from my lips.

From every point the invader is assailing us; the roll of the drum is now a familiar sound, and wakes the echoes in places forever strange to it before; the earth is trembling beneath the tramp of marching squadrons; the roar of the cannon; the crash of the musketry, the groans of the wounded and dying are familiar sounds. We may be conquered but never subdued; this beautiful banner shall wave over us while one arm has strength to strike a foe; though smoke and dust and blood may stain it, but dishonor shall never tarnish it.

Accept, then, fair lady, our thanks for this high testimonial of your estimation of our company, and receive from me, in behalf of the company, this pledge, that till the last arm has fallen nerveless, and the last heart has ceased to beat, will it become a trophy to our enemies.

CHICOT COUNTY, Ark., October 24, 1861.[167]

To one who has not attempted the calculation, the value of the voluntary contributions to the army, made by the patriotic women of Arkansas, would almost exceed belief. In a late number of the *Chicot Press* is a list of one lot sent to the Chicot Rangers. The list is half a column long. It enumerates blankets, overcoats, coats, pants, drawers, shirts and various other articles. The whole value must be several thousand dollars. Going home one evening last week, we met five wagons heavily laden with clothing for the volunteers. These were from the southern part of the State. Every county has contributed more or less and each has nobly done its duty. The value of the articles sent from Pulaski county has been estimated at $18,000. The goods already sent could not be bought with a quarter of a million of dollars. Here and elsewhere, the patriotic women have taken the blankets from their beds and sent them to the soldiers. In Johnson county, the merchants offered premiums to the young ladies who made the best or most jeans, and other woolen goods, and the result was that large quantities of excellent goods were brought in, made up and sent to the soldiery.

MEMPHIS, Tenn., October 27, 1861.

A Card.[168]

Camp Johnston, at Edgewood Church,
Editors *Appeal*: Permit me through the columns of your paper, in behalf of the officers and soldiers of the 12th Arkansas regiment, publicly to express the esteem and regard we feel toward the founders and members of the Edgewood Hospital Association, who have done so much for the benefit of the sick of this regiment. Some *four* weeks ago we changed our camping ground to this place, for convenience of water and dryness of ground. We came bringing upward of one hundred sick men with us, some with intermittent fever, some with dysentery, but by far the greater majority with that pest of our army, *measles*. The ladies, ever mindful of

---

167 *Arkansas True Democrat*, October 24, 1861, Little Rock, Ark.
168 *Memphis Daily Appeal*, November 2, 1861, Memphis, Tenn.

suffering humanity, seeing our destitute condition, with an energy and patriotism worthy the cause we advocate, without delay, organized themselves into a society called the "Edgewood Hospital Association." That excellent lady, Mrs. MacLean, whom we all love and delight to call "our mother," was chosen president, and Mrs. Waddell, whose talent and energy gained her the title of captain among the soldiers, secretary. Edgewood Church was converted to the use of the sick, and every want that necessity demanded was promptly attended to by them. They personally superintended the preparation of such food as was deemed suitable for sick men, after supplying all deficiency from their own tables.

They have personally nursed the soldiers with the same kindness and attention they would have bestowed upon their own kindred under different circumstances; but when the hospital has been so crowded that none others could be admitted, they have taken them to their own homes, often subjecting themselves to great inconvenience for their sake, and the welfare of the Confederacy we are fighting for.

They have furnished our soldiers with upward of one hundred flannel shirts, numerous pairs of socks, which their own hands have constructed - all this have they done for us, and much more that no estimate can reach, no mind calculate - the smile, the look, the word of encouragement held out to the sick, disheartened and dispirited man. Such attention, such kindness and devotion to our soldiers speak volumes for the success of the South.

Truly, no country can be unsuccessful, no matter how great the odds against them, when such loyalty as disregards all personal consideration is thrown aside, and but one common sentiment animates the breast of every person. Long shall we remember these ladies, and when the 12th Arkansas regiment shall meet the enemy of their country in the deadly strife of battle, may the ladies of this association be their watch word, and their deeds of valor recompense them for all their kindness. Again, long live these ladies, for they will never cease to live in the hearts of the officers and soldiers of the 12th Arkansas regiment.

Respectfully,
R. G. Jennings,
Surgeon of the Regiment.

HOLLY SPRINGS, Ark.,
October 28, 1861.[169]

Editor True Democrat: In order that the devotion of the citizens of Holly Springs and vicinity to the cause of liberty and right, may be more generally known, and particularly of the ladies, I send you a list of clothing, with the request that you give it a place in your paper. All the clothing described has been presented without charge, and has been forwarded to Capt. E. P. Chandler's company, 12th Arkansas regiment, and consists of the following articles, viz: 8 overcoats, 66 jean coats, 86 pairs jeans pants, 35 pairs linsey drawers, 44 pairs cotton drawers, 42 jeans vests, 12 knit shirts, 56 linsey and flannel shirts, 59 hickory shirts, 34 home knit comforts for the neck, 159 pairs socks, 42 pairs gloves, knit by the ladies, 44 blankets, mostly homemade, and 12 coverlets.

Almost all of the above articles have been spun, wove and made by the fair hands of the wives, mothers, sisters and sweethearts of those who have enlisted in said company. Can a people so united and devoted ever be conquered? Never, while the God of justice continues to rule among the inhabitants of the earth.

Yours, etc.,
Thomas Peterson.

LITTLE ROCK, Ark.,
October 31, 1861.[170]

The Arkansas penitentiary has been made a useful institution during the present war. Among the articles turned out during the summer were wagons, harness, tents, cartridge boxes, belts, knapsacks, camp chests, stools and cots, caissons, etc. Besides these a large lot of army clothing were made up and a great many shoes for soldiers. Mr. Ward, the energetic contractor, tells us that by spring he will have turned out 10,000 pairs of boots and shoes for the soldiers. These were sold to the State at cash prices and payment taken in war bonds. A great deal of difficulty has been experienced in getting a supply of leather. The most of our readers are aware that the penitentiary was leased for a term of years, with a view to the introduction of machinery to spin and weave cotton goods. For this purpose an appropriation was made for the

---

169 *Arkansas True Democrat*, November 21, 1861, Little Rock, Ark.
170 *Arkansas True Democrat*, October 31, 1861, Little Rock, Ark.

erection of buildings for the factory and additional cells for the prisoners. But the breaking out [of] the war checked this enterprise and the contractor has wisely set the convicts to work making such things as were needed by the troops. There are about 120 convicts in the prison now.

LITTLE ROCK, Ark.,
November 5, 1861.[171]

A banner recently presented to a volunteer infantry company in southern Arkansas, has inscribed on it the new popular phrase, "Here's your mule."

VAN BUREN, Ark.,
November 5, 1861.

Arkansas Intelligence.[172]

The *Van Buren Press* has the following interesting information respecting the steam cotton mill now in full operation in that place. The mill has two sets of wool cards, which can card 300 pounds per day; 1808 spindles, which can turn out 500 pounds of cotton yarn per day. They have no looms except for making seamless sacks. They are also grinding from 100 to 150 bushels of corn and wheat per day.

LITTLE ROCK, Ark.,
November 7, 1861.

Let Us Rejoice.[173]

What say our patriotic citizens to having a jubilee tomorrow night, in honor of the secession of our gallant sister State.[174] Let the loud-mouthed cannon peal forth its thunder tones; let the soul-stirring notes of martial music add enthusiasm to the joyous event; let gladsome shouts go

---

171   *Daily State Journal*, November 5, 1861, Little Rock, Ark.
172   *Memphis Daily Appeal*, November 5, 1861, Memphis, Tenn.
173   *Daily State Journal*, November 6, 1861, Little Rock, Ark.
[174]   Missouri seceded on October 31, 1861, which was passed by a "rump" legislature called in Neosho, Mo. The convention was called into session by Governor C.F. Jackson. Jackson was previously removed from public office by the Missouri State convention.

up from patriot throats till the welkin rings, and let glittering lights from an hundred houses illumine the happy scene. A people who have struggled so valiantly in the cause of God and the Right, as have the Missourians, deserve all the gratulation and homage a generous brotherhood can offer. They adopted for their watchwords the cheering notes of Bozarris to his gallant Greeks when battling against the servile Ottoman:

"Strike - till the last armed foe expires;
Strike - for your altars and your fires;
Strike - for the green graves of your sires;
God and your native land!

LITTLE ROCK, Ark.,
November 7, 1861.

Exiles.[175]

Col. R. H. Johnson -

Sir: There is quite a large number of persons who have come, and are coming, to this State from Virginia, Maryland, Kentucky and Missouri, who claim to be exiles and driven from their homes. In some cases, a poor man, with a large family, is seen seeking a new home. His family must be supported and it may be necessary for him to stay and procure them the means of support. But there are others, men without families, or those having relatives in the State with whom their families reside, who come here and sit down in inglorious ease while their State is overrun by the hirelings of Lincoln. They call themselves exiles, but of all white livered cowards, they bear the palm. These fellows turn their backs upon their own State, leaving the brave men and patriotic women to defend it - they skulk from danger and like cravens as they are attempt to magnify the dangers from which they ran. They sit here and see Arkansas going to Virginia, Kentucky or Missouri, to drive the invaders back, and yet, profess to be intensely patriotic. Shame upon such libels upon humanity. If they have not the spunk to fight, let them go back and act as cooks, teamsters or in some situation where there is but little danger. If there is a despisable object it is the coward who has deserted his country in the hour of her peril and greatest need. What is worse

---

175 *Arkansas True Democrat*, November 7, 1861, Little Rock, Ark.

about these fellows, is the fact, that they put on immense airs, and some of them are hardly upon our soil before they are seeking offices. The Executive who appoints such a man to office, or the elector who votes for one, deserves to be executed. It requires very little to make us believe that such poltroons would seek safety in Lincoln's camp, if Arkansas or Texas had not been open to them. Let us mark these fellows, and if they will not go and fight for their homes and native land, let us show our appreciation of their conduct by holding them in deserved scorn and detestation.

Yours truly,
P.R.

LITTLE ROCK, Ark.,
November 8, 1861.

Complimentary.[176]

At a meeting of the Little Rock Grays, the following resolutions were unanimously passed, 8th November, 1861.

Resolved, 1st, That we acknowledge our sincere gratitude to the noble and patriotic ladies of Little Rock for their liberal contribution of clothing to the company.

Resolved, 2d, That knowing their former exertions in behalf of the southern soldiers, and the difficulty at this late day to procure materials, we appreciate more fully their generous gift.

Resolved, 3d, That in defence of a country boasting of such women, and in defence of women whose self-sacrificing acts shed a luster upon the early pages of the South, we feel that every hardship is a holy duty, and every suffering is an offering to them and the country.

Resolved, 4th, That independence, when our arms have achieved it on bloody fields, will be still dearer to us when reflect, in after years, upon the heroic sacrifices of our patriotic women.

Resolved, 5th, That to Mrs. Matilda Johnson, Mrs. R. H. Johnson, Mrs. J. B. Johnson, Mrs. T. J. Churchill, Mrs. I. A. Jordan, Mrs. J. D. Adams, Mrs. Thos. R. Welch, Mrs. Gov. Fulton, Mrs. Martin, Mrs. Maria Stevenson, Mrs. G. D. Sizer, Mrs. Adamson, Mrs. Bertrand, we tender our special thanks.

Resolved, 6th, That the Ladies Soldier's Aid Society of Little Rock,

---

176   *Arkansas True Democrat*, November 21, 1861, Little Rock, Ark.

is entitled to our lasting gratitude, and for remembering us among the many thousands whom they have clothed, we tender them especially our thanks.

Resolved, 7th, That in honor of the ladies of Little Rock, we now adopt the name of the "Little Rock Grays," and pledge ourselves to maintain its honor on every battle field we may tread.

Resolved 8th, That we tender our thanks to Mrs. M. F. Trapnall for the beautiful banner presented to us before leaving Little Rock last June, and as upon its silken folds is embroidered the "crown of victory," so that emblem we have chosen to follow and entered the service of our country, never to return until victory crowns our arms.

Resolved 9th, That to the Sisters of Mercy, of Little Rock, for the interest shown us in embroidering our flag, and the zeal they have displayed in the holy cause for which we battle, have our humble but sincere thanks.

Resolved, 10th, That to Henry C. Ashley and Richard H. Johnson, we also acknowledge a debt of obligation which we can never repay, save that we offer our lives for that glorious independence for which they have so assiduously labored, and to achieve which they have so generously contributed.

Resolved, 11th, That for the honor of our city, as well as country, we enlisted for the whole war, and that in the night alarms, when the "long roll" summon us in storm, in dark and rain, to form and await the enemy; our wearied and benumbed limbs are strengthened and our hearts are cheered by the reflection that we are battling for the rights of those who have been so kind and thoughtful of us.

Resolved, 12th, That our thanks are due to Wm. R. Miller, Kinnear & Hughes, J. W. Woodward, and other kind friends who have aided us.

Resolved, 13th, That we tender our thanks to Jas. B. Moore, esq., for bringing our clothing to us, and shall ever remember, with gratitude, his efforts in behalf of the "Little Rock Grays."

Resolved, 14th, That the city papers be requested to insert the above resolutions.

1st Lieut. Franklin,
Com'dng Little Rock Grays,

1stArk's Battalion, Chairman,
2nd Lieut. Geo. Moore, Acting as Secretary.

LITTLE ROCK, Ark.,
November 21, 1861.[177]

At a parade of the "Dallas Rifles," in their company grounds, on the evening of the 28th inst. the following proceedings were had:

Capt. F. J. Cameron called the company to order when Lieut. M. M. Duffie offered the following resolutions, which were unanimously adopted.

Whereas, Through the agency of our fellow countryman, Hon. Jo. Gray, and the exertions of our friends of Dallas county, the "Dallas Rifles," 6th regiment Arkansas volunteers, have been supplied with clothing for the winter, be it

Resolved, That the "Dallas Rifles" return their profound thanks to their friends, and the ladies especially, for their personal efforts in behalf of the company, that such citizens do as noble a part in their country's defence as they who go to battle, and with such friends the soldier will not falter in the discharge of the most arduous duties, for he knows that there are those at home who not only watch with anxiety their condition but will also greet their return with the dawn of peace, ready to twine the laurel of honor upon the victor's brow, for the Arkansas boys will return victors *or return not at all.*

Resolved, That the untiring efforts of the ladies in behalf of the "Dallas Rifles," prove that they like the mothers of the first revolution, are fired with a truly Spartan zeal, and that they kindle a like ardor in the breast of every soldier who wears a garment from the fair hands who plied the shuttle or the needle in its construction.

Resolved, That the "Dallas Rifles" assure their fair friends, no garment sent shall cover a coward's heart, but hearts willing to brave the dangers of "flood and field," to be worthy of the mothers, the sisters and friends left behind them.

Resolved, That the proceedings be published in the "Arkansas *True Democrat.*"

Thos. A. Wiley, O. S.
Cave City, Ky., October 28th, 1861.

---

177 *Arkansas True Democrat*, November 21, 1861, Little Rock, Ark.

CAMP BEAUREGARD, Ark.,
Nov. 21, 1861.

Magruder Guards.
Thanks.[178]

J. W. Walker, Esq. - It again becomes my pleasing duty, as Captain of the Magruder Guards, to acknowledge the receipt for the company under my command, of *another* dozen heavy wool undershirts from your hands. Such an act of kindness from one who can count no relative amidst the ranks bespeaks a heart overflowing with generosity. With many thanks, I remain,

Very truly yours,
F. W. Hoadley,
Capt. Magruder Guards.

LITTLE ROCK, Ark.,
November 28, 1861.[179]

Twenty-seven prisoners, members of a secret Lincoln organization, from Van Buren county, were brought to this city yesterday and lodged in jail for safe keeping, until tried by the civil authorities. Forty others are said to be on the way, and the names of the whole clan known, also their secret signs and pass words, which were divulged by a young man who was ignorantly initiated into the order. The most judicious and available means should be adopted to rid the country of such traitors. Our Police and Home Guard should, in the meantime, be on the alert otherwise we may suffer at the hands of the friends and sympathizers of those arrested. Such was the case in Texas some years ago, under similar circumstances.

LITTLE ROCK, Ark.,
December 11, 1861.[180]

The ball given last night by the colored population for the benefit of our volunteer soldiers, was a very creditable affair, and realized quite a handsome sum. We stepped in to take a look about 9 o'clock, and were much pleased with the gaudy show of fine dresses and happy faces that

---

178 *Daily State Journal*, November 24, 1861, Little Rock, Ark.
179 *Daily State Journal*, November 29, 1861, Little Rock, Ark.
180 *Daily State Journal*, December 12, 1861, Little Rock, Ark.

greeted us. We thought if old *Lincoln* and his fanatical crew could only have seen that spectacle, their minds would have been greatly illuminated as to the condition of our slave population.

LITTLE ROCK, Ark.,
December 15, 1861.

More of the Conspirators.[181]

Seventy-seven additional prisoners were brought in yesterday from the county of Searcy, being a part of that gang of jayhawkers or conspirators whose nest was first discovered and broken up in Van Buren county a few weeks ago. This foul conspiracy which was the work of a fanatical old free-will Baptist preacher, aided by a few hoary headed old sinners, who have been long living in crime and wickedness among the barrens of our northern border counties, has been thoroughly broken up by the vigilance and prompt action of the loyal citizens of those counties. One of the most lamentable features connected with its development and discovery is the fact that a great many good, but simple minded young men, were seduced and deceived by those wicked old sinners, into a crime which they now sadly, but perhaps too late, lament. The law will be rigidly enforced against them, and, in all probability, the neck of the last one of them will swing by the halter, as a warning to all future traitors and conspirators.

FORT SMITH, Ark.,
December 17, 1861.

Troubles in the Indian Territory.[182]

We learn from late Fort Smith papers that affairs are becoming very complicated, not to say alarming, in the Indian territory. Opothleyholo, the Yankee abolition leader of the Creeks, Cherokees and Seminoles, had gathered a force of three or four thousand around him, and was

---

181 *Daily State Journal*, December 15, 1861, Little Rock, Ark.
182 *Daily State Journal*, December 17, 1861, Little Rock, Ark.

threatening Col. Cooper with his little force of three small regiments. The Indians were flocking to the standard of Opothleyholo, and it was thought that he had Cooper in rather a tight place - Should he overcome Cooper and disperse his forces, the Indian territory will be, for a time at least, effectually lost to us. It seems strange indeed, while such great and momentous interests are thus menaced in the Indian Territory, that the forces of McCulloch which were raised with an especial view to the protection of that country, should be slumbering in inglorious ease in their winter quarters upon the Arkansas river. We cannot comprehend the policy of such course.

LITTLE ROCK, Ark.,
December 17, 1861.

The Conspirators.[183]

The case of the seventy-eight prisoners who were brought down from Searcy county, a few days ago, on the charge of being implicated in the Jayhawking conspiracy which has recently come to light, in that county, was brought before the Military Board on Saturday, and thoroughly investigated. While it was admitted that there was a secret bound association in that region of country called the "Peace and Home Protection" Association, it could not be made to appear that its objects contemplated any more criminal intent than to ensure them against the hostilities of an invading army. The leaders of this movement, doubtless contemplated ulterior objects of a much more criminal character, but the majority of their followers were doubtless ignorant of those purposes, many of them, in fact, being under the impression that they were doing creditable service to their country. They manifested on the investigation of their case, much regret and mortification for the position in which their acts had placed them. They protested their loyalty and devotion to their country, and agreed, if they were released, to testify their devotion by volunteering in the Confederate service for the war. Every consideration of patriotism and humanity plead in their favor; they were accordingly released, and forthwith formed themselves into a company, elected their officers from those who had arrested and escorted them as a

---

183 *Daily State Journal*, December 17, 1861, Little Rock, Ark.

guard from their native county, and were sworn into the service of the Confederate States "for and during the war." The scene which followed their release, the touching remarks of the Governor and their solemn enlistment into the Confederate service was a very affective and impressing one. We hope as we doubt not, that they will prove true and faithful, as well as valiant soldiers in the service of their country.

LITTLE ROCK, Ark.,
December 25, 1861.

Christmas Day.[184]

What hallowed associations cluster around the memories of this sacred day! Of all the bright sunny recollections that gladden the retrospect of childhood's hours, those connected with this joyous holiday are the brightest. The bounteous favors of good old Santa Claus; the beautiful presents - pledges of parental love and tokens of a yet more tender passion; gay dresses and gorgeous toys, fire crackers, Christmas trees, sumptuous dinners, family re-unions - these are some of the things that always connect themselves with the recollections of Christmas. It is a happy day to childhood, a joyous occasion to the young, and even old age is cheered and rejuvenated by its lively scenes. It is the day of all others that revives the sweet sad memories of the past; the day of all others when we miss absent friends and yearn for the comforts of "home, sweet home." Oh! to the sad heart tossed upon the rough billows of tempestuous life, away from home and loved friends, what associations of mingled joy, sadness and regret does this day bring! How the heart aches with the recollections with which it is burdened, and pines for the old homestead, and the friends who gathered around the family hearth when last the sacred circle was formed.

To how many such sad hearts did the light of this joyous day unfold its morning glory? Think of the vast numbers who are now encamped upon the cold tented field, yielding up the pleasures and comforts of home and even offering up their bodies a willing sacrifice upon the altar of their bleeding country. Poor soldiers! How the sympathies of our hearts should reach out to them laddered with our most earnest prayers

---

184 *Daily State Journal*, December 25, 1861, Little Rock, Ark.

for their safety and protection.

Five hundred thousand brave, noble gallant sons of the South, that last Christmas were enjoying the festivities of this day, amid the sweet comforts of home, are now far away from home, exposed to the cold winds of winter, the rigors of camp, and the perils of a soldiers life. Poor fellows, we owe them a debt of gratitude which the homage of years could not redeem. They have interposed their faithful breasts, a living rampart to shield us from the destroyers advance, and to protect us in the enjoyment of our rights. They are heroes and patriots, whose brows should be crowned with the evergreen chaplets of our undying gratitude. Brave hearts, may the pangs which you have suffered in dread suspense and anxiety for your country's safety, never be increased by the still sharper pangs of a people's ingratitude; may all the sufferings you have so patiently and nobly borne, be more than compensated in the praise and gratitude that shall ever welcome and congratulate you as conquering heroes - as saviors of your native land.

www.ingramcontent.com/pod-product-compliance
Lightning Source LLC
Chambersburg PA
CBHW031338040426
42443CB00006B/381